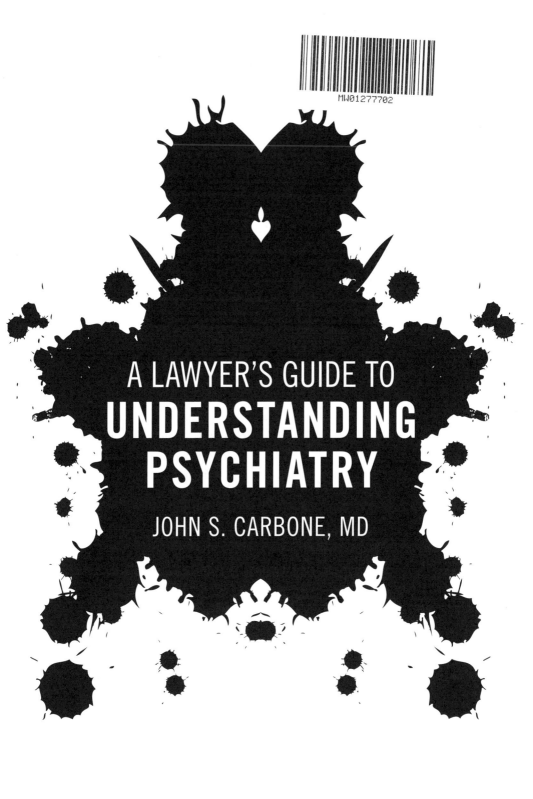

A LAWYER'S GUIDE TO
UNDERSTANDING
PSYCHIATRY

JOHN S. CARBONE, MD

Cover design by Kelly Book/ABA Publishing.

16 15 14 13 13   5 4 3 2 1

Library of Congress Cataloging-in-Publication Data
Carbone, John S. (John Stephen), 1962-
A lawyer's guide to understanding psychiatry / John S. Carbone
    p. cm.
    Includes bibliographical references and index.
ISBN 978-1-61438-594-3
1. Forensic psychiatry—United States. 2. Insanity defense—United States. 3. Insanity (Law)—United States. 4. Evidence, Expert—United States. I. Title.
KF8965.C37 2012
314'.1502434—dc23   2012025173

Dedication

Caporale Cipriano Carbone (1879-1948), 11th Reggimento Bersaglieri, Regio Esercito Italiano (Royal Italian Army), Peking 1900.

Sapper Gilbert J. Gove (1884-1974), 505th field company of Royal Engineers, 57th (2nd West Lancashire) Division, XI Corps, First Army, British Expeditionary Force, Ypres, 1917.

Major Ralph Carbone (1911-2002), medical corps, 34th Bomb Squadron, 17th Bomb Group (medium), Twelfth Air Force, United States Army, Anzio 1943.

Contents

Acknowledgments

Shakespeare allowed that brevity is the soul of wit, and nowhere is this more applicable than in apportioning thanks for an endeavor as large as writing a book. As the process spans months, and though Oscar winners might try, it is impossible to name in a minute or two everyone who impacted the final product. So while it is important to recognize those who shone especially brightly, such affirmations inevitably fall short. They are neither all-inclusive nor fully reflective of the sincere appreciation for labors expended.

In roughly chronological order, I owe gratitude to Ludwell Johnson, PhD, professor of history emeritus at the College of William & Mary. Professor Johnson was an early and significant influence on my academic pursuits. I am proud to count him among my close friends to this day.

Four colleagues in particular from the school of medicine at the University of Virginia—Nicholas Kambouris, MD, PhD; Lew Rowe, MD; David Harrison, MD; and David Wages, MD, PhD —remain a source of both light-hearted relief and serious consultation. Nowhere else have I been honored with the company of a more accomplished yet unpretentious group of professionals and brethren.

Former colleagues at Dorothea Dix Hospital in Raleigh include David Hattem, PhD; Valerie Brooks, PharmD; and Nancy Laney, PhD The mental health staff with whom I work at the North Carolina Department of Correction include Mark Mattioli, MD, DFAPA.; Anna Jamieson, MD; Laura Yates, LCSW; Beth Ridgway, MD; Betty Gardner, RN; Leslie Quick, MA; Linda Cross, RPh; Sally MacKain, PhD; and Wanda Thompson. My compadres have indulged me on a near-daily basis with their efforts to maintain our collective sanity while tilting at the windmills of mental illness, with their invaluable editorial input, and often with both.

A special thanks is very much in order to my dear friend from days in residency, Sally Andersen Stacy, SPHR, with whom I lost touch many years ago but with whom I was fortunate to reconnect shortly after this work was commenced. Hearing from her again was a delight in itself, and she also demonstrates with her good humor and wise counsel that sharpness of mind diminishes not a whit over the passage of two decades.

My friends Monika Vainoriene, MD; Enrikas Vainorius, MD; Sergei Chernikov, PhD; and Tatiana Chernikova, PhD, deserve more than mere words of appreciation. For many a delightful evening of companionship, reassurance, and good conversation, I say *ačiu labai! Большое спасибо!* in the hope that I can reciprocate in days to come.

The members of the local chapter of the Horseless Carriage Club—the Whites, the Minges, the Harleys, the Landeses, and others—deserve recognition as a font of camaraderie and much-needed stress reduction. There is nothing quite like chugging along a two-lane country road in a convoy of Tin Lizzies. It relaxes the soul and puts life in perspective. They are kind and hospitable to a person. And of that group, thanks are especially owed to Brandy Strickland for subduing my natural tendency to use five words when one will suffice.

I am indebted as well to Rick Pazskiet, JD, Deputy Director of American Bar Association Publishing, for his year of encouragement and assistance. Without his belief in my abilities and proposal, none of this would have come to fruition.

Needless to say, my mother, Jean Carbone, RN, my wife, Jurgita Šuliokaite-Carbone, MD, and my children—Daniel Carbone, Suzanne Carbone, and Anna Maria Cicero—remained unflagging, the former as both therapists and supporters and the latter as fan club members, during this long and arduous process. To them I express my heartfelt and loving gratitude.

—JSC, Cary, North Carolina, May 21, 2012

Chapter 1

Introduction

A mental disorder is a clinically significant behavioral or psychological syndrome or pattern that occurs within an individual and that is associated with present distress or disability or with a significantly increased risk of suffering death, pain, disability, or an important loss of freedom.

—*Diagnostic and Statistical Manual*
Fourth edition, text revision[1]

Psychiatry is not . . . an exact science, and psychiatrists disagree widely and frequently on what constitutes mental illness.

—Justice Thurgood Marshall
Ake v. Oklahoma, 1985[2]

In autumn of 2010, I received a phone call at my office from an assistant attorney general in Raleigh. I knew this individual from previous professional interactions, and after we exchanged pleasantries, he proceeded to tell me about a case on which he was work-

---

1. _____. DIAGNOSTIC AND STATISTICAL MANUAL OF MENTAL DISORDERS, 4th ed., text revision. Washington, D.C.: American Psychiatric Association, 2000, p. xxi.
2. 470 U.S. 68, 81.

ing that involved a former offender with a fresh charge and upcoming court date. The offender was thought to have a serious personality disorder. The assistant attorney general asked me a number of questions about personality disorders in general and borderline personalities in particular, and what one might expect in dealing with an individual so afflicted. While prefacing my remarks with the disclaimer that I obviously did not know the person in question, I explained the subtleties of personality disorders and their potential impact on proceedings. We had an interesting discussion, and I thought that the questions he posed were insightful, given that, to my knowledge, he had no previous training in, or specific professional exposure to, psychiatric evaluation and treatment.

Personality disorders can be a difficult concept to grasp, and after we had hung up, I found myself wondering if I could have done a better job, on the spur of the moment, of explaining the topic. Psychiatry is complicated even for seasoned clinicians, and competent practitioners can honestly have differing opinions—and often do—when discussing diagnoses and treatments. Being an unrequited academician at heart, I decided after that phone call that, given the frequency of such inquiries and the importance in clearly disseminating answers to my legal brethren, it might be useful to try to compose a work that would explain some of the basic facets of mental health practice, and write it in a way that would be both informative and enjoyable to read.

I thought about this for several days, and finally floated my idea to the publishing section of the American Bar Association. The ABA staff was tremendously supportive, and this manuscript is the outgrowth of our subsequent discussions and collaboration.

My book is not meant to cover all things psychiatric. Not only would such a tome be overwhelming in size, but it would also overwhelm with details that are likely not pertinent to most legal situations. Instead, in looking back on my consultations, presentations, and writings over the years, I believe there is demand for an entertaining and educational introduction to mental health that is written in plain English. After reading this book, my legal audience will still need to consult with mental health professionals when a situation so dictates; what I hope a legal practitioner will gain from this book, however, is a better *basic* understanding of, and working familiarity with, the situations and terminology that they will often encounter in dealing with patients and clinicians. Armed thus, they will possess sharpened abilities to frame questions and identify pertinent facts.

This treatise is organized into seven main sections. The first outlines the evolution of nomenclature and classification of mental illness. From the earliest times there has been a need to classify human illnesses in understandable terms. At first, superstitious descriptions—vague ill-humors and otherworldly possessions—were used to recount what we have come to see as mental disorders. However, since all early efforts at management were empirical (based on observation alone), attempts at classification, when they did occur, revolved as much around potential interventions as they did around causation, which was unknown. In A.D. 100, the Greek physician Pedanius Dioscorides composed *Materia Medica Libri Quinque,* which documented a number of "treatments" for conditions that resembled delirium, depression, anxiety, and dementia.[3] The Persian physician Ibn Sina did likewise in *Al-Qanun fi al-Tibb,* or *The Law of Medicine,* which he composed in A.D. 1100. Sina's work described conditions that today we know as schizophrenia, mania, melancholia, and dementia.[4] These quasi-scientific efforts indicated a nascent understanding that human interventions, rather than those of idols and deities, can possibly yield beneficial results.

Going beyond the studies of Dioscorides, Ibn Sina, and early medical scholars, the *Diagnostic and Statistical Manual (DSM)* has been embraced by modern clinicians as the canon by which mental disorders are classified and subsequently treated. Yet, while comparing antiquated works with *DSM* at first seems a paradox, understanding how the *DSM* evolved from earlier efforts at classification

---

3. DIOSCORIDES' DE MATERIA MEDICA: A NEW ENGLISH TRANSLATION. Johannesburg, IBIDIS Press, p. 33 (Osbaldeston, Tess Ann, transl.). Dioscorides's text was used in western European universities until the late 16th century.

4. Youssef, H.A., Youssef, F.A. & Dening, T.R., *Evidence for the Existence of Schizophrenia in Medieval Islamic Society,* HISTORY OF PSYCHIATRY, vol. 56, no. 7 (1996), pp. 55–62. Ibn Sina's text was used in western European universities until the mid-17th century and had been translated by that time into Latin, French, English, and Chinese.

is essential to grasping commonly encountered diagnostic situations and controversies that arise to this day.

The book's second section addresses the manner in which clinical information is gathered and analyzed by mental health practitioners to arrive at postulated diagnoses, while the third and fourth sections discuss commonly encountered states of disorder, including the neuroses (e.g., depression, anxiety), the psychoses (e.g., schizophrenia), and the personality disorders. Attorneys will be particularly interested in understanding how some of these disease states can potentially impact *mens rea,* and thus diminish the capacity to form intent.

The fifth section reviews the serendipitous discoveries that led to our current array of available psychotropic medications. With the advent of more refined pharmacotherapy in the mid-twentieth century, psychiatry was supposed to have been delivered from the quackery of the Dark Ages into the Age of Science. Americans' use of psychiatric medications is at an all-time high, and while there is good evidence that many agents can be life-saving, much of the world of psychopharmacology remains poorly understood. Issues addressed in this section include what is actually known about the pathophysiology of mental illness (i.e., the so-called chemical imbalance theories), the postulated mechanisms of action of medications currently at our disposal, the wonders of the placebo effect, the real differences among many psychiatric medications, widespread off-label prescribing practices, and common and serious drug side effects. This discussion also includes a review of other available treatment options, including psychotherapy and electroconvulsive therapy (ECT).

The sixth section deals with the manners in which frank malingering or over-endorsement of symptoms can occur and how they can be detected. This discussion includes information about so-called trendy diagnoses (where the author interjects his experiences). These are often at the root of attempts at fabrication. Multiple personality disorder, adult attention-deficit disorder, and post-traumatic stress disorder come to mind.

The seventh section of the book focuses on risk assessments in legal settings. This last chapter is unlikely to calm the waters of this controversial subject; the author instead wishes to illustrate what we do know about the ability of practitioners to predict future dangers, and what scholars, legislators, attorneys, judges, and juries have subsequently said about the practice. In doing so, it is hoped that those relying on expert testimony will be better armed with objectivity, and will thus be free of the varying and ill-conceived expectations that the legal system has frequently created.

Remember, this work is not a one-stop reference. While I have liberally cited both scholarly and lay sources, there is within these pages much clinical opinion, though I have strived to make note of contentious issues where honest differences exist among practitioners. As mentioned above, this tome is not wholly inclusive of all things psychiatric, and thus there are some intentional omissions.

For example, there are no specific discussions of child psychiatry, eating disorders, dementia and delirium, or issues involving developmental disabilities, as these conditions fall outside the scope envisioned for this book.

Additionally, I have avoided specific discussion of chemical abuse except as it impacts other areas of mental health that are addressed. Many aspects of psychiatry remain controversial, and substance dependency is among the most controversial. Benjamin Rush, M.D., who authored *An Inquiry into the Effects of Ardent Spirits upon the Human Body and Mind*, was one of the first to offer the alcoholism-as-malady postulate.[5] "[D]runkenness," he wrote in 1805, "resembles certain hereditary family and contagious diseases." Yet the idea that substance addiction is like diabetes or cancer is relatively recent; it was preceded by, and has since been accompanied with, the seemingly simple view that some individuals freely choose to overindulge and the rest of the population does not.[6] It is interesting to note that acceptance of the disease model of chemical abuse became more widespread at approximately the same time that diagnostic categories were expanding like kudzu in the *DSM*. Some say that the perception of addiction as an illness will eventu-

---

5. Miller, N. & Chappel, J.N., *History of the Disease Concept*, Psychiatric Annals, vol. 21, no. 4 (April 1991), p. 198.

6. *See* Traynor v. Turnage, 485 U.S. 535; *see also* Goff, J.L., *Alcoholism: Disease or Willful Misconduct?*, J. of Psychiatry and Law, vol. 18, no. 59 (1990), p. 89.

ally go the way of the dodo bird, while others staunchly maintain that belief.[7] Time, and not this treatise, will tell.

The continuum of psychiatric care in twenty-first-century America includes acute inpatient wards, crisis stabilization units, 23-hour admission units, partial hospitalization programs, therapeutic foster care, respite programs, residential services, mobile crisis teams, intensive outpatient services, home health services, traditional office-based outpatient practices, and community mental health centers.[8] Add to this jumble that many providers suffer from what Csernansky presciently calls "furor diagnosticus" and "furor therapeuticus" (the frenzies to reach a *DSM* diagnosis and treat, aggravated by time constraints placed by third-party payers), and it is little wonder that mental health care can prove to be a confusing maze to all but the most initiated.[9] This book hopes to serve as a road map.

Trying to make sense of the above has been a challenge, and yet the objectives remain relatively straightforward: to discuss and simplify the most common facets of basic mental health evaluation and management that a legal professional might expect to encounter. I hope that, having read this work, the reader will find it to have been a success.

7. Warner, Jessica, *Addiction Fatigue Syndrome: The End of an Intoxicating Idea*, THE GLOBE AND MAIL, Dec. 17, 2010, at p. 9.

8. Schreter, Robert, *Alternative Treatment Programs*, PSYCHIATRIC CLINICS OF NORTH AMERICA, vol. 23, no. 2 (June 2000), p. 339.

9. CSERNANSKY, JOHN. SCHIZOPHRENIA: A NEW GUIDE FOR CLINICIANS. N.Y.: Marcel Dekker Inc. (2002), p. 21.

Chapter 2

Whirlwind Historical Observations on Western Psychiatry, or How We Came to Have the Diagnostic and Statistical Manual

> For Jesus had commanded the evil spirit to come out of the man. Many times it had seized [the man], and though he was chained hand and foot and kept under guard, he had broken his chains and had been driven by the demon into solitary places.
>
> —*The Gospel of Luke*, First Century A.D.[1]

> I have read every definition [of insanity] which I could [find], and never was satisfied with one of them, and I have endeavored in vain to make one satisfactory to myself. I verily believe it is not in human power to do so.
>
> —Lord Blackburn to Parliament
> Late Nineteenth Century[2]

1. _____. *The Gospel of Luke*. New International Version Bible. Grand Rapids, Mich.: Zondervan (1984), 8:29.
2. Cook, W.G. Insanity and Mental Deficiency in Relation to Legal Responsibility. N.Y.: E.P. Dutton & Co. (1921), p. 1.

Taxonomy is the science of classification, and nosology is, more specifically, the science of classification of diseases. Though nosology and medical therapies have progressed unevenly over the years, they have largely advanced in tandem, as healers have asked not only from what condition a person suffers, but also how to cure it. Treatment approaches to mental illness will be examined in more detail later. For now, the focus will be on the language used to describe observations, expressly psychiatric, which changed in ways that practitioners as recently as 100 years ago could not have anticipated. While the need to describe illnesses has become readily apparent over time, there has been little agreement on nomenclature. Early attempts suffered from over-simplification, wholesale ignorance, and basic lack of accuracy. Yet in order to understand the controversial and fluid nature of our current diagnostic regimen, one must know the history of the numerous failed attempts to codify mental illnesses.

The convoluted tale is neither easy to recount nor always readily apparent. Bear with me as the story is told, since the evolution has culminated, albeit imperfectly, in two references with which the reader will become intimately familiar: the *Diagnostic and Statistical Manual (DSM)* and the mental and behavioral disorders section of the *International Classification of Diseases (ICD)*.

Long before Sigmund Freud analyzed the subconscious or scientists discovered the neurotransmitter serotonin, there were witches and demons and celestial events. Ancients believed that the lunar body exerted an influence on human behavior. Comets, too, were viewed with fear and trepidation. Science, as we know it, did not exist. The unknown and unknowable were clouded in superstition and explained as emanating from magic, and for the ancients, that sufficed. Unfortunately for the ill, the myths were sometimes accompanied by "treatments"—if that term can be used—that were unpleasant at best, and more often dangerous. For example, trephining—the drilling of holes into the skull to release evil spirits—was performed in a number of antediluvian societies, likely on those with frightening mental changes.

By A.D. 400, one finds the first known attempts to systematically examine and codify mental illness. The Greek philosopher Plato classified madness into four varieties: prophetic (governed by the god Apollo), ritualistic (by Dionysus), poetic (by the Muses), and erotic (by Eros).[3] We also have Plato to thank for championing the belief that female mental instability originates from a wandering uterus that must somehow be forced back into its proper anatomic location in the body.[4] How this recalcitrant womb was to be properly repositioned in a hysterical ancient, though, remains uncertain.

Hippocrates, a contemporary of Plato, is thought to have gone one step further with his hypothesis that the brain is in fact the organ of thought and that mental illnesses were to be understood in terms of disturbed bodily function rather than as reflections of anger from deities or demons.[5] Hippocrates's work was later expanded by the Roman physician Galen in A.D. 100. Galen introduced a new conceptualization of four humors that regulated personality and behavior by their varying concentrations and combinations (i.e., the humor of blood, being warm and moist; phlegm, being cold and moist; yellow bile, being warm and dry; and black bile, being cold and dry).[6] Accurately or not, Hippocrates is often credited with being the first to attempt to develop nosology for mental illnesses in the Western tradition.

By A.D. 900, a relatively elaborate psychiatric nosology was developed by the Arab physician Najab ud-din Unhammad. He posited nine distinct categories of affliction, comprising 30 mental diagnoses in total. His descriptions included those conditions that today would be labeled as obsessive-compulsive disorder, delusional

---

3. LYONS, A. & PETRUCELLI, R. MEDICINE, AN ILLUSTRATED HISTORY. N.Y.: Abradale Press (1987), p. 195.

4. _____, *Do All Men Think All Women Are Like This?*, INSIDE UVA, vol. 20, no. 19 (Nov. 15, 1990), p. 12.

5. LYONS & PETRUCELLI, *supra* note 3, at p. 214. It was long held by the ancients that the presence of epilepsy was somehow protective against developing a mental illness; of course, this is not the case. *See also* Bender, K.J., *Bidirectional Relation Between Schizophrenia and Epilepsy, in* PSYCHIATRIC TIMES, Oct. 6, 2011, p. 12, for a discussion of insurance data illustrating that the likelihood of schizophrenia occurring in patients with epilepsy is eight times greater, and the likelihood of epilepsy occurring in those with schizophrenia is six times greater.

6. BUTCHER, JAMES, ET AL. ABNORMAL PSYCHOLOGY, 13th ed. Boston: Pearson Education, Inc. (2007), p. 29.

disorder, depression, and mania.[7] A few decades later, fellow Arab Ibn Sina wrote *Al-Qanun fi al-Tibb*, which describes conditions consistent with schizophrenia, depression, mania, dementia, and, interestingly, passive but not active male homosexuality.[8]

The Islamic world did a better job of codifying disease than its European counterparts. As late as the sixteenth century, the Swiss physician Felix Platter offered a classification of the insanities that was still based in part on the supernatural: *defatigatio* (the insomnias), *imbecilitas* (mental retardation and the cognitive debilities), *consternatio* (the febrile deliriums and catatonic states), and *alienatio* (the catch-all for dementias, alcoholic stupors, love and jealousy, melancholic states, hypochondriacal obsessions, demonic possessions, manias, and tremors).[9] Not surprisingly, Platter's nosology never really caught on.

Though lacking any modern understanding of the root causes of mental illnesses, the Islamic world was also more advanced than its European counterparts in managing those so afflicted. Available evidence suggests that dedicated asylums for the mentally ill—the genesis of a public mental health system—appeared in the greater Caliphate before they did on the Continent. A hospital that housed those with mental disorders was operating in Baghdad as early as A.D. 700. Other asylums appeared thereafter in Cairo, Damascus, and Fez.[10]

When Europe did establish dedicated asylums for the mentally ill, without any scientific foundations for the effort, the result was rarely idyllic or particularly therapeutic. St. Mary's of Bethlehem was founded as a public hospital in London in 1247 and evolved quickly into an asylum. Abuses of patients at "Bethlem," later "Bedlam," became so notorious that its poorly enunciated name has since

7. MILLON, THEODORE. MASTERS OF THE MIND: EXPLORING THE STORY OF MENTAL ILLNESS FROM ANCIENT TIMES TO THE NEW MILLENNIUM. N.Y.: John Wiley & Sons (2004), p. 38.

8. Youssef, H.A., et al. *Evidence for the Existence of Schizophrenia in Medieval Islamic Society.* HISTORY OF PSYCHIATRY, vol. 7, no. 25 (March 1996), pp. 55–62.

9. LYONS & PETRUCELLI, p. 456.

10. INTERNATIONAL PUBLIC HEALTH: DISEASES, PROGRAMS, SYSTEMS, AND POLICIES (Merson, M.H., et al. eds.). Boston: Jones and Bartlett (2005), p. 356.

become synonymous with chaos and tumult.[11] Demand for warehousing of the mentally ill increased, and for generations a number of private "madhouses" existed in the British Isles to compensate for lack of space at the few public asylums then in existence. Unfortunately for the stricken, the care at private facilities was probably no better than at Bedlam. These madhouses, sometimes located in the back rooms of a physician's home or freestanding larger structures holding several hundred patients billeted in cramped quarters, provided custodial care and little if any therapy for those individuals deemed unmanageable. As one English physician observed as late as 1809, "[i]t is a painful recollection . . . the number of [patients] I have seen who, after having suffered a disarrangement of mind and undergone the brutal operation of spouting [force-medicating by oral tube] in private [houses] for the insane, have been restored to their friends without a front tooth in either jaw!"[12]

Elsewhere in Europe, it was just as bad or worse. Johann Reil, a professor of medicine at the University of Halle, also recorded as recently as the early nineteenth century that "these [asylums are filled with] fools who laugh and . . . torture themselves without reason. Like criminals we lock these unfortunate creatures into mad-cages, into antiquated prisons, or put them next to the nesting holes of owls in desolate attics over the town gates or in the damp cellars of jails."[13]

~~~~~~~~~~~~~~~~~~~~~~~~~~~~~~

Whether a man of uncommon prescience or merely morbid preoccupation, a haberdasher named John Graunt, when not making hats in seventeenth-century London, turned to gathering census and disease data. His efforts apparently stemmed from the desire of the London city fathers to develop a method by which future outbreaks of bubonic plague might be discovered before spreading. Graunt's opus, *Natural and Political Observations Made*

---

11. LEGAL ASPECTS OF HEALTH CARE ADMINISTRATION (Pozgar, George. ed.). Boston: Jones and Bartlett (2007), p. 2.

12. SHORTER, EDWARD. A HISTORY OF PSYCHIATRY: FROM THE ERA OF THE ASYLUM TO THE AGE OF PROZAC. N.Y.: John Wiley & Sons (1997), p. 5.

13. *Id.*, p. 7.

upon the Bills of Mortality (1662), later became the framework for the modern fields of demography, epidemiology, and public health, and yielded the earliest known life expectancy charts. Though the envisioned early warning system was never implemented, Graunt remained intrigued. He wanted to determine if accurate statistics could be collated and analyzed concerning disease states and mortality in general. Despite the initial success of these statistical efforts, many prominent individuals of the day argued against any perceived usefulness of such information, saying that the difficulty of producing a uniform classification schema for diseases rendered Graunt's categories meaningless. Undeterred, Graunt continued his efforts for several years until his own untimely death, though his theories did not expire with his corporeal self, as the reader will shortly learn.[14]

Others, both contemporary and subsequent to Graunt, were more sanguine regarding efforts at better classification. In the seventeenth century, English physician Thomas Sydenham developed the concept of syndromes—clusters of signs and symptoms that are seen together in certain disease states. Swedish scientist Carl Linnaeus contributed with the elegant system of binary nomenclature, a means of cataloguing organisms by genus and species that is used to this day. In the eighteenth century, Frenchman Francois Bossier Sauvages de Lacroix published his treatise *Nosologia Methodica* (1763), a lengthy pre-modern work on the organization of human pathology (2,400 ailments in all) that is still considered a landmark. That was followed six years later by the similarly named *Synopsis Nosologiae Methodicae* of Scotsman William Cullen.[15] The first diagnostic textbook of what would ultimately become psychiatry in North America was written in 1812 by Benjamin Rush, one of the signers of the Declaration of Independence. The U.S. census of 1840 was the first to include per-

---

14. NATURAL AND POLITICAL OBSERVATIONS MADE UPON THE BILLS OF MORTALITY (Willcox, Walter, ed.). Baltimore: Johns Hopkins Univ. Press (1939), p. 22.

15. _____. "William Cullen." ENCYCLOPÆDIA BRITANNICA ONLINE. *Available at* http://www.britannica.com/EBchecked/topic/146062/William-Cullen (retrieved Jan. 23, 2011).

sons with mental illnesses, although they were filed under the demeaning categories of "lunatic" and "idiot."[16, 17]

Still, not everyone saw much point in analyzing the mentally ill. Said one prominent physician and author in the late 1830s:

> It is not pretended that any classification [of mental illnesses] can be rigorously correct, for such divisions have not been made by nature, and cannot be observed in practice. . . . We shall often find [the diagnostic categories] running into one another, and be puzzled to assign to a particular disease its proper place.[18]

Furthermore, such indifference to the mentally ill came from no less august a figure than the prominent nineteenth-century French psychiatrist Benedict Morel, the superintendent of the asylum at Asile d'Aliénés de Maréville. Morel stated in his work *Traité des Maladies Mentales* that mental illness is nothing more than the natural and expected end-result of progressive hereditary degeneration, which for the individual results in insanity and dementia, and for the family results in "extinction through idiocy."[19] No other classification was really necessary, he held.

John Graunt the haberdasher would yet have the last (posthumous) laugh over the naysayers. A then-unknown statistician named William Farr was hired by the General Register's Office of England and Wales at the beginning of Victoria's reign of in the late 1830s. Farr was tasked with advancing the work that Graunt had left off more than a century before, along with making the best of the still-imperfect medical classification templates then available. Farr knew

---

16. *See also* Bloch, Sidney, *A History of Psychiatric Ethics*, in Psychiatric Clinics of North America, vol. 25, no. 3. Phila.: W.B. Saunders Co. (Sept. 2002), p. 511, for a discussion of simplistic 19th-century efforts to attribute all psychiatric illness to a single disease entity called "mental alienation."

17. *Available at* http://www.census.gov/prod/www/abs/decennial/1840.html (retrieved March 19, 2011).

18. Ray, Isaac. A Treatise on the Medical Jurisprudence of Insanity. Boston: Charles Little and James Brown (1838), p. 71.

19. Conti, N.A., *Benedict Augustin Morel and the Origin of the Term 'Dementia Praecox,'* Vertex, vol. 14, no. 53 (2003), pp. 227–31.

that, without a uniform system of classification, a single reported disease entity might be described by three or four different commonly employed terms, and then each term might be applied to more than one disease state.

By the early 1850s, Farr had developed his own classification system, building upon Graunt's, that clustered all illnesses under one of five broad umbrellas: epidemic diseases, constitutional diseases, localized diseases arranged by anatomical site, developmental diseases, and conditions that were the result of trauma. At first, the goal of these efforts was to more accurately compile mortality statistics. Farr, though, realized that it was ultimately desirable "to extend the same system of nomenclature to diseases which, though not fatal, cause disability in the population and . . . [the] armies, navies, hospitals, prisons, lunatic asylums, public institutions of every kind, and sickness societies." Farr's work was championed by no less a figure than Florence Nightingale, who urged that Farr's classification system be adopted throughout medical circles in the United Kingdom.[20, 21]

~~~~~~~~~~~~~~~~~~~~~~~~~~~~~

Despite advances toward a modern, evidence-based approach, there were continued lapses into pseudoscience and quackery. An example would be the classification efforts of mental illnesses by means of phrenology. To understand this practice, one must turn the clock back centuries to a time when human anatomy was entirely mysterious and forbidden. The previously cited Galen produced in A.D. 100 a number of medical and anatomical works that were the standard for more than a millennium. His studies were rife with errors because the Romans outlawed human dissection. Thus, Galen's writings were based instead on his work with dead apes.[22] When the revered father of modern anatomy, Andreas Vesalius, set out to produce a more accurate reference in the sixteenth century, he is suspected of having used illicitly obtained human remains

---

20. STATISTICIANS OF THE CENTURIES (Dupaquier, Michel, et al. eds.). N.Y.: Springer-Verlag (2001), pp. 163–66.

21. *Id.*

22. *Available at* http://vesalius.northwestern.edu/essays/animalanatomy. html (retrieved April 3, 2011).

from graveyards and ossuaries, rather than animal carrion, to create his classic *De Humani Corporis Fabrica*.[23]

Vesalius may have been the most renowned grave robber, but he certainly was not the first, nor the last. In addition to a long history of pilfering for specimens, there are even known instances where agents were offered handsome payments to commit homicides to provide fresh bodies for anatomists. Communities often went so far as to post guards around graveyards to prevent "resurrectionists" from snatching corpses until such time that freshly interred bodies were decomposed past their useful shelf life. Yet the legal supply of bodies—usually made up of those executed for committing murder—represented a mere trickle.

An interesting statistic comes to us from 1825: in that year, anatomical schools in the British Isles dissected 592 corpses, but in that same year there were fewer than 60 court-ordered executions, illustrating quite a specimen gap.[24] And while it has not been expressly admitted, Harvard's medical school is said to have been located in Boston, away from the main Cambridge campus, for better access to the poorhouses and asylums and their potential bounty of unclaimed corpses.[25]

In the nineteenth century, laws were finally passed in both the United Kingdom and the United States that allowed individuals to donate their bodies to science. Unfortunately, if the demand for the stolen dead thus lessened, the practice of stealing bodies did not disappear, largely because a dead body at the turn of the twentieth century could still fetch over $35 on the black market.[26] As late as 1890, W.H. Wathen, dean of a medical school, told a reporter from the *Chicago Tribune*, "[t]he gentlemen [on a recent cemetery raid across the border in Indiana] were acting not for the Kentucky School of Medicine nor for themselves individually, but

---

23. O'MALLEY, C.D. ANDREAS VESALIUS OF BRUSSELS, 1514–1564. Berkeley, Cal.: Univ. of Cal. Press (1964), p. 19.

24. *Available at* http://www.executedtoday.com/category/where/scotland/ (retrieved July 3, 2011).

25. HEALTH LAW AND BIOETHICS (Johnson, Sandra, et al. eds.). N.Y.: Wolters Kluwer (2009), p. 147.

26. LARSON, ERIK. THE DEVIL IN THE WHITE CITY. N.Y.: Vintage Press (2004), p. 150.

for the medical schools of Louisville, to which the human subject
is as necessary as breath to life."[27] Just three weeks later, the stu-
dent-physicians of Louisville were at it again, attempting to rob a
grave at the State Asylum for the Insane in Anchorage, Kentucky.
"Yes, the party was sent out by us," a senior school official said.
"We must have bodies, and if the State won't give them to us we
must steal them. The winter classes were large and used up so
many [cadavers] that there are none for the spring classes." With
amazing moxie, the official added, "[t]he Asylum Cemetery has
been robbed for years, and I doubt if there is a corpse [left] in it. I
tell you we must have bodies. . . . If we can't get them any other
way we will arm the students with Winchester rifles and send them
to protect the body snatchers on their raids."[28]

Here at last is the convergence of stolen corpses and psychiatric
classification. One facet of anatomy that was apparent to
dissectionists throughout the centuries was the marked variations
of human body size and shape. Lacking a clear understanding of
disease causation, many clinicians fell back upon the notion that
there must be a predictable relationship between the outward appearance of an individual and inner traits and characteristics. Such
theories stretched back as far as Aristotle. This belief—known as
physiognomy—formed the basis of some nineteenth-century efforts
at psychiatric nosology. Some held that facial characteristics could
be diagnostic of mental illness.[29] In a related vein, Franz Gall championed the science he called cranioscopy, or phrenology, the belief
that the inner workings of the brain could be discerned by examining not merely the face, but the bumps and general contours of a
person's skull. This would have been laughable had phrenology
not attracted a number of prominent adherents, starting around 1800
in Vienna and gaining strength throughout Europe and in America
as the century progressed.[30]

Worse yet, becoming fully "proficient" at phrenology required
a supply of many variations of sample skulls, leading to a brisk

27. *Id.*, referencing the CHICAGO TRIBUNE, Feb. 27, 1890.
28. *Id.*, referencing the CHICAGO TRIBUNE, Mar. 24, 1890.
29. LYONS & PETRUCELLI, *supra* note 3, at p. 485.
30. DICKEY, COLIN. CRANIOKLEPTY: GRAVE ROBBING AND THE SEARCH FOR GENIUS.
Cave Creek: Unbridled Books (2009), p. 6.

business in recently buried human remains when grave robbing for general anatomical dissection purposes was on the wane. Especially targeted were those of renown or those with heads that were particularly interesting in appearance. Gall himself had a sizable collection of skulls, by some counts numbering well into the hundreds, almost all of which were obtained illicitly.[31] Perhaps most amazing, some very famous people of the day lost parts or all of their skulls to those wishing to study them to determine features that might indicate genius, criminality, or insanity; among those subsequently headless individuals were Josef Haydn, Francisco Goya, Emanuel Swedenborg, Sir Thomas Browne, Elizabeth Roose, Wolfgang Amadeus Mozart, and Ludwig von Beethoven.[32] While phrenology was eventually discredited as pseudoscience, it proved to be a macabre detour on the road to a truly scientific system of diagnosis and classification of mental conditions.

~~~~~~~~~~~~~~~~~~~~~~~~~~~~~~~

A meeting of the International Statistical Institute was convened in Chicago in 1893, and, given past failures, one is excused for expecting nothing new to have come from this gathering. However, at the conference was a French physician, Jacques Bertillon, who presented his own system built upon the anatomical approach espoused by Farr a generation earlier. The classification that Bertillon proposed later inspired the publication of the *International List of Causes of Death*. At the urging of prominent officials, the parameters of Bertillon's system were adopted by several international and municipal public health entities at the turn of the twentieth century.

At its annual meeting in 1898, the American Public Health Association recommended that Bertillon's system be reviewed, updated, and re-published at least once every decade.[33] Others agreed, and the French government convened the First International Conference for the Revision of the *International List of Causes of Death* in 1900. Twenty-six national delegations attended. The resulting

31. *Id.*, p. 30.

32. *Id.*, pp. 15, 16, 154, 184.

33. *Available at* http://www.who.int/classifications/icd/en/HistoryOfICD.pdf (retrieved May 28, 2011).

revised reference consisted of 179 distinct disease categories, including some that were primarily psychiatric. Consistency, however, did not occur overnight. Still there were efforts at promulgating separate diagnostic schema in the United States, which continued at the same time as, and in contradiction with, those promising efforts involving Bertillon's contributions.

The pressing need to understand and organize mental illnesses only increased. The slaughterhouse that was the Great War produced many psychiatric casualties, those suffering from what today we might call post-traumatic stress disorder, generalized anxiety, major depression, or even amnesia. Allied forces were dealing with damaged psyches on an unprecedented scale; for example, by the Armistice of 1918, one-seventh of all disability discharges from the British Army were for mental illness. Of 200,000 soldiers on the U.K. pension list after the war, 20 percent were classified as suffering from the ill-defined "war neurosis."[34] The breakdown of American casualties was similar. This influx of wounded served again as an impetus to adopt a better and more uniform psychiatric classification system.

Yet it remained elusive; one widely circulated American psychiatric textbook from the 1920s stated:

> Unfortunately, there are many systems of classification in use, most of them possessing certain advantages of their own. But the practical consequence is that the layman, who has no knowledge of the good reasons that exist for variations in the methods of classification, is misled into thinking that two alienists [i.e., psychiatrists] are not in accord, even when there is only a divergence in nomenclature.[35, 36]

With the entry of the United States into World War II in 1941, American psychiatrists once again faced a tremendous tide of mental health cases from both potential enlistees and wounded service

---

34. Hales, Robert & Jones, Franklin, *Military Combat Psychiatry: A Historical Review*, PSYCHIATRIC ANNALS, vol. 81, no. 17, Aug. 1987, p. 525.

35. SINGER, H.D. & KROHN, WILLIAM. INSANITY AND LAW, A TREATISE ON FORENSIC PSYCHIATRY. Phila.: Blakiston's Son & Co. (1924), p. 77.

36. *Id.*, p. 79.

members. "There [is] a need to account accurately for all causes of morbidity," claimed one period text, "hence the need for a suitable diagnosis for every case seen by the [armed forces] psychiatrist, a situation not faced in civilian life. Only about 10 percent of the total cases seen [fall] into any of the categories ordinarily seen in public mental hospitals. [Non-civilian] psychiatrists [find] themselves operating within the limits of a nomenclature specifically not designed for 90 percent of the cases handled."[37]

Unfortunately, persistent misperceptions of disease causation—and what conditions even constituted distinct pathology rather than aspects of other ailments—continued to hamper efforts at classification. For example, as late as 1944, E.D. Loewenstein, a prominent infectious disease researcher of the day, still maintained that schizophrenia was caused by tuberculosis bacteria lodging in the smallest blood vessels of the brain and central nervous system, a theory of causation long since disproven but which at that time still counted adherents.[38]

By the late 1940s in the United States, there were three primary psychiatric taxonomies in common usage—one for civilians, one in the military for active duty personnel, and one in the Veterans' Administration system.[39] At the same time, the newly created World Health Organization had assumed responsibility for the competing *Manual of the International Statistical Classification of Diseases, Injuries, and Causes of Death*, the incarnation of Bertillon's original efforts from the 1890s.[40]

Eschewing both Bertillon's classification system and the other competing efforts in the United States, a committee on nomenclature and statistics of the American Psychiatric Association (APA)

---

37. _____. DIAGNOSTIC AND STATISTICAL MANUAL [OF] MENTAL DISORDERS. Washington, D.C.: American Psychiatric Ass'n Mental Hospital Service (1952), p. vi [hereinafter referred to as DSM].

38. BELLAK, LEOPOLD. DEMENTIA PRAECOX. N.Y.: Grune & Stratton (1947), p. 39. The belief that tuberculosis contributed to the genesis of schizophrenia was a red herring due to the large, albeit unrelated, number of psychiatric patients in sanatoriums worldwide who were also TB-positive.

39. DSM, p. vii.

40. *Available at* http://www.who.int/classifications/icd/en/HistoryOfICD. pdf (retrieved May 25, 2011).

began developing a taxonomic reference specifically for use in the public sector. After many drafts and a vote of the membership, the result was the *Diagnostic and Statistical Manual* (*DSM*) in 1952, drawing in large part from U.S. Army references from World War II. The *DSM* foreword said, in part, "[t]he development of a uniform nomenclature of disease in the United States is comparatively recent. In the late [1920s], each large teaching center employed a system of its own origination, no one of which met more than the immediate needs of that local institution. . . . There resulted a polyglot of diagnostic labels and systems, effectively blocking communication and the collection of medical statistics."[41, 42]

The *DSM* is 132 pages long and lists 106 discrete mental conditions. Diagnostic categories include acute brain disorders (e.g., infections); chronic brain disorders (e.g., senility); mental deficiencies; psychotic disorders; psycho-physiologic disorders (e.g., hypochondriasis); neurotic disorders; personality disorders; and conditions that are transient and situational (e.g., drunkenness).[43] The *DSM* became the first widely promulgated manual of mental disorders to include a glossary of terminology, as well as an appendix illustrating how to segue old-fashioned diagnostic phrases into this new and previously un-encountered rubric.[44]

Reception to the *DSM* was generally favorable in the profession, and 16 years after what would prove to be the first of many editions, the American Psychiatric Association revised its *DSM,* creating the *DSM-II.* Though similar in many regards, *DSM-II* employed colloquial English more than had its predecessor, making it an easier read for those not medically or psychoanalytically trained. Though the task force on *DSM* stated at the time that "mental disorders are [in fact] a subset of medical disorders," it added that "each of the mental disorders [herein] is conceptualized as a clinically significant behavioral or psychological syndrome."[45] Paradoxically, many

---

41. DSM (I), p. v.
42. *Id.*
43. DSM (I), pp. 2–8.
44. DSM (I), p. 89.
45. Mayes, R. & Horwitz, A.V., *DSM-III and the Revolution in the Classification of Mental Illness,* J. OF THE HISTORY OF BEHAVIORAL SCIENCE, vol. 41, no. 3 (2005), pp. 249–67.

of the symptomatic elements of specific disorders in both *DSM* and *DSM-II* are vague, in part reflecting a continuing lack of hard empirical data and professional agreement.

This issue of an absence of empirical data is perhaps reflected best by the controversy surrounding *DSM-II* for which the work is arguably most remembered. Following heated demonstrations by gay rights activists at psychiatric conferences in the early 1970s, the sixth printing of *DSM-II* in 1974 suddenly dropped homosexuality from its list of mental disorders, instead choosing to employ a classification labeled "sexual orientation disturbance," one that applied only to individuals who were emotionally distressed by their sexuality, not the orientation per se.[46]

While many lamented what was viewed as the subjugation of dispassionate scientific analysis to special interests of the day, cultural controversies in medical labeling are actually nothing new. In the American South in the nineteenth century, there had once existed a diagnosis of drapetomania, from which slaves were said to suffer when they inexplicably wanted to run away to freedom![47] There was also an antebellum diagnosis of dysaethesia aethiopica, known alternatively as rascality, which was an apparent lack of work ethic ascribed by racist whites to free persons of color.[48] And historical precedents aside, the controversy over homosexuality was not to be the last time politicization charges would be leveled at the psychiatric profession; concerning sexual paraphilias (e.g., sado-masochism, exhibitionism, pedophilia), Dr. Robert Spitzer, chairman of two task forces on *DSM* revisions, argued against their removal from the index of mental disorders, *not on scientific grounds,* but by saying that "it would be a public relations disaster for psychiatry."[49]

---

46. _____. Homosexuality and Sexual Orientation Disturbance: Proposed Change in DSM-II, Dec. 1973, p. 44. Approved by the Board of Trustees of the American Psychiatric Association. APA Document Reference no. 730008.

47. Cartwright, Samuel. *Diseases and Peculiarities of the Negro Race*, DEBOW'S REVIEW—SOUTHERN AND WESTERN STATES, vol. XI (New Orleans, 1851) (reprinted by AMS Press, Inc., New York, 1967). *Available at* http://www.pbs.org/wgbh/aia/part4/4h3106t.html (retrieved Nov. 28, 2011).

48. *Id.*

49. Kleinplatz, P.J & Moser, C., *Politics versus Science: An Addendum and Response to Drs. Spitzer and Fink*, J. OF PSYCH. AND HUMAN SEXUALITY, vol. 17, no.

Throughout the 1960s and 1970s, there were continuing efforts to synchronize *DSM* nomenclature and coding with that of the *International Classification of Diseases*. Such coordination remained problematic, not only because two separate bodies worked on the respective references, but also because *DSM* usually classifies disorders by symptoms, while *ICD* tends more toward causation. In a related vein, the foreword of the 1968 *DSM-II* states that "in preparing [the *DSM-II*] the [American Psychiatric Association] committee had to make adjustments within a few of the *ICD* categories to make them conform better to U.S. usage. Decisions were also made regarding certain diagnoses that have not been generally accepted in U.S. psychiatry. Some of these diagnoses have been omitted here, while others have been included and qualified as controversial."[50] Critics felt that the APA's efforts to adjust to "U.S. usage" or delete diagnoses that had not been "generally accepted in U.S. psychiatry" gave the unmistakable appearance of cultural bias and regionalism.

The *DSM-II* contains 182 disorders in its 119 pages. There are diagnostic categories for mental retardation, psychotic and nonpsychotic organic brain syndromes, psychoses not attributable to physical conditions, psycho-physiologic disorders, neurotic disorders, and personality disorders. There is also an odd section titled "Certain Other Nonpsychotic Mental Disorders," representing an

---

3/4 (2005), pp. 135–39; *see also* Frances, Allen, *Solving the Problem of Questionable Diagnoses Grandfathered into DSM*, PSYCHIATRIC TIMES, Feb. 10, 2011, p. 16. And in fairness to "the other APA," the American Psychological Association advocated earlier than their psychiatric brethren for the removal of homosexuality from the diagnostic canon because of a lack of objective research to suggest that it was in fact a disorder. *See* Conger, J.J., *Minutes of the Annual Meeting of the Council of Representatives, Proceedings of the American Psychological Association for 1974*, AMERICAN PSYCHOLOGIST, no. 30 (1975), pp. 620–51.

50. _____. DSM, 2d ed. Washington, D.C., The Committee on Nomenclature and Statistics of the American Psychiatric Association (1968), p. viii. It is unfortunate that delving further into the authoring of both DSM and DSM-II is not now possible. The location of the papers of both task forces is unknown, and a collection of possibly related documents from the Office of the Medical Director of the APA of that era are inaccessible and represent "several hundred completely un-analyzed [and] un-processed boxes," according to an April 2010 email from the archivist of the APA.

unwieldy clumping of both homosexuality (at first) and various afflictions of chemical dependency.[51]

Work began on the *DSM-III* in 1974, will revisions were still being made to the later printings of the *DSM-II*. Efforts were redoubled to emphasize the science behind the process; Dr. Spitzer promised that the work would be "a defense of the medical model as applied to psychiatric problems." The president of the American Psychiatric Association, Jack Weinberg, M.D., went further, stating unequivocally that the book would "clarify to anyone who may be in doubt that we regard psychiatry as a specialty of medicine."[52] The foreword of the work even noted, "[t]he development of this manual over the past five years has not gone unnoticed; in fact, it is remarkable how much interest (alarm, despair, excitement, joy) has been shown in successive drafts of this document."[53]

The *DSM-III* was finally published in 1980, and it is significant for having the first classification system ostensibly based on objective clinical evidence rather than subjective practitioner consensus.[54] Terminology was once more adjusted, with quasi-psychoanalytic terms such as "neurosis" being placed in parentheses after terms thought to be more scientific, such as "disorder." Recognizing inherent shortcomings, however, the foreword of the *DSM-III* states that "although this manual provides a classification for mental disorders, there is no satisfactory definition that specifies precise boundaries for the concept of 'mental disorder'. . . . In [the] *DSM-III* there is no assumption that each mental disorder is a discrete entity with sharp boundaries between it and other mental disorders, as well as between it and no mental disorder."[55]

---

51. DSM-II, pp. 5–13.

52. *Available at* http://www.nybooks.com/articles/archives/2011/jul/14/illusions-of-psychiatry/?pagination=false (retrieved Dec. 14, 2011).

53. _____. Diagnostic and Statistical Manual of Mental Disorders, 3d ed. Washington, D.C.: American Psychiatric Association (1980), p. 1.

54. Csernansky, John. Schizophrenia: A New Guide for Clinicians. N.Y.: Marcel Dekker Inc. (2002), p. 31.

55. DSM-III, pp. 6–7. Perhaps one reason that blurred boundaries exist is because causation of mental illness remains elusive. As recently as 2005, both Drs. Robert Spitzer and Michael First suggested that "little progress has been made toward understanding the patho-physiological processes and etiology of

In 1987, only seven years after its initial appearance, a new version of the *DSM-III* was published, *DSM-III-R* (revised) instead of the logical *DSM-IV*. Categories in *DSM-III-R* were renamed, deleted, added, and shuffled, and some significant alterations in diagnostic criteria were seen. Many new diagnoses were proposed, but not all were approved for inclusion. As the requirements for inclusion of new categories had by then become more stringent, a paradox existed in that some of the proposed diagnoses that were ultimately rejected for *DSM-III-R* may have enjoyed more supporting clinical data than that available for many of the grandfathered diagnoses already in the *DSM* canon. This fact was not lost on *DSM* polemicists, some of whom argued that maintaining the status quo, even with less-stringently vetted diagnoses, was preferable to a rushed revision. Others held that in order to bolster the empirical foundation of the *DSM-III-R*, weeding must take place to reject questionable diagnoses and to dispel any notion that all diagnoses were created equally and deserved identical protection.[56]

Perhaps most telling, Dr. Spitzer later criticized his own task forces' efforts, claiming that both *DSM-III* and *DSM-III-R* led to the medicalization of up to 30 percent of the population, covering individuals who may not, in fact, have had any serious mental problems.[57] This statement was trumpeted by those who had been arguing for years that the pharmaceutical industry was encouraging such disease-mongering and trying to get more variants of normal turned into pathology so that medications could be developed and used to

---

mental disorders. If anything, the research has shown the situation is even more complex than initially imagined, and we believe not enough is known to structure [any] classification of psychiatric disorders according to etiology." *See* Spitzer, Robert & First, Michael, *Classification of Psychiatric Disorders*, J. OF THE AMERICAN MEDICAL ASS'N (Oct. 19, 2005), pp. 1898–99.

56. Frances, Allen, *Solving the Problem*; *see also* Phillips, James, *DSM-5: When to Change and When Not to Change*, PSYCHIATRIC TIMES, Jan. 25, 2011, p. 3, for an interesting discussion on whether pedophilia should be considered a psychiatric disorder or simply socially unacceptable behavior.

57. Curtis, Adam, interview of Dr. Robert Spitzer seen in the documentary "The Trap," part II (March 2007), beginning at 34:10. *Available at* http://www.archive.org/details/AdamCurtis_TheTrap (retrieved on Nov. 28, 2011).

combat those perceived illnesses.[58] A former president of the American Psychiatric Association, Steven Sharfstein, M.D., made a comment acknowledging that the process had "allowed the bio-psychosocial model to become the bio-bio-bio model."[59] In a journal article that appeared in 1984, George Vaillant, M.D., a professor of psychiatry at Harvard University, perhaps put it best when he stated that the *DSM-III* represented nothing more than "a bold series of choices based on guess[work], taste, prejudice, and hope."[60]

Such criticism didn't dissuade the *DSM* authors. In 494 pages, *DSM-III* totalled 265 distinct diagnoses. Then, in *DSM-III-R*, there were 292 diagnoses in more than 567 pages. Both works in sheer volume outstripped the relevant sections of the *International Classification of Diseases*. For example, whereas in the ninth edition of the *ICD* there was one category to encompass all of "frigidity and impotence," in the *DSM-III-R* there were headings for seemingly overlapping conditions, including hypoactive sexual desire disorder, sexual aversion disorder, female sexual arousal disorder, male erectile disorder, inhibited female orgasm, inhibited male orgasm, premature ejaculation, dyspareunia, vaginismus, and sexual dysfunction not otherwise specified.[61]

The *DSM-IV* arrived in 1994. It was the outgrowth of more than six years of effort involving an exhaustive review of empirical data and published literature, the input of more than 1,000 clinicians and a dozen workgroups and subcommittees, scores of advisors and consultants, and numerous professional societies and organizations (and, for the first time, a team of allied psychologists). *DSM-IV* represented the largest effort of its kind up to that point. Again

---

58. *See* Frances, Allen, *Drug Companies Peddle Female Sexual Dysfunction*, PSYCHIATRIC TIMES, Feb. 14, 2011, p. 9. Questionably valid surveys have suggested that up to half of American females may "suffer" from "Female Sexual Dysfunction," which for many people is arguably nothing more than normal variations in sex drive with aging. However, this has not prevented the pharmaceutical industry from considering if medication options may exist for this imaginary epidemic.

59. Sharfstein, S., *Big Pharma and American Psychiatry: The Good, the Bad, and the Ugly*, PSYCHIATRIC NEWS, vol. 40, no. 16, Aug. 19, 2005, p. 4.

60. *Available at* http://www.nybooks.com/articles/archives/2011/jul/14/illusions-of-psychiatry/?pagination=false (retrieved Dec. 4, 2011).

61. Mayes & Horwitz, *supra* note 45.

disorders were added, deleted, and reorganized. But those wishing to employ the book for diagnostic, clinical, research, or administrative purposes from any discipline were sternly cautioned in the text that appropriate use of the reference parameters required extensive clinical training and "cannot simply be applied in a cookbook fashion."[62] And interestingly, though it took until the publication of the *DSM-IV*, the obvious is again stated, if without fanfare: "there is no assumption that each category of mental disorder is a completely discrete entity with absolute boundaries."[63]

The target audience for the *DSM*s expanded as well. While originally aimed at psychiatrists, later *DSM*s grudgingly stipulated that anyone with "appropriate clinical training and experience" can render a *DSM* diagnosis. Nowhere is it stated that four years of medical school and later residency must be completed, even though many of the diagnostic categories were then, and are still, laced with medical considerations.[64] Increasingly, the *DSM*s became the reference of first resort for insurance companies, hospital administrators, courts, prisons, government agencies, the medical world at large, and the general public. Factoring in this expanding status, the 1995 edtion of the *DSM-IV* appeared in a corollary version titled *DSM-IV-PC* (primary care), a recognition that nonpsychiatric health-care providers in the community see as much, if not more, mental illness than do psychiatrists. The *DSM-IV-PC* lists those disorders that are most likely encountered in a family practice setting, presented by means of nine basic algorithms (depressed mood, anxiety, unexplained physical symptoms, cognitive disturbances, problematic substance use, sexual dysfunction, sleep disorders, weight change and eating problems, and psychotic symptoms). These algorithms employ language that is easier to understand, and they are additionally populated by clustering symptoms that commonly present together.[65]

---

62. _____. DIAGNOSTIC AND STATISTICAL MANUAL OF MENTAL DISORDERS, 4th ed. Washington, D.C.: American Psychiatric Association (1994), p. xxxii.

63. *Id.*

64. _____. DIAGNOSTIC AND STATISTICAL MANUAL OF MENTAL DISORDERS, 4th ed., text revision. Washington, D.C.: American Psychiatric Association (2000), p. xxxii.

65. _____. DIAGNOSTIC AND STATISTICAL MANUAL OF MENTAL DISORDERS, 4th edition, primary care. Washington, D.C.: American Psychiatric Association (1995), pp. 8–27.

In 2000, yet another iteration of the *DSM* was published. As was the case with *DSM-III* and *DSM-III-R*, the new release could have been titled *DSM-V*, but was instead labeled *DSM-IV-TR* (text revision). Both releases were huge; *DSM-IV* tops out at 297 disorders listed over 886 pages, while *DSM-IV-TR* ballooned to 365 disorders over a whopping 943 pages. However, the oft-stated goal of synchronizing the contents with the *ICD* remains unfulfilled. This is all the more strange when one realizes that Medicare, Medicaid, and other third-party payers currently require modified *ICD-9* codes for purposes of documentation and reimbursement.[66]

Furthermore, there are still frequent complaints that the *DSM* as presently structured, despite its size, lacks reliability because there remains too much room for subjective clinical input. Such a view is bolstered by oft-repeated anecdotes that, within the last several generations, mental health practitioners have been far more likely to diagnose minority patients at state hospitals with schizophrenia, while white patients suffering from similar symptoms have been documented as having manic-depressive disorder. The arbitrary boundaries between conditions and between pathology and normalcy can be powerful if not carefully monitored and judiciously applied.[67] This is further complicated by the near-constant rearrangements, deletions, and additions to the *DSM*. And meta-analyses suggest that attempts to demonstrate "natural boundaries" between related *DSM* syndromes, or between a *DSM* syndrome and a perceived normal state, have repeatedly fallen short. All of these problems in organizing material suggest that the complaints have some merit.[68]

In another issue relating to suspected diagnostic artifice, criticisms have been directed at the cultural component of modern psychiatric practice, as many hold that the *DSM* publications promulgate

---

66. Rubenstein, Sarah, *Feds Delay ICD-10 for Two Years*, WALL ST. J., Jan. 15, 2009, p. 11.

67. CARLAT, DANIEL. UNHINGED: THE TROUBLE WITH PSYCHIATRY—A DOCTOR'S REVELATIONS ABOUT A PROFESSION IN CRISIS. N.Y.: Free Press (2010), pp. 54 and 140.

68. Dalal, P.K. & Sivakumar, T., *Moving Towards ICD-11 and DSM-5: Concept and Evolution of Psychiatric Classification*, INDIAN J. OF PSYCHIATRY, vol. 51, no. 4 (2009), pp. 310–19.

an orientation that is decidedly Western European and North American to the exclusion of all else. Opponents of this Euro-Americentric approach are frustrated about the large number of non-Western psychiatric conditions that have been left out of the *DSM*s and relegated to footnotes and appendices (Amok, Ataque de Nervios, Boufee Delirante, Dhat, Hwa-Byung, Koro, Latah, Locura, Mal de Ojo, Pibloktoq, Qi-Gong, Rootwork, Sangue Dormido, Shenkui, Susto, Taijin Kyofusho, and Zar are all said to be mental states arising in non-Western societies).[69] Others hold that culture-specific diagnoses are nothing more than a nod to political correctness, are rarely used in day-to-day practice, and have little objective evidence to support their unique existence or need for inclusion.

Keep in mind, too, that the near-constant expansion of *DSM* diagnoses and diagnostic criteria can produce many other unintended consequences. Take, for example, the situation surrounding Asperger's syndrome. Prior to 1994, there was no separate *DSM* entry for Asperger's (the social isolation and eccentricities that are thought to represent a less devastating form of autism). There was an entry for autism, but it dealt with those individuals suffering from the most severe symptoms. Some doctors as far back as the 1940s had suggested that a milder version of autism was being seen clinically, but didn't fit the diagnostic criteria then in use. A few studies supported this assertion. Dr. Allen Frances then guided Asperger's through the editorial process, and it was included in *DSM-IV*. Predictably, the number of adolescents being thus labeled markedly increased in subsequent years. Articles began to appear that discussed the "new epidemic" of Asperger's that was sweeping the nation. Frances has been asked about this, and while he continues to espouse that the disease state exists, he has also acknowledged that the diagnosis is now being used in expansive ways never originally intended. When asked to elaborate, Frances has suggested that many children and adolescents who were previously deemed socially awkward but otherwise doing adequately well in school can now be given the diagnosis of Asperger's Syndrome, at which time "[they] get into a special program where they may get $50,000

---

69. Kleinman, A., *Triumph or Pyrrhic Victory? The Inclusion of Culture in DSM-IV*, HARVARD REVIEW OF PSYCHIATRY, vol. 6, no. 4 (1997), pp. 343–44; *see also* DSM-IV-TR, p. 902.

a year worth of educational services."[70] Advocacy groups are en-
raged at this suggestion, and they counter that the diagnosis is being seen more today because of increased awareness and decreased
social stigma and that the change in diagnostic criteria is reflective
of awareness, and not causative in and of itself.[71]

Another example of unintended consequences appeared in the
New York Times in December 2010. An article stated that over the
previous decade, more college students in the United States were
being diagnosed with mental illnesses. The incidence of psychiatric disorders among those seen by university mental health services
was once approximately 16 percent of all enrolled students, and
more recently it had been noted near 44 percent. In 2000, 17 percent of college students were prescribed psychotropic medications
nationwide, but by 2010 that figure had risen to 24 percent. The
Times article suggested that perhaps newer medications have allowed those with more severe symptoms to attend college, or that
the mental health staff serving students are doing a better job of
recognizing conditions that once festered just below the surface.
Without solid data to support either contention, there is a much more
plausible third option: overdiagnosis. As noted in an op-ed piece in
the *Psychiatric Times*, "[p]sychiatric illness is elusive and difficult
to define and there are no biologically-based laboratory tests. The
presence or absence of any given mental disorder is determined by
a checklist of symptoms establishing thresholds that are necessarily
to some extent fallible and arbitrary. Requiring the presence of six
symptoms rather than five (or a duration of four weeks rather than
two) can dramatically change the rates of a disorder, . . . who gets
diagnosed as ill, [and] who is considered normal."[72]

---

70. Spiegel, Alix, *What's a Mental Disorder? Even Experts Can't Agree*,
on "All Things Considered," National Public Radio (Dec. 29, 2010). *Available at* http://www.npr.org/2010/12/29/132407384/whats-a-mental-disorder-
even-experts-cant-agree (retrieved on Nov. 28, 2011).

71. Schneider, Sarah, *Allen Frances Gave Us the Asperger's 'Epidemic'
Just Like Al Gore Gave Us the Internet*, SHIFT JOURNAL, Jan. 6, 2011, *available
at* http://www.shiftjournal.com (retrieved on Aug. 29, 2011).

72. Frances, Allen, *Are College Students Getting Sicker? No, Diagnoses
Change Faster Than People*, PSYCHIATRIC TIMES, Jan. 11, 2011, p. 12.

Having quickly summarized almost 3,000 years of Western efforts to understand and codify the possible dysfunctions of the 100 billion nerve cells that compose the human brain,[73] we have finally reached the end of this long journey.

Well, not exactly. . . .

The new *DSM-5* is to be published in May 2013 (note the unexplained official change from Roman to Arabic numeration). A task force has been laboring at this endeavor now for several years, and there is already concern that the deadline may not be met. The project espouses some noble goals, most notably that *DSM-5* workgroups must find ways to better deal with co-occurring symptoms and vague diagnostic criteria. Predictably, drafts that have been informally floated among professional communities generated a lot of controversy. It is impossible to pick up a professional journal and not see an op-ed piece on this subject. Even some psychiatrists and academicians who have been involved in the drafting process have criticized the work product and the relative secrecy and lack of empirical foundation that is perceived in its genesis.[74]

Before one assumes that all *DSM-5* critics are anti-psychiatry, be aware that in the March 2011 issue of the *Psychiatric Times*, an editorial by Dr. Frances himself refutes efforts by those intent on using his regular critiques to support attacks on the profession. Dr. Frances stated firmly in that column that his criticisms of diagnostic inflation reflect concern that psychiatry may have strayed across its boundaries, resulting in too much diagnosis and treatment of those

---

73. CARLAT, *supra* note 67, at p. 75.

74. Frances, Allen, *DSM-5 Badly Off Track*, PSYCHIATRIC TIMES, June 26, 2009, p. 5; *see also* Schatzberg, Alan, et al., *American Psychiatric Association Response to Frances Commentary on DSM-5*, PSYCHIATRIC TIMES, June 29, 2009, p. 8; *see also* Granados, Alex, and Stasio, Frank, *Defining Mental Health*, on "The State of Things," National Public Radio, Feb. 24, 2011, in which it is noted that up to 10% of the American Psychiatric Association's annual budget comes from sales of the DSM, and that suggestions that the profession should delay the next edition until more supporting clinical data is available is not met with much enthusiasm. *Available at* http://wunc.org/tsot/archive/sot022411B.mp3/view (retrieved on March 4, 2011).

not actually ill. His critiques, he maintained, should not be construed as a wholesale condemnation of the discipline.[75]

Whether accurate or not, charges of diagnostic inflation and the accompanying secrecy have been directed at the *DSM-5* process for years, once more raising the specter of bias, preference, and politicization. While it is impossible to know for certain at this juncture what will be contained in the final manuscript that goes to print, rough drafts that have been circulated show a mixture of relatively noncontroversial changes accompanied by some that are raising eyebrows.

In conclusion, here is a list of some of the more perplexing proposals that have been floated to date. Many fear that these categories, and others like them, reflect conditions that are either very common in the general population or else represent the dilution of diagnostic criteria for determining existing disorders. Either way, if adopted, such revisions will almost certainly result in more people being given psychiatric diagnoses.[76]

☑ **Addiction Disorders.** Some drafts have recommended eliminating the distinction between substance abuse and substance dependence (i.e., the line between episodic misuse and physiologic habituation and withdrawal). Instead, there would be a newly unified category for both "abuse" and "dependence," called "addiction." If approved, this would serve only to eliminate the valuable clinical line between those who intermittently binge and those who experience continuous compulsive abuse with physiologic and psychological dependence.

---

75. Frances, Allen, *Defending Psychiatry from Reckless Attacks*, PSYCHIATRIC TIMES, March 31, 2011, p. 1.

76. Frances, Allen, *Opening Pandora's Box: The 19 Worst Suggestions for DSM-5*, PSYCHIATRIC TIMES, Feb. 11, 2010; *see also* website of the APA regarding DSM-5 at http://www.dsm5.org; Marin, R.S., *Apathy:Neuropsychiatric Syndrome*, J. OF NEUROPSYCHIATRY AND CLINICAL NEUROSCIENCE, no. 3, 1991, pp. 243–54; Granados & Stasio, *supra* note 74, where it is posited that fewer than 40% of those who may be diagnosed with Psychosis Risk Syndrome might eventually develop a diagnosable psychotic disorder.

☑ **Apathy Syndrome.** This proposed diagnostic category potentially shares signs and symptoms with major depression. The gray zone here seems very large indeed. Additionally, there are no interventions indicated for this condition, so treatment modalities would likely be those already widely and commonly used for depressive states and personality disorders.

☑ **Attention Deficit Disorder.** The first proposed change to this entity has been to allow the diagnosis to be given based solely on the presence of enumerated symptoms, and not on the requisite impairment or clinical significance that is now listed in *DSM-IV-TR*. This new policy would result in a larger gray zone. A second proposal has been to reduce by almost half the number of symptoms that are required to diagnose ADD in adults. Many of the seemingly nonspecific symptoms that lead to a diagnosis of adult ADD have overlapped with other conditions or with variants of what could easily be considered normalcy. How many individuals—especially those in dead-end, unfulfilling jobs in the age of downsizing—have not felt restless and distracted in the workplace? It is highly debatable if a need exists for decreasing the threshold of diagnosis for a condition that may not even be a disorder. Specificity of diagnosis would be reduced, and many more false positives would result.

☑ **Autism Spectrum Disorder.** Asperger's Syndrome would disappear as a separate heading and instead would be collapsed into this newly reunified category. At first, given the controversy over the expansion of Asperger's, this consolidation might appear beneficial. However, some have argued that a return to the days when a single diagnosis was used to describe all individuals with autism-type symptoms, regardless of degree of impairment, will unnecessarily stigmatize those with a less-debilitating degree of affliction. It is felt that this change might again fuel an epidemic of those with loosely defined symptoms that suggest autism but vary widely in severity.[77]

---

77. McQueen, M.P., *Health Costs: More Autism Coverage*, WALL ST. J., March 6, 2011, p. B-8.

☑ **Behavioral Addictions.** It doesn't take a mental health professional to see where this might lead. Next in line could easily be a generalized Internet addiction. Then recall the number of celebrities and other public figures who, once caught in embarrassing illicit liaisons, perform the expected mea culpa through the media and admit themselves to inpatient treatment for so-called sex addiction. The slippery slope to BlackBerry and email addiction, shopping addiction, shoe addiction, workplace addiction, video game addiction, Facebook addiction, and many other addictions is easy to imagine, especially if a meaningless "not otherwise specified" catch-all is applied. Many of these behaviors are in reality (damaging) lifestyle choices, and turning such choices into diagnosable pathology would present those with little or no self-discipline with a ready-made excuse for such indulgences. It would be only a matter of time until such ill-conceived diagnoses found their way into forensic settings.

☑ **Binge-Eating Disorder.** Classifications currently exist that address those who suffer with eating disorders. However, some clinicians and researchers have held that a new diagnostic category such as this would have a rate of prevalence in the general population approaching 6 percent. This percentage could easily increase if the diagnosis were to become trendy. Those (millions of) individuals who "binge eat" once a week for three months would suddenly find themselves with a mental disorder.

☑ **Complicated Prolonged Grief Reaction.** *DSM-5* changes may allow for those grieving a death and subsequently experiencing decreased interest in previously pleasurable activities, crying spells, sleep and appetite disturbances, and decreased concentration to have a diagnosable mental disorder. Imagine losing a loved one and *not* potentially having this sort of reaction to the loss. That is not to say that those who are experiencing grief may not require outside assistance and support. Instead, because of the tremendous variation in individual coping, a change such as this promises to turn grief into pathology and to elevate the number of mental illness false positives. The pharmaceutical industry would be close behind.

☑ **Generalized Anxiety Disorder (GAD).** It has been proposed that the necessary time frame for this diagnosis be decreased from the current six months to three months. It has also been proposed that associated symptoms necessary for the diagnosis be changed from the current three out of six to a less stringent one out of four. There are no data currently available to tell how much the incidence of GAD would rise if these changes are approved, but it seems inarguable that rates would increase. Keep in mind that the symptoms of GAD are already nonspecific and very common in the general population, since they merge imperceptibly into the expectable worries of everyday life and the normal reactions to common stressors.[78]

☑ **Hypersexuality Disorder.** Pick up any women's magazine (or, increasingly, any men's magazine) and one will notice that the quality of sexual relations—what is too much, what is too little, what is "normal"—continues to generate countless articles. There is no satiating the prurient interests of the public to know how they stack up in the bedroom against their neighbors. *DSM-5* may provide commentary on this issue, even though no study has identified an "ideal" frequency regarding intercourse. This proposed diagnosis would nicely segue with the gift to the excuse-seekers found in the behavior addictions section above. It would also present a forensic accident-waiting-to-happen.

☑ **Male-to-Eunuch Gender Identity Disorder.** This would include those individuals who seek castration because they feel they are neither male nor female. It is unknown how prevalent this state may be in the general population, and including this condition without more clinical data seems rushed and ill-advised.

☑ **Minor Neurocognitive Disorder.** This proposed diagnostic category is notable because its elements are premised on

78. Frances, Allen, *DSM-5 Will Medicalize Everyday Worries into Generalized Anxiety Disorder*, PSYCHIATRIC TIMES, April 11, 2011, p. 19.

nonspecific symptoms of reduced cognitive performance that are common (some would say ubiquitous) in people 50 and older. In the hopes of preventing a blossoming of false positives, a proposal has been made to require cognitive testing to confirm that the individual, in fact, does have decreased cognitive abilities. The problem arises in trying to determine a meaningful reference point (an especially thorny problem given the allegations that have already been leveled at the *DSM*s for having fuzzy diagnostic boundaries).

☑ **Mixed Anxiety Depressive Disorder.** This category would ultimately identify nonspecific findings that are highly prevalent in the general population. It could become one of the most widely employed diagnoses in any future editions of the *DSM*. It could well yield another epidemic of mental affliction, becoming a tempting target for pharmaceutical marketers in the process. Some recent studies have questioned the efficacy of antidepressants for conditions other than severe major depression (more on this later), and the placebo effect for those in this diagnostic category could be quite high.

☑ **Paraphilic Coercive Disorder.** This proposal would serve little more than to expand the potential pool of sex offenders who would then be eligible for indefinite civil commitment and "treatment" because they have a "mental disorder." Like a bad check bouncing, this condition was first proposed for inclusion in *DSM-III-R* under the label of "paraphilic rapism"; it was ultimately rejected the first time around because of the difficulty of differentiating in any reliable manner between rapists whose actions are the result of a paraphilia (an obsession with an unusual sex practice) and rapists who are motivated by other factors, such as power and control, misogyny, and anger. Given the propensity of sociopaths to deceive (in this case, regarding sexual fantasies), coupled with the lack of any reliable objective parameters, the diagnosis would have to be based on behavior combined with subjective claims that would be nigh impossible to refute.

☑ **Parental Alienation Disorder.** This is a term coined in the early 1980s to describe the condition of a child or adolescent who constantly belittles and insults one or both parents without justification or apparent provocation. Originally seen—little wonder!—in the context of child custody disputes, it has never been a part of the official legal or medical lexicon, and with good reason. Existing diagnoses, such as oppositional defiant disorder, conduct disorder, or even adjustment disorder, can describe this phenomenon when it is encountered without the need for additional and meaningless diagnostic codes.

☑ **Pedohebephilia.** This may take the prize for the most poorly written and unworkable of all of the diagnostic proposals for *DSM-5*. It is postulated that this condition could expand the definition of pedophilia to include pubescent teenagers. The continued misuse of diagnoses by some lawyers and the courts would predictably follow. Make no mistake, sexual interactions with underaged individuals should be discouraged as a matter of decency and public policy. This end, however, should be accomplished by adult or juvenile criminal adjudication and sentencing that reflect the seriousness of the offense, not by reliance on psychiatric diagnosis and fiat.

☑ **Personality Disorders.** It has been proposed that five currently employed personality disorders be eliminated from the *DSM-5*: the paranoid, the narcissistic, the histrionic, the dependent, and the schizoid. All are well known and time tested clinically within mental health circles. The taxonomic replacements for these disorders remain to be seen.

☑ **Psychosis Risk Syndrome.** This is a worrisome diagnostic proposal. It would result in labeling those deemed *at risk* for developing a disease before symptoms of the disease actually occur, if they occur at all. False positives would be high. Many more individuals would wind up taking antipsychotics preemptively, with all of the risks inherent with use of that particular class of medication.

☑ **Seasonal Affective Disorder.** This is a "disorder" that has worked itself into the public consciousness, and yet it has never been a part of the *DSM* canon. While some individuals experience a subjective increase in depressive symptoms as the light of day gets shorter and the nights get longer, the problem is that the net that this diagnosis potentially casts (capturing those with winter blahs and cabin fever) would likely be very wide indeed, especially when the situational disappointments and sadness around the winter holidays are factored into the equation.

☑ **Suicide Disorder.** This represents a noble but possibly misguided stand-alone diagnosis. It is suggested that anyone with at least one suicide attempt within the past 12 months would qualify (though defining what constitutes a suicide attempt might prove tricky as well). At present, suicidality is reflected as an aspect of other disorders, such as major depression, bipolar disorder, borderline personality disorder, and schizophrenia. Proponents of this stand-alone approach maintain that such a designation would put practitioners on notice that a person may be at elevated risk. Those opposed to additional (and possibly redundant) diagnostic categories maintain that good documentation will reflect this aspect of presentation without need for additional diagnostic categories.[79]

☑ **Temper Dysregulation Disorder.** There is concern in psychiatric circles in recent years over the number of children who are being given bipolar disorder diagnoses, and this proposed classification is an apparent attempt to cut down on the overuse of the bipolar designation. Unfortunately, there do not appear to be any signs or symptoms of dysregulation that are unique to this supposed entity. What in effect might occur is increased medicalization of childhood, adolescent, and even adult temper tantrums. It is hard to see how this diagnosis would avoid becoming widely identified in just about every age group in the population.

---

79. Otto, M.A., *DSM Workgroup Examines Proposed Separate Diagnosis for Suicide Disorder*, CLINICAL PSYCHIATRY NEWS, April 22, 2011, p. 5, referencing observations published earlier in the AMERICAN JOURNAL OF PSYCHIATRY (2002; 159:1746–51) and the BRITISH JOURNAL OF PSYCHIATRY (1998; 173:531–5).

Use of medication would potentially ensue, along with all the risks attendant to that treatment option. Misapplication of the diagnosis would also provide a much-desired blanket excuse and discourage personal accountability for all manner of inappropriate behaviors.

Take-Home Pearls

- Beginning in the unrecorded past, mental illness was cloaked in superstition and mythology, and up until the late 1940s there was no unified and universally accepted nosology in the United States regarding mental illnesses.
- Created by the American Psychiatric Association, the *DSM* was designed to help psychiatrists, but it is now used by a number of allied professionals, including those with no formal training in mental health (e.g., administrators and insurance executives). Despite the admonition by earlier *DSM* task forces that the work not be used in cookbook fashion, that is, in many cases, exactly what is occurring.
- While quality improvement is desirable in theory, "improvements" in the *DSM* series have arguably been sporadic, stemming from a sense of urgency often felt in the psychiatric profession to do something rather than do nothing.
- The number of identified *DSM* diagnoses has increased by more than 300 percent (from 106 diagnoses in the *DSM* to 365 diagnoses in the *DSM-IV-TR*). This explosion of diagnostic criteria, simultaneously precise and vague, has allowed new and relatively untested categories into the psychiatric canon, expanding the numbers of those who are deemed to be suffering from a mental disorder. Despite advances in neuroscience, psychiatry continues to rely on a diagnostic system defined by behavioral syndromes as opposed to one based on knowledge of etiology and pathophysiology.

- Politics unfortunately has played a role in past editions of the *DSM*, with social agendas butting against dispassionate examination of the human condition.
- Some in the field have posited that "our diagnoses are subjective and expandable." This allows us to loosen parameters and create new diagnoses in ways that would be impossible in other fields of medicine.
- The future role—and unintended consequences—of *DSM* revisions remain uncertain. This is especially true in regard to the growth in diagnosable states; the symbiotic relationship between new and revised diagnoses and pharmaceuticals, the courts, and third-party payers; and efforts to synchronize fully with the *International Classification of Diseases*.

Chapter 3

Pursuing the Diagnosis

> The mental health professions have a track record of advancing diagnostic categories that lack clear underlying unity based on scientific evidence, but that, nonetheless, have the effect of responding to popular needs and aggrandizing the power and authority of mental health professionals.
>
> —Eric Dean[1]
>
> For every complex question, there is an answer which is clear, simple, and wrong.
>
> —H.L. Mencken[2]

According to the American Medical Association, in 2006 there were 633,000 actively employed physicians in the United States. Of that number, slightly more than 5 percent, or roughly 32,000 individuals, identified themselves as psychiatrists.[3] As with most specialties, though, the ranks of psychiatry are not uniformly distributed nationwide. There is a noticeable trend of many specialists congregating in non-rural areas and at large academic or tertiary-care medi-

---

1. DEAN, ERIC. SHOOK OVER HELL: POST-TRAUMATIC STRESS, VIETNAM, AND THE CIVIL WAR. Cambridge: Harvard University Press (1997), p. 1.

2. *Available at* http://www.qotd.org/ (retrieved on Nov. 28, 2011).

3. _____. PHYSICIAN CHARACTERISTICS AND DISTRIBUTION IN THE UNITED STATES. American Medical Ass'n (2007), *available at* http://www.bls.gov/oco/ocos074.htm (retrieved on May 4, 2011).

cal centers, leaving other swaths of the country relatively underserved. Even so, unforeseen emergencies occur without concern for available resources, and psychiatric problems obviously can and do arise in locations and at times when a psychiatrist is not available.

Furthermore, as most nonpsychiatric physicians already know, a considerable degree of co-morbidity exists between psychiatric and physical illnesses; patients may come to the office with one set of complaints, only to have other issues arise during evaluation. For this reason, a working familiarity with aspects of mental health, and how to competently manage scenarios in which they present, is crucial to all providers. This theme of working familiarity should be stressed to students and practitioners of both medicine and law.

So before we proceed in the discussion of specific disease entities, just how *does* one arrive at a psychiatric diagnosis in the first place?

Despite what numerous nonpsychiatrists may think, arriving at diagnoses is not achieved by divination that can be surreptitiously performed, like mind reading, while the unassuming subject chats at a cocktail party (though certainly hints of psyche can be revealed in any setting). Many laypersons believe that a psychiatrist is "analyzing" them while merely exchanging social pleasantries. If only it were that easy! Instead, a psychiatric diagnosis is determined by employing an organized approach that requires the study of all available information, both subjective and objective. The imperfections of the *DSM*s notwithstanding, diagnosing can at times be a cookbook process, albeit one requiring considerable attention to detail. This process becomes second nature to a clinician after having done it a few hundred times.

A thorough psychiatric evaluation, possibly resulting in a *DSM* diagnosis, begins with an interview. Psychiatric interviews can be insight-oriented, symptom-oriented, or a combination of the two; focusing on symptoms is probably more commonly employed at first, as *DSM*s deal with symptoms. A more analytic and insight-oriented approach can be utilized later, once the clinician has a general feel for what is ongoing.[4]

---

4. Othmer, E. & Othmer, S. The Clinical Interview Using DSM-IV-TR: Fundamentals, vol. 1. Washington, D.C.: American Psychiatric Publishing, Inc. (2002), p. 14.

In either event, the evaluation process, starting with the interview, should include the following elements:

History of the Current Symptoms

Also known as History of Present Illness, or HPI, this is an examination of why a person has decided to see a clinician. Is the person in distress? If so, for how long has the distress been present, and under what circumstances? Is the person seeking help of her own free accord, or at the urging of another? Is the subject under a court order? The more one digs, the more one may find complicating issues that are not initially readily apparent. The reader might be surprised to learn just how many times pending legal charges are discovered when the digging commences, and, naturally, those seeking a clinician under the threat of court action sometimes present in a manner not wholly dispassionate.

When possible, the clinician should record exact quotes from the person being evaluated. This is not yet the time and place to analyze, but merely to document. At this stage in the process, one is collecting data, and this first part of gathering information will direct the clinician on how to conduct the balance of the investigation.

Past Medical History

Psychiatry may be the red-headed stepchild of medicine, but that does not negate the familial relationship. Having worked in the past as a community psychiatrist in an underserved region in Appalachia, I can attest that many times one uncovers previously unknown, or undertreated, medical conditions while performing a psychiatric evaluation. Some conditions might impact the mental health of patients and some apparently do not, but in either event it is imperative for psychiatry to remain true to its medical roots.

During the gathering of the past medical history, or PMH, the psychiatrist asks about former and current medications, past surgeries, past medical hospitalizations, the presence of allergies and intolerances to any substances, and whether home remedies have been attempted or are still being used. Many people take herbs and roots and other over-the-counter supplements that they do not reveal as part of their medical history unless specifically asked. The information from this section will also guide the organic work-up (labs) that will be ordered.

Past Psychiatric History

In the past psychiatric history, or PPH, the clinician inquires about visits to community mental health centers, cultural or spiritual providers, and inpatient psychiatric units. The clinician also asks about treatment for conditions that are related to mental health but that might have been provided by family practitioners, OB-GYNs, physician extenders, or practitioners of pain management or alternative medicine. It is vital at this juncture also to inquire about previous thoughts of doing harm to oneself or others, or actual attempts. Not all thoughts or acts of violence prove the presence of a mental illness, but where there is smoke, there is often fire.

Another important aspect of past presentation involves previous emergency department visits. In 2005, there were more than 115 million emergency visits in the United States, and while the number of individuals in that year whose primary complaint involved mental health is estimated to have constituted less than 4 percent of the total, the ranks of those who come to an emergency department for psychiatric reasons, in both relative and absolute terms, are increasing.[5] In one study of visits to an emergency department for any reason in a given 12-month period, the prevalence of symptoms suggestive of a psychiatric disorder was found to be 26 percent, whether or not the person went specifically for that reason. And of that 26 percent, more than half had symptoms potentially diagnostic of a single psychiatric disorder, while more

---

5. Kunen, Seth & Stamps, Leighton, *Psychiatric Comorbidity in Emergency Department Patients: Why Is It Being Missed by ED Physicians?*, PSYCHIATRIC TIMES, vol. 25, no. 12, Oct. 1, 2008, p. 11; *see also* STEFAN, SUSAN, *Emergency Department Assessment of Psychiatric Patients: Reducing Inappropriate Inpatient Admissions*, MEDSCAPE. *Available at* http://www.medscape.com/viewarticle/541478 (retrieved on July 17, 2011); *see also* Dhossche, Dirk, *Suicidal Behavior in Psychiatric Emergency Room Patients*, SOUTHERN MEDICAL JOURNAL, March 1, 2000. *Available at* http://www.medscape.com/viewarticle/410512 (retrieved on July 17, 2011).

than a third had symptoms potentially diagnostic of two or more psychiatric disorders.[6] Thus, the history of emergency department visits is a key area to look for pertinent information that is often forgotten or intentionally omitted when the clinician merely asks, "Why are you here?"

Psychosocial and Family History

This part of the information gathering delves into developmental milestones of the person being evaluated, along with notable findings regarding family members. Does the person have siblings, and if so, do any of them suffer from medical or psychiatric illnesses? Was abuse of any sort present in the household while growing up? Was the family intact? Were caretakers transient during formative years? Was substance abuse ongoing? What was the background of the person's parents, children, and other biological relatives? Were friends made (and kept) easily while growing up? Was there any known history of fire-setting, prolonged bedwetting, vandalism, or cruelty to animals? Has the person been employed, and if so, have symptoms interfered with functioning in the workplace or led to the loss of employment?

This line of questioning can yield pertinent information. During my residency, a middle-aged woman once was brought to the hospital's crisis unit by concerned coworkers. She was restless and agitated, and she acknowledged a number of ongoing life stressors, including a messy divorce and mounting financial problems. She was experiencing weight loss, decreased sleep, subjective headaches, and crying spells. Had it stopped there, I might have diagnosed an adjustment disorder with mixed emotional features, or perhaps a mild or moderate depression, depending on the length and intensity of impairment. But the patient continued with her story, and the more I heard of it, the odder it became.

She said that she came from a large family of very modest means, and that one of her sisters had begun dating a man who came from "old money" and a high social stature. Not wanting to scare off her potential beau with working-class roots, her sister (according to the

---

6. *Id.*

patient) had pretended to be from European royal stock and had essentially disowned—at least in public—her many nearby blue-collar family members, instead treating them like hired hands and day laborers when their paths crossed. The patient went on to relate a convoluted tale whereby the snubbed family members, my patient included, had to resort to sending secret coded messages when they desired communication with the sister, who had by then married this old money suitor. The family would not have been able to exhibit any degree of familiarity in public and still maintain the charade.

This added information sounded delusional indeed, and I began treating the patient with both mood stabilizing and antipsychotic medications to address her presentation. While the medication calmed her and allowed her to sleep, her story regarding the family dynamic did not change. I was finally able to gain additional information from other sources, including relatives, and as unusual as it sounds, I learned that the patient was telling the truth all along. The patient was genuinely exhibiting depressive symptoms because of life stressors, but her sister had in fact married a much older man of means and did in fact hide her own working-class roots by denying that she had siblings while maintaining that the *doppelgängers* who were often seen working the fields nearby were merely hired hands. An elaborate and intentional fantasy world had been woven in which my patient was only one of the bit players. Needless to say, had I not investigated the story with the patient's family and checked her social background, I might well have continued to treat her with ever-increasing doses of antipsychotic medications, all the while wondering why no real progress in her "delusion" could be noted!

Physical Examination with Review of Systems

The physical examination documents what a doctor observes, while the review of systems, or ROS, documents those difficulties of which a patient complains. The physical exam and ROS for a psychiatric evaluation should be no less thorough than one performed by family practitioners or general internists, but regrettably that is often not the case. For example, a state psychiatric hospital at which I once worked had preprinted physical examination forms, complete with a simple body silhouette, that the psychiatrist on-call could complete by drawing arrows or circling words under headings for each body part or system to describe the patient's physical state (e.g., "pale," "tremulous," "obese," "rash"). This slipshod approach, with its failure to record vital information, resulted in a lot of exams of little use. Not only is this protocol not very professional but, given the number of co-morbid physical and psychiatric illnesses, it increases the likelihood that concomitant conditions will be missed. For example, are there distended veins around the umbilicus or perhaps swollen hemorrhoids? There might be liver disease and an unstated history of alcoholism. Are there swollen lower extremities? There could be congestive heart failure complicating the presentation. Is there a tremor? That will raise concerns about Parkinson's disease, medication side effects, or alcohol withdrawal.

A thorough ROS potentially enhances the value of any documented physical findings by recording what is actually bothering the patient and motivating her to seek treatment. Paradoxically, though, many times facets of the physical examination that appear significant to the physician will not even be related by the patient in the ROS. Nevertheless, all of this is pertinent to eventual treatment decisions.

Mental Status Exam

Arguably the single most important and specialty-specific facet of a psychiatric evaluation is the mental status exam, or MSE. Documenting an MSE enables a clinician to expound on a patient's clinical presentation in a way that illustrates nuances far more thoroughly than do raw laboratory data, physical findings, and basic reviews of systems.

A common trap set for medical students and residents occurs when an attending psychiatrist asks the unwary trainee to formulate an MSE on a catatonic and mute patient. The trainee will often reply with a few fumbled words, and then blurt out, "I can't say much else about her, since she won't talk to me." This is wrong. Remember, the exam is to give a complete picture of the objective clinical presentation, and the catatonic subject gives a wealth of information without uttering a single word. Keep in mind that it is such descriptive information, well documented in detail, that will not only allow a patient to obtain the help that she needs, but will also protect the practitioner by supporting treatment decisions should others later second-guess.

The MSE should be committed to memory for all who work in mental health. It includes objective information concerning the appearance, cognitive abilities, mood, insight and judgment, reality testing, communication abilities, and behavior of the patient. The presence of restlessness and distractibility, and the level of cooperation shown, are important additional observations, as is the apparent comprehension of the situation by the patient. Thoughts of violence are also to be addressed and documented at this point.

Thus, a well-apportioned mental status exam might read like this:

> The patient is a 54-year-old Caucasian male, appearing markedly older than his stated age, who is seated in the examination room when approached by the examiner. He extends his hand in greeting in a manner that seems forced and strained. He appears ill at ease and fidgets during the interview, although he remains seated throughout. He is wearing what appears to be gym clothes that are tattered and stained, his hair is shoulder-length and uncombed, he has strong body odor, and he does not appear to have bathed recently. A tattoo of a skull is visible on the left forearm, along with a Confederate flag on the right forearm. He shows no frank psychomotor agitation nor does he demonstrate any psychomotor retardation. Other than general restlessness in his chair, the patient demonstrates fair impulse control and attention span, though with poor eye contact throughout. Speech is without pressure or latency noted and is of normal volume and tone, and the patient uses several slang vulgarisms during the interview in an impolite and inappropriate manner. Affect is sullen, without much spontaneous range evident. He denies any neuro-vegetative perturbations at present. Mood is "okay, I guess." Thought processes are notable for some loosening of associations

and flight of ideas, though with easy redirectability, after which the patient expresses apologies for getting off track. There is no delusional thought content readily apparent. The patient appears to exhibit some insight into his current situation regarding identified social stressors, though he appears confused regarding how he came to be in the emergency department this evening. Quality of judgment is uncertain at present. He denies suicidal and homicidal ideation and fully contracts concerning destructive acts. He expresses future orientation during the interview. He additionally denies any adverse reactions or side effects referable to his medication.

Note that "mood" is what the patient tells you, in his own words, whereas "affect" is what you observe in a patient's facial expression. Note too that "future orientation" refers to expressions of outlook that indicate planning for days yet to come; a person with suicidal intent will often exhibit no future orientation, as they do not envision themselves being around long enough to see something through to its logical conclusion. ("I don't know what is going to happen . . . it's all meaningless. . . .")

What, exactly, is "insight"? In the vernacular it denotes a degree of awareness of a situation or state (with "judgment" being the ability to make a decision or act on that awareness). In psychiatry, though, insight is more nebulous and has a somewhat checkered past. Many individuals who are given a diagnosis of a major mental illness—a psychotic thought disorder, for example—do not necessarily accept that they are, in fact, ill. In mental health circles this would be considered a lack of insight into the nature and severity of the disorder in question. But many patient advocates insist that, as applied, the concept of "absent insight" is nothing more than the description of a patient who does not agree with the doctor's proffered diagnosis. Many advocates further hold that psychiatry is the only field of medicine in which refusal of (diagnosis and) treatment is held to be evidence per se of the presence of the illness!

Despite not having a universally accepted contextual definition, psychiatrists and psychologists continue to employ the term "insight" in clinical settings. A professional descriptor—the tongue-twister *anosognosia*—was even coined for use in the *DSM* as a synonym for poor insight.[7, 8] While lack of insight often presages poor judgment (and a likely need for close monitoring for safety), the opposite is not always true, as the apparent presence of insight does not always ensure sound judgment. A challenging situation involves a patient who does not believe a diagnosis—that is, if she lacks insight, she would be less likely to cooperate with any suggested treatments for the condition, which would add greatly to the task of caretaker and healer.

A vital facet of the mental status examination concerns documentation of words or actions that suggest thoughts of suicide. A word on suicide prevention contracts, alternately known as contracts for safety, is therefore appropriate. When I was in my psychiatric residency in the late 1980s, we were reminded repeatedly that at no time were we to interact with a patient without making note of the presence or absence of discernible thoughts of her doing harm to herself or others. Suicide, more than any other outcome of clinical practice, was the fear constantly in the back of our minds, as no psychiatrist wants to experience the guilt and self-recrimination—not to mention the devastation for the patient and family—of somehow having missed the warning signs of such an impending act.

One easy way to document absent destructive ideation, we were reminded, was to ask a patient if she would assure the interviewer—in essence, contract—that if she were having thoughts of self-violence, she would speak to a staff member before acting on any such thoughts. Though we were young and naïve, it did not take long before we realized that patients can sometimes be purposely vague or misleading, especially those who want to do harm. What good, we wondered, was such an extracted promise? Our faculty members were quick to remind us that, far from being some sort of binding agreement in the legal sense, the contract for safety is nothing more than a professional term of art reflecting that the question of self-harm has been raised with a patient deemed at possible risk. We were told that, in the event of an act of violence, professional

<hr />

7. Aviv, Rachel, *Annals of Mental Health: God Knows Where I Am*, THE NEW YORKER, vol. 87, no. 15, May 30, 2011, p. 57, *referencing* the BRITISH J. OF MEDICAL PSYCHOLOGY.

8. *Id.*

accountability hinged on having documented evidence that the subject of suicide had been discussed. Foreseeing, we were reminded, can be the crux of liability, and it would be difficult to refute that something was potentially foreseeable if it were never discussed.

Those who do not support the use of the contract for safety offer a litany of retorts, including, as noted above, that it is not a binding contract, that it is not an ironclad defense against malpractice, that it can be misapplied, that it can put a decision-making burden on a fragile patient, that it can give a clinician a false sense of security, that it renders the patient-provider relationship adversarial from the beginning, and so on.[9] I would agree that the contract for safety, applied incorrectly, is ill-advised and hardly a defense against an action in malpractice. One can easily appreciate that saying "but the deceased contracted for safety, Your Honor . . ." is a poor excuse in the absence of other professional assessment and documentation. Put another way, a patient's refusal to contract can be very telling, but willingness to contract is no absolute guarantee that nothing bad will happen.

Given this, if the contract for safety is employed as *one aspect* of a thorough evaluation and is coupled with the exercise of good clinical judgment based on available information and recorded accordingly, then even with its limitations, I hold that a contract for safety can illustrate that the clinician paid close attention to the seriousness of the situation at hand. While it may prove to be but a single important part of a thoughtful and well-documented mental status evaluation, it has saved many a clinician from later auditors and attorneys who wish to second-guess the clinical decisions made.

Testing, Both Laboratory and Psychometric

Testing is necessary for diagnostic assessment, treatment decisions, treatment monitoring, and, of course, research.[10] One of the

___

9. Knoll, James, *The Suicide Prevention Contract: Contracting for Comfort*, PSYCHIATRIC TIMES, March 1, 2011, p. 13.

10. KAPLAN, HAROLD & SADOCK, BENJAMIN. COMPREHENSIVE TEXTBOOK OF PSYCHIATRY, 5th ed. Baltimore: Williams & Wilkins (1989), p. 527. Some individuals hold that science has progressed to the point that lab tests for biomarkers can discern the presence of certain psychiatric conditions much the same as does a blood test for diabetes. For an affirmative view, *see* Akiskal, Hagop, *Biomarkers*

first tests to complete—and certainly one of the simplest—is actually considered to be a subset of the Mental Status Exam. The Folstein Mini-Mental Status Examination (MMSE) is a well-established noncommercial instrument containing questions and simple instructions that can be completed in less than 10 minutes, and that gives a good, albeit basic, overview of a patient's cognitive abilities. Thirty points is a perfect score; lower scores are not diagnostic, but rather suggest degrees of cognitive dysfunction and the need for further focused evaluation. Serial MMSEs are particularly helpful should the clinician later be asked to defend a treatment decision based on the presumption of impaired cognition.

The MMSE

- **Questions on orientation:** What is the (year) (season) (date) (day) (month)? *5 points.* Where are you now located (state) (country) (town) (building) (floor)? *5 points.*
- **Questions on registration:** Repeat three common words that are a noun, an adjective or verb, and an abstract principle (e.g., *ball, truth, red*), and then ask the patient to repeat the words after you have said them; give 1 point for each correctly repeated word. *3 points.*
- **Questions on attention and calculation:** Have the patient count backward from 100 in increments of seven. Alternatively, have the patient spell "world" backward. For completing five incremental steps correctly, *5 points.*
- **Question on recall:** Ask for the three common words named above after a five-minute delay. Give 1 point for each correctly remembered word. *3 points.*

---

for Mental Disorders: A Field Whose Time Has Come, PSYCHIATRIC TIMES, vol. 28, no. 11, Nov. 8, 2011, p. 14; for a jaundiced view, *see* Kaplan, Arline, *Blood Tests for Schizophrenia and Depression: Not Ready for Prime Time*, PSYCHIATRIC TIMES, vol. 28, no. 11, Nov. 8, 2011, p. 14, and also Carlat, Daniel, *A Blood Test for Depression? Really?*, The Carlat Psychiatry Blog, Aug. 15, 2011. *Available at* http://carlatpsychiatry.blogspot.com (retrieved Dec. 21, 2011).

> - **Questions on language:** Hold up a pencil and a wrist-watch and ask for their names. *1 point for each.* Repeat the following verbal phrase: "No ifs, ands, or buts." *1 point.* Follow a simple three-step verbal command: "Take a paper in your hand, fold it in half, and put it on the floor." *3 points.* Read and obey the following statement written on paper: CLOSE YOUR EYES. *1 point.* Write a complete sentence on any subject. *1 point.* Copy a simple design provided by the examiner (e.g., intersecting circles). *1 point.*

The MMSE has been criticized in some quarters for favoring those who have higher baseline educational levels or IQs, and especially those with innate math, reading, and spelling skills. There are ways to adjust for illiterate, semi-literate, and literate patient populations, however. One adjustment would be to ask a patient to recite the days of the week backward instead of the numerical counting exercise.[11] Keep in mind, though, that the MMSE is described as a "basic overview of cognitive abilities." It is diagnostic of no specific condition, but is rather indicative of the need for further, and more detailed and calibrated, assessments for certain illnesses when red flags are noted.

Psychological tests in general are those that employ tasks or written responses to determine the correlation, if any, between a test-taker and a normative group. The normative group is usually a cohort of persons with a known level of emotional or cognitive functioning, or those with a specific mental disorder. Examples of such instruments include IQ tests, personality inventories, and a host of examinations designed to uncover evidence of specific constellations of symptoms (or, for that matter, evidence of the faking of those symptoms). There are many psychological testing instruments available that are inarguably more sensitive and specific than the MMSE. While a full discussion of all of such tests is beyond the scope of this work, suffice it to say that for just about any purported

11. _____, *Modified MMSE Screens More Accurately for Dementia*, CLINICAL PSYCHIATRY NEWS, vol. 38, no. 8, Aug. 2010, p. 18.

condition there is a tool—perhaps proprietary, perhaps not—that can be employed for diagnostic purposes.

The reader should keep in mind that none of these tests is, in and of itself, diagnostic. Diagnoses are best determined after conducting a thorough review of all available data and after completing one or more clinical interviews. A psychological testing result is therefore just one facet of an overall evaluation, albeit a highly persuasive one.

As for tests of the nonpsychological variety, there are no definitive rules concerning which ones are "required." Some tests are used much more often than others during the course of a physical work-up. Lab tests, when ordered, should ideally establish or exclude a diagnosis, assist in the choice of therapy, and monitor treatment benefits or side effects.[12] Unfortunately, many clinicians still use the shotgun approach to testing, which actually yields little except higher health-care costs. Although one needs the categorical criteria of the *DSM* for guidance, keep in mind that psychiatric illnesses such as schizophrenia are essentially diagnoses of exclusion, given that no specific laboratory tests exist that establish such a diagnosis (i.e., one should rule out all medical conditions that may have secondary psychotic symptoms before assuming that a schizophrenic-appearing person is, in fact, schizophrenic).

The following list is not meant to be exhaustive, but measurements that can be seen as part of a physical work-up can include:

- Vital signs and physical parameters, including blood pressure, pulse, respiratory rate, weight, and height, all of which are usually performed at the time of a physical examination;
- Hematology and chemistry labs, including a comprehensive metabolic panel that measures electrolytes, fasting blood sugar, and kidney function; a complete blood count with differential that measures numbers of red and white blood cells and platelets and examines the shape and size of cells;

---

12. *Psychiatric Evaluation of Adults*, APA Practice Guidelines for the Treatment of Psychiatric Disorders (McIntyre, J.S. et al. eds). Washington, D.C.: American Psychiatric Ass'n (2000), p. 15.

vitamin B12 and folate levels, as deficits are strongly corre-
lated with both physical and mental changes; triglyceride
and cholesterol levels; a coagulation assay to reveal any
blood clotting problems; liver enzymes to suggest damage
from ingested substances or an infectious process; a blood
gas measurement if questions of tissue oxygenation exist;
and urine analysis;

- Microbiology labs, including examination of blood, cervi-
cal smears, sputum samples, and fluid from the central nervous system to reveal evidence of malignancies and
microbes;

- Endocrine assays, including a thyroid panel, a measurement
of reproductive hormones, and a cortisol level;

- Genetic testing for conditions such as Down syndrome,
Klinefelter's syndrome, Turner's syndrome, and Fragile X
syndrome;

- A pregnancy test for *all* pre-menopausal female patients;

- Toxicology assays, including a urine drug screen, a serum
drug screen, and measurements of any medication blood
levels that might be too high;

- Serology and immunology labs, including detection in the
blood or body fluids of any antibodies suggestive of the
presence of, or exposure to, infectious agents;

- Cardiac tests, including an electrocardiogram (EKG) and a
Holter monitor to look for evidence of impaired heart muscle
oxygenation or abnormal rhythms, which can affect systemic blood flow;

- Radiographic imaging, including a CT scan, MRI and fMRI
scans, a chest X-ray, and a mammogram, all to look for
evidence of tumors, bleeding, reduced blood flow, anatomical injuries and abnormalities, and the presence of
foreign bodies;[13]

---

13. *See* Chowdhury, Uttom, et al., *Clinical Implications of Brain Imaging in
Eating Disorders*, THE PSYCHIATRIC CLINICS OF NORTH AMERICA, vol. 24, no. 2, June
2001, p. 229, for an interesting discussion on how patients with anorexia nervosa
often demonstrate sulcal widening on head CT and MRI, whereas those with
bulimia are divided regarding that finding; *see also* Argyropoulos, Spilios, et
al., *Brain Function in Social Anxiety Disorder*, THE PSYCHIATRIC CLINICS OF NORTH

- Electrophysiology studies, including an electroencephalo-gram (EEG) to examine brain waves, and a polysomnograph to reveal evidence of altered sleep patterns;
- Completion of the Abnormal Involuntary Movement Scale (AIMS), a checklist that records the presence and progres-sion of neurological side effects of certain psychiatric medi-cations. Tardive dyskinesia, for example, is a serious complication of long-term use of antipsychotics, character-ized by involuntary movements that are purposeless, rhyth-mic, and repetitive, and that can involve the tongue, muscles of the face, arms, jaw, legs, and trunk. The AIMS can pick up early evidence of tardive dyskinesia.

Keep in mind that the focused clinician does not conduct the "million-dollar work-up" blindly, a common mistake of trainees, new doctors, and the ill-informed. Ordering laboratory tests or psychological screens en masse and without thoughtful assessment is not only counterproductive and directionless, but wastes precious finite resources.[14]

Differential Diagnosis

A differential diagnosis is the final step of the initial mental health evaluation. The clinician synthesizes the available findings (i.e., the interview, available past records, physical examination, review of systems, and testing results) into a laundry list of those conditions that might explain the presentation, from the most likely

---

AMERICA, vol. 24, no. 4, Dec. 2001, p. 708, for a discussion on the manner in which neuro-imaging can provide information on structural abnormalities as well as specific areas of brain activation in anxiety conditions, both at rest and during specific tasks; Roberts, Michelle, "Experts May Have Found a Way to Detect Alzheimer's Years Before Symptoms Appear," BBC News, Dec. 22, 2010, *referencing* the ANNALS OF NEUROLOGY, for information on the use in research of lumbar puncture in conjunction with head CTs and MRIs for the early detection of Alzheimer's disease. Admittedly, the use of imaging and laboratory testing in the diagnosis of certain psychiatric conditions remains an as-yet elusive goal of the mental health profession.

14. KAPLAN & SADOCK, *supra* note 10, at p. 528.

to those that are uncommon but still possible. Think of this as a worksheet from which the clinician will proceed in an attempt to determine or eliminate possible conditions. Nothing about it is cast in stone, and it tends to be fluid, with some possible conditions being eliminated rather quickly as more data is collected and collated, and other possible conditions being added when further supportive information is obtained.

After formulating a differential diagnosis, it is advisable for the clinician to explain in the patient's chart her thought processes and why one putative diagnosis is more likely than others. The goal should be to competently analyze the data that is available and proceed accordingly, and this is a process that evolves over time. Many a patient completes the initial evaluation with one diagnosis postulated, only to have one or more diagnoses added or deleted as more is learned during subsequent visits. This is not unexpected, but because of this potential fluidity, good documentation is essential. Having one's thought processes committed to the record helps to clarify the reasons for certain treatment decisions.

A rush to judgment must not occur. A telling example of this unfortunate phenomenon occurred during my second year of residency, and it is worth repeating as a cautionary tale. A college student was admitted to the psychiatric unit at the end of the semester with what appeared to be a first-time psychotic break. She was 20 years old and had no known history of mental disturbances. When I first examined her, she was disorganized, restless, irritable, and speaking in a nonsensical manner, unable to give me any meaningful history. Her roommates, who had called 911, told me that she had been "okay, but a little stressed" until the reading period for exams had commenced, when they noticed a rather sudden change in her previously unremarkable behavior. The roommates denied any knowledge of the patient having sustained head trauma, and they said she never drank or used drugs. True enough, a head CT was unremarkable, and her urine showed no traces of any of the common recreational drugs of abuse.

A rush to judgment would have supported a primary psychotic process. This young woman was the right age for a first-time psychotic break, and the lack of restful sleep, poor dietary intake, and other stressors commonly associated with college exams might have been the trigger for that break. Recreational drugs were apparently not to blame, and her presentation by all measures looked schizophrenic. However, after a day in the hospital she began to clear and then provided a crucial part of missing history. Yes, she had been stressed by upcoming exams, and no, she was not getting enough sleep as a result. But she said she had caught a cold while studying and was self-medicating with an over-the-counter agent, Nyquil, to relieve symptoms. The patient admitted to reading the dosing recommendations, but she believed that "if some is good, more is better." Accordingly, she had considerably overdosed on Nyquil, not with suicidal intent, but to clear her nasal passages and also to get herself into the deeply restorative sleep that was eluding her.

Nyquil contains acetaminophen to relieve pain and fever, dextromethorphan for cough suppression, and the anticholinergic doxylamine to reduce sinus congestion. In modest amounts, medications with anticholinergic properties can dry nasal secretions and produce sleep without serious side effects. In excessive amounts, however, they can produce delirium that closely mimics the mental status changes of a primary psychotic process. Although I lost contact with the student shortly after her discharge, I never heard of her having further difficulties that necessitated psychiatric intervention, so I am left with the belief that too much Nyquil did in fact cause her sudden deterioration. That was almost 25 years ago, but I have long remembered how a rush to judgment in that case would have resulted in a very incorrect diagnosis.

Documentation

Once all data is gathered and analyzed, and tentative diagnoses are determined, the *DSM IV-TR* stipulates that the information be documented in the now-familiar "five axes" format that was first developed for *DSM III*. All mental disorders and other conditions that may be a focus of clinical attention are listed under Axis I; if one is uncertain about a diagnosis, the prefix "r/o" (for "rule out") or the suffix "provisional" is often employed. Under Axis II are listed the personality disorders and mental retardation. Under Axis III are listed general medical conditions. Axis IV lists any psychosocial stressors that may be contributing to the clinical presentation (e.g., divorce, bankruptcy, death in family). And Axis V pertains to the Global Assessment of Functioning (GAF), a 100-point scale delineating in approximate terms how well the patient is coping with the situation at hand, and how adequately she is able to attend to activities of daily living. While all five axes are important, Axes I through III are the most commonly documented in most psychiatric charts.

Take-Home Pearls

- Many conditions can present clinically in ways that mimic one another. It is imperative that a good physical evaluation be undertaken to ensure that an occult physiologic process is not mistaken for a primary psychiatric disorder.
- A thorough psychiatric evaluation should include a detailed interview that investigates the history of present illness, the past medical history, the past psychiatric history, and the psychosocial and family histories. There should also be a physical examination with review of systems, and testing of both the psychological and laboratory varieties as clinically indicated.
- The mental status exam should describe in great detail the manner in which a patient clinically presents. Any evidence of dangerousness or suicidality should be documented in the mental status exam as well.
- When the clinician has obtained all available data, a differential diagnosis is formulated, listing, in decreasing order of likelihood, the conditions that might explain the patient's presentation. From that point, additional clinical observations will serve to confirm or refute disorders of the differential diagnosis until the clinician is comfortable that the patient has been thoroughly evaluated and treatment is proceeding correctly.

Chapter 4

The Neuroses
and the Psychoses

> The diseases of the mind are more numerous, and more destructive, than those of the body.
>
> —Cicero[1]
>
> There is no question that the problem of anxiety is a nodal point at which the most various and important questions converge, a riddle whose solution would be bound to throw a flood of light on our whole mental existence.
>
> —Freud[2]
>
> Insanity, even in its mildest forms, involves the greatest suffering that physicians have to meet.
>
> —Kraepelin[3]

The neuroses encompass the mood and anxiety disorders. These, along with the psychoses, comprise the lion's share of the conditions listed under Axis I in the *DSM-IV-TR*. They are significant

---

1. MENNINGER, KARL. THE HUMAN MIND. New York: Alfred Knopf, 1947, p. 3.

2. Kessler, Ronald, et al., *The Epidemiology of Generalized Anxiety Disorder*, THE PSYCHIATRIC CLINICS OF NORTH AMERICA, vol. 24, no 1, March 2001, p. xi.

3. Othmer, Ekkehard & Othmer, Sieglinde. THE CLINICAL INTERVIEW USING DSM-IV-TR: FUNDAMENTALS. Washington, D.C., American Psychiatric Publishing, Inc., vol. 1, 2002, p. 1, *referencing* LECTURES ON CLINICAL PSYCHIATRY, 2d edition (1906).

sources of morbidity and mortality, and they are not uncommon. Despite this, they can still present descriptive challenges to both the public and the profession.

Consider the millions afflicted with any one of the depressive-spectrum ailments. Such individuals not only experience significant debilitation and likelihood of premature death, but they are also at increased risk for more than a single episode of the disorder. Without long-term follow-up treatment and medication, up to 80 percent of individuals suffering from major depression, for example, eventually experience a relapse. One recent study showed that, even with ongoing treatment, almost one in five of those diagnosed with major depression has another episode within five years.[4,5]

The numbers involved and the incontrovertible public health impact notwithstanding, vocabulary remains problematic, as words that are commonly used in public discourse do not easily segue into precise professional terminology. A clear example of this is the generic term "depression." It is a frequently spoken word that means different things to different people. How many use "depression" to describe how they feel when in a soulful or disappointed state that actually has nothing to do with the devastating biochemical condition?[6] I suspect that just about everyone has done this. In some ways, "neurosis" was an easier term for psychiatrists to employ, as it never gained popularity in common parlance.

It may seem odd that, as an experienced board-certified psychiatrist, I long ago gave up directly asking any of my patients at the time of initial evaluation if they were depressed. This is because that word has lost much of its intended meaning. In many clinical situations I can almost guarantee that such a question will elicit an affirmative answer, even though objectively there may be little or no evidence to support the claim. This is because patients are replying to my inquiry with the layman's definition of "depression." The

4. Solomon, D.A., et al., *Multiple Recurrences of Major Depressive Disorder*, AMERICAN JOURNAL OF PSYCHIATRY, vol. 157, no. 2, Feb. 1, 2000, pp. 229–33.

5. Moon, Mary Ann, *Worldwide Bipolar Disorder Prevalence Estimated at 2.4%*, CLINICAL PSYCHIATRY NEWS, March 7, 2011, p. 7, *referencing* ARCHIVES OF GENERAL PSYCHIATRY (2011, 68: 241-51).

6. "Depression," MERRIAM-WEBSTER'S MEDICAL DICTIONARY. Springfield: Merriam-Webster Mass Market, Inc., 2006, p. 118.

same applies when individuals are described by nonprofessionals as suffering from "nerves" or, pejoratively, as being "crazy." The savvy modern clinician has had to learn other, less-direct ways by which to glean the necessary information without relying solely on the prevalent and often faulty jargon.

~~~~~~~~~~~~~~~~~~~~~~~~~~~~~~

According to current *DSM* nosology, mood disorders include major depression; bipolar disorder types I and II; dysthymic disorder; cyclothymic disorder; those substance-induced; those due to a general medical condition; and those not otherwise specified. Included in this list should also be the adjustment disorders with depressive features. Regarding all of these conditions, a common thread is the presence of the symptom that we broadly term "depression."

As we review *DSM* diagnostic elements, a certain logical pattern will emerge, one that is organized and comforting to the clinician and student. Whether that organization actually reflects reality remains debatable. With that in mind, I have simplified the language of the diagnostic criteria for conditions found in the *DSM-IV-TR*; for example, for a diagnosis of **major depression**, there must be:

A. Five or more of the following symptoms that have been present during the same two-week period and represent a change from the previous level of functioning, with at least one of the symptoms being either (1) or (2). The symptoms present must cause clinically significant distress or impairment in social or occupational functioning.
 (1) depressed or irritable mood,
 (2) markedly diminished interest in or pleasure regarding almost all activities,
 (3) significant change in weight when not attempting to gain or lose weight,
 (4) too much or too little sleep,
 (5) physical agitation or slowing, observable by others and not merely subjective feelings of restlessness or dragging,
 (6) fatigue,
 (7) feelings of worthlessness or inappropriate guilt,
 (8) diminished ability to concentrate, and

> (9) thoughts of death, a suicide attempt, or a specific plan
> for committing suicide.
> B. The symptoms do not better fulfill the criteria for bipolar
> disorder, active substance abuse, a general medical condi-
> tion, or bereavement after the loss of a loved one lasting
> less than two months.

Not to diminish the seriousness of major depression, but a lot of the above elements have a subjective component, and a certain amount of time must pass before the symptoms can fulfill the criteria. Unfortunately, what passes in the outpatient setting for mild to moderate depression, I suspect, is often situationally driven sadness, most likely time-limited, and does not justify chemical (prescription) intervention. Even so, such a condition would not necessarily prevent the diagnosis of major depression from being accurate under the *DSM* template.

If the criteria for major depression can be faulted for requiring a relatively short symptom duration before diagnosis, **dysthymic disorder** runs to the other extreme. In lay terms, the best way to envision dysthymia is to think of Eeyore in *Winnie the Pooh*. Adapted from the *DSM-IV-TR*, the **simplified criteria for dysthymic disorder** are:

> A. Depressed or irritable mood, as indicated either by subjec-
> tive account or observation of others, for at least two years,
> causing clinically significant distress or impairment in so-
> cial or occupational functioning.
> B. The presence, while feeling depressed or irritable, of two or
> more of the following:
> (1) too much or too little appetite,
> (2) too much or too little sleep,
> (3) low energy,
> (4) low self-esteem,
> (5) poor concentration or difficulty making decisions, and
> (6) feelings of hopelessness.
> C. During the period of the disturbance, the person has never
> been without the symptoms in (A) and (B) for more than
> two months at a time.

D. During the period, the symptoms are not better explained by the presence of a major depression or another mood disorder; a chronic psychotic disorder; active substance abuse; or a general medical condition.

To echo concerns about the diagnosis of major depression, there is much subjectivity in the above criteria. Psychological testing can assist, but given the absence in psychiatry of confirmatory laboratory tests, it still boils down to the clinical judgment of the care provider.

Vignette #1: The patient is a 44-year-old black male who presents to his primary care physician complaining of "not feeling good" for the past _____. While there has been some waxing and waning of his emotional state over that period of time, the patient denies having felt at his pre-morbid baseline since the onset of symptoms. The patient denies any specific stressors at home or work, though he admits to having difficulty concentrating on office projects and getting tasks completed on time. The patient also reports that his coworkers have made note that he seems more irritable than usual. He states that his sleep has been fragmented over this period, and he is conscious of waking up numerous times during the night, though not to urinate. He frequently feels fatigued during the day. Usually one who enjoys food sometimes to excess, the patient's appetite has also decreased, and he has lost an unspecified amount of weight over the period in question. He owns a race car that he hand-built 20 years ago and is his pride and joy, but he has ignored it and his racing friends since feeling so poorly. With encouragement, the patient admits that at times, he really doesn't care if he lives or dies, though he disavows any thoughts of doing harm to himself. There is no history of drug or alcohol abuse, and his physical examination and lab tests are entirely within normal limits.

The duration of the above symptoms was purposely left blank to illustrate that, depending on the selected time frame, the above scenario could suggest a single episode of major depression, a major depression that has recurred several times over the course of several years, or else dysthymic disorder. It is the clinician's call.

In many ways, **bipolar disorder** is easier to detect. Even medical students who cannot tease out the subtleties of other mood disorders can usually recognize the classic symptoms of the bipolar state. There is rarely any overlooking the person in full-blown mania.

So, the diagnosis of bipolar disorder is a no-brainer? Not exactly.

According to practice guidelines of the American Psychiatric Association, successfully making a bipolar diagnosis involves analysis that is both cross-sectional (i.e., current features of presentation) as well as longitudinal (i.e., the history of symptoms over time).[7] The two bipolar subtypes are conditions that can span a lifetime, and those so diagnosed experience wide-ranging frequencies of active symptoms, everything from rapid-cycling in a matter of hours and days to experiencing prolonged periods of normal mood for months and even years in between periods of instability.

The **simplified criteria for bipolar disorder type I** requires the presence of *mania* only. In the *DSM-IV-TR*, mania is defined as a distinct period of abnormally and persistently elevated, expansive, or irritable mood lasting at least one week (or any duration if hospitalization is necessary). It must result in marked impairment in social or occupational functioning, and it must be accompanied by

---

7. *Psychiatric Evaluation of Adults*, APA PRACTICE GUIDELINES FOR THE TREATMENT OF PSYCHIATRIC DISORDERS (McIntyre, J.S., et al. eds.). Washington, D.C., American Psychiatric Association, 2000, p. 43. It is worth asking how one gets longitudinal data in children who have not been in existence long enough to have a lengthy time line of symptoms. In 2000, NIMH director Steven Hyman convened a roundtable of 19 psychiatrists to determine whether use of the term "bipolar disorder" for children was even appropriate. The group opined that the disorder exists but offered no practical advice on how to diagnose or treat it. This vague report encouraged a mini-industry in ways to identify the condition in minors. Books—some pop-psychology—were quickly published, the diagnosis skyrocketed, and a lot of kids were put on medication. This is alarming because controlled clinical trials of psychotropics in this juvenile population are very limited, but the side effects of the medications are very real. *See* Sanghavi, Darshak, *Manic Panic: Why Are More and More Children Being Diagnosed with Bipolar Disorder?*, SLATE, Nov. 4, 2010. *Available at* http://www.slate.com/articles/health_and_science/medical_examiner/2010/11/manic_panic.html. Retrieved Dec. 24, 2011.

three or more of the following findings: grandiosity, decreased need for sleep, increased and pressured speech, racing thoughts, distractibility, agitation, and impulsive actions without concern for possible consequences.

[Note that the descriptor of hypomania applies also in a period of elevated, expansive, or irritable mood, with the presence of three or more of the elements enumerated for mania. In the case of hypomania, however, symptoms need to have lasted only four days and do not require hospitalization (if hospitalization is needed, the individual by definition would be manic, not hypomanic). Neither mania nor hypomania can be due to active substance abuse, a general medical condition, or a psychotic disorder.]

But what about concommitant symptoms of depression? While the diagnosis of bipolar disorder type I at first requires only the presence of mania, over the span of the disease, there will almost always be cyclical recurrences of depressive symptoms, manic symptoms, mixed symptoms, and hypomanic symptoms, and sometimes psychotic symptoms at the very extremes, all to varying degrees. That initial diagnosis, however, requires the mania. If the depressive symptoms come first, it is impossible to discern the condition from major depression or another mood disorder, unless or until the mania at some point follows.

Unlike type I, to meet the **simplified criteria for bipolar disorder type II,** one must see both:

A. a history of one or more episodes of major depression, and
B. a history of one or more hypomanic episodes. (Remember: if you have even one episode of mania, it's not type II, it's type I.)

Note that an initial hypomanic episode by itself, before any depression is seen, is not diagnostic of bipolar disorder type II, as mania is for type I. If such a scenario were to occur, though, it would put the astute clinician on notice that a bipolar predisposition was likely brewing.

What if a person has repeated and frequent episodes of hypomania and depressive symptoms over the years, resulting in distress or impairment, but the depressive symptoms do not quite meet the criteria for major depression, as required for the diagnosis of bipolar disorder type II? That person would then be diagnosed with **cyclothymic disorder,** best described as a watered-down version of bipolar disorder type II with even more subjectivity inherent.

The reader should note that some of the diagnoses above would be excluded if mood symptoms occur in the context of active substance abuse or a general medical condition. What happens diagnostically when such mood symptoms do occur in that context? Adapted from the *DSM-IV-TR*, the **simplified criteria for substance-induced mood disorder** are:

A. Prominent and persistent disturbances in mood—either depressive or elevated—that predominate and are the cause of clinically significant distress or impairment.
B. Evidence from the history, physical examination, or laboratory findings that the symptoms in (A) developed during or shortly after substance intoxication or withdrawal, or are related to known medication use.
C. The mood disturbances are not better explained by a disorder that is not related to substance use.

Adapted from the *DSM-IV-TR*, the **simplified criteria for mood disorder due to a general medical condition** are:

A. Persistent disturbances in mood—either depressive or elevated—that predominate and are the cause of clinically significant distress or impairment.
B. Evidence from the history, physical examination, or laboratory findings that the symptoms in (A) are the direct physiologic consequence of a general medical condition.
C. The mood disturbances are not better explained by another mental disorder or due to a state of delirium.

While a considerable degree of subjective clinical judgment has been suggested up to this point, the following discussion briefly describes two of the most subjective entities in the *DSM* canon: the adjustment disorders (specifically those with depressed mood) and those diagnoses employing the descriptor "not otherwise specified" (NOS).

Here is a dirty little secret of clinical psychiatry: if one is seeing an individual for treatment, a diagnosis is needed for coding and billing purposes, and yet if the clinician is not certain about the individual's struggles, the problem can almost always be safely labeled as an adjustment disorder. This is because the criteria for adjustment disorders are rather nonspecific, and the clinical state is usually not very severe and thus almost never in need of hospitalization. The clinician is not misleading with such a diagnosis, but instead falling back on what, in the opinion of many, is a catch-all category more useful in dealing with third-party payers than in providing much disorder-specific treatment. Adjustment disorders are time-limited and, in the experience of many, respond equally well to almost any type of psychotherapy, and sometimes they go away on their own.

Adapted from the *DSM-IV-TR*, the **simplified criteria for an adjustment disorder** are:

A. The development of emotional or behavioral symptoms in response to an identifiable stressor occurring within three months. (Just about everyone can think of at least one stressor from the past three months!)
B. These symptoms result in either distress in excess of what would be expected or significant impairment in social or occupational functioning.
C. The symptoms are not better explained by another Axis I disorder, an exacerbation of a preexisting mental disorder, or bereavement.
D. Once the stressor (or its consequences) has terminated, the symptoms do not persist for more than an additional six months.

Adjustment disorders come in different flavors: those with depressed mood, with anxiety, with mixed anxiety and depression, with disturbance of conduct, with mixed disturbance of emotions and conduct, and unspecified. Cynically, they are ideally suited to the worried well who are in therapy for generalized life dissatisfaction and in need of a diagnostic code.

Finally, a word on the descriptor "NOS." Diagnoses that are "not otherwise specified" indicate those situations in which clinical findings exist, but do not fulfill the diagnostic criteria for a specific category. For example, if five elements are needed to make a diagnosis, but only four are present—and yet those four are significant—NOS is appropriate to employ. There exists depression NOS, mood disorder NOS, and bipolar disorder NOS for those cases in which the presentations fall just short. While there is certainly a role for NOS diagnoses, it is sometimes a (lazy) catch-all description, employed at times in lieu of a thorough examination and an exhaustive multi-volume chart review by harried clinicians.

~~~~~~~~~~~~~~~~~~~~~~~~~~~~~

Concerning the anxiety disorders, Freud did not address the concept of "nerves" by that term, but I hear about nerves a lot in my practice. This is arguably the most commonly used colloquialism for all that has to do with anxiety. Unfortunately, it is also freely used to describe depression and, at times, psychosis. It seems to be the ubiquitous word in nonprofessional circles for just about anything that is amiss emotionally.

In the nineteenth century, "hysteria" was bandied about much like "nerves" is today. Hysteria was said to be a condition in which reality was experienced as inferior to the dream state; this is why many doctors felt that reading novels was dangerous, especially for young women—it encouraged the dream state. Noted medical commentators of the day said that if a girl were given a novel by age 15, she would be a hysteric by age 20.[8] Novels, though, were not the only danger; no less a luminary than Sir Benjamin Brodie—surgeon and physiologist to whom the 1858 edition of *Grey's Anatomy* was dedicated—posited that "female children are being kept indoors in warm rooms and over-educated . . . and this is producing an entire generation of hysterics."[9]

A popular medical text of the mid-nineteenth century described hysteria thusly:

---

8. *Do All Men Think All Women Are Like This?* INSIDE UVA, vol. 20, no. 19, Nov. 15, 1990, p. 12.

9. Watson, Thomas. LECTURES ON THE PRINCIPLES AND PRACTICE OF PHYSIC. Phila.: Blanchard and Lea, 1853, p. 24.

[It] most generally occurs in females between 15 and 30 years of age. The hysteric fit commences with coldness and shivering over the whole body, a quick but fluttering pulse, and an acute pain in the head. Some pain is also felt in the belly, generally on the left side. From this a ball seems to move with a grumbling noise through the abdomen. Thence, after various evolutions, it rises into the stomach and then into the throat, where it seems to remain for some time, and . . . to cause a feeling of suffocation. . . . Sometimes there is a singular combination of sobbing, crying, laughing, and shrieking in the midst of the fit. . . . The insensibility in hysteria is usually incomplete, the patient having some consciousness of what is going on around her.[10]

While many clinicians did not think it possible, by the early twentieth century, men were finally regarded as capable of becoming hysterics; in WWI, shell shock was held to be the male version of female hysteria.[11]

According to *DSM-IV-TR* nosology, anxiety disorders include panic disorder, both with and without agoraphobia; agoraphobia without panic disorder; phobia, both specific and social; obsessive-compulsive disorder; post-traumatic stress disorder; acute stress disorder; generalized anxiety disorder; those due to a general medical condition; those substance-induced; and those not otherwise specified. **Substance-induced anxiety disorder** and **anxiety disorder due to a general medical condition** have parameters that are parallel to those seen in the analogous mood disorders, except that the resulting symptom is one of anxiety and not depression or mania.

---

10. Coates, Reynell. Popular Medicine. Phila.: Carey, Lea, and Blanchard Publishers, Inc., 1838, pp. 482–83. Is this fanciful? Not in an age in which understanding of mental illness and disease causation was largely absent. From the *Newcastle Recorder* in March 1857 came the following indignant letter to the editor: "On Friday last [near Montreal, Quebec], two young ladies were taking a drive round the mountain. They wore bonnets attached to the backs of their heads. The cold wind penetrated to the brain [and] one of them died almost immediately after her return to the town, the other becoming insane. . . . Let me ask, is it not high time for the fathers of families to interfere and insist upon the abolishment of attire so very dangerous?" *See* The Newcastle Reporter, vol. 1, no. 6, March 26, 1857, p. 2.

11. *Do All Men Think All Women Are Like This?, supra* note 8.

Next is **generalized anxiety disorder,** one of the most common of the anxiety diagnoses. Also known in some circles as generalized worry disorder in recognition of the cardinal feature, it first appeared in *DSM-III* as a means to separate the diagnostic clumping of severe panic with lesser anxiety symptoms.[12]

Adapted from the *DSM-IV-TR*, the **simplified criteria for generalized anxiety disorder** include the following elements:

A. Anxiety producing clinically significant distress or impairment that occurs for at least six months, usually concerning a variety of events or activities (e.g., work or school performance).
B. The anxiety is associated with three or more of the following symptoms: (1) restlessness, (2) fatigue, (3) poor concentration, (4) irritability, (5) musculoskeletal tension, (6) sleep disturbances.
C. The symptoms are not better explained by another anxiety disorder, another Axis I disorder for which anxiety is a prominent symptom, a general medical condition, or a developmental disorder.

More than 10 percent of the U.S. population say that they are chronic worriers to the point that activities of daily living are affected.[13] However, diagnosable anxiety symptoms probably exert a measurable impact on approximately 7 percent of the U.S. population.[14]

Agoraphobia is defined as "the abnormal fear of being helpless in a situation from which escape may be difficult or embarrassing [and] that is characterized initially by anticipatory anxiety and finally by avoidance of open or public spaces [altogether]."[15]

Adapted from the *DSM-IV-TR*, the **simplified criteria for agoraphobia without history of panic** are:

---

12. Kessler, *supra* note 2, at p. 19.
13. *Id.*, *supra* note 2, at p. 20.
14. *Id.*
15. _____. "Agoraphobia," MERRIAM-WEBSTER'S MEDICAL DICTIONARY. Springfield: Merriam-Webster Mass Market, Inc., 2006, at p. 37.

A. The presence of agoraphobia, but without ever having actually met the criteria for panic disorder.
B. The symptoms are not better explained by substance use or
   a general medical condition.

Adapted from the *DSM-IV-TR*, the **simplified criteria for panic
disorder with agoraphobia** are:

A. Recurrent unexpected panic attacks, with concern about
   having additional attacks, worry about ramifications of another attack, or a significant change in behavior because of
   the attacks, lasting for at least one month.
B. The presence of agoraphobia.
C. The panic attacks are not better explained by substance use,
   a general medical condition, or another anxiety disorder.

The similarities between these two conditions can be considerable, especially when the heightened anticipatory anxiety is taken
into account.

Vignette #2: The patient is a 61-year-old divorced white
male who presents with a greater than 20-year history of
avoidance of crowded public places. Years ago, in a large
shopping mall near his home, he suddenly experienced intense fear that he would be unable to get out of the mall
(though there were no barriers to the well-marked exits).
He dropped his shopping bag and ran outside in an agitated
state, and since then has not returned to any sort of shopping mall, theater, or civic arena. Just thinking of being in
such a situation can precipitate intense anxiety, and the patient was greatly disturbed when he had to miss his only
son's college graduation for fear of the crowds at the cer-
emony. The patient is otherwise healthy and does not use
any substances, confirmed by drug screen. After two decades of anticipatory worry about being stuck in a public
place without an avenue for escape, five years ago the patient began to experience panic symptoms even though he
was safely in his own house. Without apparent precipitants

his pulse would race, and he would become short of breath and sweaty, feeling as though he were suffocating. The first time this happened he was alone and feared he was having a heart attack. Now he has panic attacks of the same nature at home at least once per week. Since then, he has curtailed all socializing for fear of having attacks in front of others. He has his groceries delivered, and except for checking his mailbox every few days, does not leave his house.

Until the patient's panic attacks began at home, this scenario would have suggested agoraphobia without history of panic. Once the panic attacks started at home, the presentation is consistent with panic disorder with agoraphobia. But depending on the intensity of the anticipatory anxiety of being in a public place, the two conditions can have much diagnostic overlap.

Adapted from the *DSM-IV-TR*, the **simplified criteria for acute stress disorder** are:

A. Exposure to, witnessing of, or confrontation by an event that involved actual or threatened death or serious injury to self or others, with contemporaneous fear, helplessness, or horror resulting.

B. Either while experiencing or after experiencing the distressing event, the individual has three or more of the following symptoms: (1) subjective numbing, detachment, or absence of emotional responsiveness, (2) the sense of being in a daze, (3) derealization (a feeling of altered reality), (4) depersonalization (a loss of sense of personal integrity or identity), (5) amnesia.

C. The traumatic event is persistently re-experienced through recurrent images, thoughts, dreams, illusions, flashbacks, or distress on exposure to reminders of the event.

D. Avoidance of stimuli that arouse memories of the event.

E. Symptoms of anxiety and increased arousal persist no less than two days and no more than four weeks, and result in clinically significant distress or impairment.

F. The symptoms are not better explained by substance use, a general medical condition, a brief psychotic disorder, or an exacerbation of a preexisting Axis I or II disorder.

When acute stress disorder persists for more than four weeks and is accompanied by additional and magnified clinical findings, including marked sleep disturbances, unexpected outbursts of anger, difficulty in concentrating, hypervigilance, and an exaggerated startle reflex, it is classified as **post-traumatic stress disorder (PTSD).** This condition has not only received an inordinate amount of controversial coverage in the lay press, but also represents what many in the field of mental health consider the paradigmatic example of a disorder involving the complex interaction of both genes and the environment.[16,17]

Obsessions are defined in the *DSM-IV-TR* as recurrent and persistent thoughts, impulses, or images that are experienced as one's own and yet are intrusive and inappropriate, cause marked anxiety and distress, and can result in subsequent attempts by the subject to ignore or suppress them. **Compulsions** are defined as repetitive behaviors that one feels driven to perform in response to self-imposed rules that are applied rigidly. These behaviors are attempts to prevent or reduce stress or some dreaded imagined outcome, but are not realistically connected with the outcome.[18]

Adapted from the *DSM-IV-TR*, the **simplified criteria for obsessive-compulsive disorder** are:

A. The presence of either obsessions or compulsions that cause marked distress, are time-consuming (more than one hour per day), and significantly interfere with the subject's normal social or occupational routine.

B. At some point the realization occurs that the obsessions or compulsions are excessive or unreasonable.

C. The symptoms are not better explained by substance use, a general medical condition, or facets of another Axis I disorder.

---

16. Grossman, Robert, *Neuroimaging Studies in Post-Traumatic Stress Disorder*, THE PSYCHIATRIC CLINICS OF NORTH AMERICA, vol. 25, no. 2, June 2002, p. 334.

17. Arehart-Treichel, Joan, *Surprising Accord Found in Psychiatric Testimony*, PSYCHIATRIC NEWS, vol. 46, no. 3, Feb. 4, 2011, p. 9.

18. Saxena, Sanjaya & Rauch, Scott, *Functional Neuroimaging and the Neuroanatomy of Obsessive-Compulsive Disorder*, THE PSYCHIATRIC CLINICS OF NORTH AMERICA, vol. 23, no. 3, Sept. 2000, p. 563.

[A facet of another Axis I diagnosis that would prove exclusory for obsessive-compulsive disorder, for example, would be the intense preoccupation with food that is common in those with active symptoms of an eating disorder.]

Finally, **phobias** are defined as "exaggerated and often disabling fears that are related to objects or situations that are often illogical and symbolic."[19] Under the *DSM* template, phobias come in two varieties: **social** and **specific.** Both involve exposure to stimuli that, when encountered, provoke intense anxiety. The fears are recognized as excessive or unreasonable and interfere with social or occupational functioning. Those individuals so afflicted will attempt to avoid the causative stimuli whenever possible, or else will be forced to endure with intense distress. With both types of phobic disorders, the symptoms cannot be better explained by substance use, a general medical condition, or by another mental disorder.

The differences between the conditions lie in the stimuli that provoke the fear. With **specific phobia,** fear is triggered by anticipation of a specific object or nonsocial setting (e.g., flying, heights, animals, receiving an injection, the presence of blood). With **social phobia,** fear is triggered by the perceived possibility of humiliation when exposed to unfamiliar people or possible scrutiny others in a public setting.

~~~~~~~~~~~~~~~~~~~~~~~~~~~~~~~~

Also known as a thought disorder, **psychosis** is defined as "a fundamental derangement of the mind characterized by defective or lost contact with reality, especially as evinced by delusions, hallucinations, and disorganized speech and behavior."[20] Keep in mind that psychosis is a symptom and *not* a diagnosis, as many conditions can yield psychosis, just as many conditions can yield mood or anxiety symptoms.

Delusions are "persistent false beliefs regarding the self or persons or objects outside the self that are maintained despite irrefut-

19. _____. "Phobia," Merriam-Webster's Medical Dictionary: Springfield: Merriam-Webster Mass Market, Inc., 2006, p. 701.

20. _____."Psychosis." Merriam-Webster's Medical Dictionary. Springfield: Merriam-Webster Mass Market, Inc., 2006, p. 737.

able evidence to the contrary."[21] Delusions, a type of psychosis, are likewise a symptom and not a diagnosis.

Hallucinations are "perceptions of someone or something with no external cause, usually arising from a disorder of the central nervous system."[22] Hallucinations can be auditory, visual, tactile, gustatory (taste), or olfactory (smell) in nature and, like delusions, are a symptom and not a diagnosis.

According to current *DSM-IV-TR* nosology, psychotic disorders include schizophrenia; schizophreniform disorder; schizoaffective disorder; delusional disorder; brief psychotic disorder; shared psychotic disorder; those due to a general medical condition; those substance-induced; and those not otherwise specified.

Substance-induced psychotic disorder and **psychotic disorder due to a general medical condition** have parameters that parallel those seen in the analogous mood and anxiety disorders, except that the resulting symptom is one of psychosis and not one of a mood or anxiety disturbance.

Among other psychotic disorders, **schizophrenia** is the one most recognized by the public, and yet seemingly very little of it is understood by laypersons (perhaps explaining why Hollywood has a poor history of accurately portraying mental illness in popular films). The illness is not uncommon; schizophrenia—literally "split mind" in Greek—typically first occurs in adolescence or early adulthood and is estimated as affecting slightly less than 1 percent of the worldwide population. It is seen with equal frequency in all races and both genders.[23]

As noted in the practice guidelines of the American Psychiatric Association:

Schizophrenia is a chronic [incurable] condition that frequently has devastating effects on many aspects of a patient's life. . . . The care of most patients [with this diagnosis] involves multiple efforts to reduce the frequency and severity

21. _____. "Delusion." MERRIAM-WEBSTER'S MEDICAL DICTIONARY. Springfield: Merriam-Webster Mass Market, Inc., 2006, p. 112.

22. _____. "Hallucination." MERRIAM-WEBSTER'S MEDICAL DICTIONARY. Springfield: Merriam-Webster Mass Market, Inc., 2006, p. 460.

23. Kapur S., *Schizophrenia*, THE LANCET, Aug. 22, 2009, pp. 635–45.

of episodes and to reduce the overall morbidity and mortality of the disorder. Many patients require comprehensive and continuous care over the course of their lives with no limits as to duration of treatment.[24]

Those with schizophrenia are considerably more likely to suffer from significant substance abuse than are other populations, and up to 10 percent of those with schizophrenia will eventually die by their own hand.[25,26]

Schizophrenia, however, is but one of many potential sources of psychosis. The differential diagnosis of a seemingly psychotic presentation certainly include schizophrenia, but also includes mood disorders with psychotic features; paranoid, schizoid, schizotypal, and borderline personality disorders; factitious disorder; and of course malingering. Medical conditions that could resemble schizophrenia include temporal lobe epilepsy and other nonconvulsive seizures, tumors, strokes, brain trauma, central nervous system infections, Alzheimer's disease, Huntington's disease, Wilson's disease, endocrine and metabolic disorders, vitamin deficiencies, and autoimmune disorders. Substances that can also cause behaviors resembling schizophrenia include stimulants, hallucinogens, PCP, anticholinergics, steroids, L-dopa, H2 blockers, alcohol, barbiturates, and heavy metals. This clearly illustrates why an individual who has thought disorganization and might be hallucinating is not to be reflexively diagnosed as having schizophrenia without a thorough organic work-up and review of available history.[27, 28]

The following three diagnoses under the psychotic disorders umbrella are best described together, as more often than not they are snapshots at different points along the same continuum. Read

24. McIntyre, *supra* note 7, at p. 305.

25. Kessler R.C., et al., *Lifetime and 12-Month Prevalence of DSM-III-R Psychiatric Disorders in the United States—Results from the National Comorbidity Survey*, ARCHIVES OF GENERAL PSYCHIATRY, vol. 51, no. 1, 1994, pp. 8–19.

26. *Id.*

27. HADDAD, JANE & COHEN, FRED. TRAINING IN CORRECTIONAL MENTAL HEALTH. Tucson: Correctional Mental Health Specialists, 1999, p. 62.

28. SCHIZOPHRENIA, A NEW GUIDE FOR CLINICIANS (Csernansky, J.G., ed.). New York: Marcel Dekker, Inc., 2002, p. 55.

first the **simplified criteria** adapted from the *DSM-IV-TR* for **schizophrenia:**

A. The presence of two or more of the following active symptoms, each present for a period of at least one month, with subsequent impairment in social or occupational functioning of at least six months: (1) delusions, (2) hallucinations, (3) disorganized speech, (4) grossly disorganized or catatonic behavior, (5) prominent negative symptoms (e.g., withdrawal into self, mutism, lack of motivation).
B. The symptoms are not better explained by substance use, in the context of a general medical condition, or by another mental disorder with psychotic features.

Now, compare with the **simplified criteria** adapted from the *DSM-IV-TR* for **schizophreniform disorder:**

A. The criteria for schizophrenia are met, except
B. The impairment in social or occupational functioning, including active phase and residual symptoms, has lasted less than six months.

Finally, compare the above with the **simplified criteria** adapted from the *DSM-IV-TR* for **brief psychotic disorder:**

A. The presence of at least one of the following symptoms for at least one day, but not exceeding one month in duration: (1) delusions, (2) hallucinations, (3) disorganized speech, (4) grossly disorganized or catatonic behaviors.
B. Following the onset of symptoms in (A), there is an eventual return to the baseline pre-morbid level of functioning.
C. The disturbance is not better explained by substance use, a general medical condition, or another disorder with psychotic features.

Notice that the number of symptoms for brief psychotic disorder (at least one) is fewer than that required for either schizophreniform disorder or schizophrenia (at least two). Notice also that, for brief psychotic disorder, a return to the baseline pre-morbid level of functioning is required following the symptomatic phase.

Vignette #3: The patient is a 23-year-old single Hispanic male. He has been brought to the emergency room by concerned friends after exhibiting unusual behaviors for the past _____. He is physically healthy and has no known history of substance abuse or any past psychiatric problems. His urine drug screen is negative. However, he now talks to people who are not present, sometimes becoming quite agitated during these conversations, and this frightens those who witness it. He also has told his family and friends that he fears the Department of Homeland Security is monitoring his apartment at night and is preparing to arrest him for crimes against humanity (he has no legal history or any past involvement with criminal elements, according to his brother). The patient has become increasingly withdrawn from his previously close circle of friends. And because of his odd behavior, he was recently fired from his job at a video store, which merely served to exacerbate his belief in conspiracies against him.

The duration above was left blank. If it said that the symptoms had been present for less than 30 days, the scenario would be most consistent with a brief psychotic disorder. If it said that the symptoms had been present for 10 weeks, the scenario would be most consistent with schizophreniform disorder. And if it said that the symptoms had been present for seven months, the scenario would be most consistent with schizophrenia, the difference in diagnoses stemming exclusively from the passage of time with a common end result. Of course, any diagnosis of a primary thought disorder is contingent on the physical evaluation revealing no other causation for the mental status changes noted.

The next disorder can also be conceptualized along a continuum, but one that instead straddles the line between the psychotic disorders and the mood disorders. Major depression and bipolar disorder, as well as **schizoaffective disorder,** can all involve mood symptoms as well as psychosis. The difference is that those individuals with major depression and bipolar disorder exhibit psychosis only at the extremes of mood (i.e., the height of mania or the very nadir of depression), whereas those with schizoaffective disorder may exhibit psychosis at any point in the mood cycle.

Adapted from the *DSM-IV-TR*, the **simplified criteria for schizoaffective disorder** are:

A. The presence of symptoms that meet the criteria for schizophrenia.
B. The concomitant presence of symptoms that meet the criteria for either major depression or bipolar disorder.
C. The presence of delusions or hallucinations for at least two weeks without any prominent mood symptoms.
D. The symptoms are not better explained by substance use, or in the context of a general medical condition.

Next is another disorder that can be conceptualized along a continuum, but one that instead straddles the line between the psychotic disorders and the personality disorders.

Adapted from the *DSM-IV-TR*, the **simplified criteria for delusional disorder** are:

A. The presence of a prominent non-bizarre delusion (i.e., involving a situation that might actually occur in real life, such as being followed, poisoned, infected, loved at a distance, of higher birth unrecognized by others, or deceived by spouse or lover) of at least one month's duration.
B. Apart from the ramifications of the delusion, functioning is not markedly impaired and behavior is not obviously odd or bizarre.
C. The delusion is not better explained by substance use, a general medical condition, another psychotic disorder, or a mood disorder.

Delusional disorders can be particularly difficult to diagnose because, aside from the delusion, behavior and level of function are not grossly impacted. Thus, it becomes the duty of the clinician to serve as a private investigator of sorts, and since the delusions involved are, by definition, non-bizarre (no Martians here), until or unless irrefutable evidence is uncovered that proves the belief system to be fantastical, the diagnosis cannot be rendered unequivocally. For illustrative purposes, go back and reread my earlier clinical anecdote in the previous chapter regarding the woman who, to retain the romantic interest of her high-society beau, persuaded her sister to play along with a faux royal background. All but the most seasoned (and fortunate) of clinicians might have felt comfortable labeling that individual as having a delusional disorder—except that the "delusion" was, in fact, entirely real.

Finally, we turn to what French psychiatrists in the nineteenth century labeled "folie à deux," or "madness of two"; this can also exist as "folie à trois," "folie à quatre," "folie en famille," or even "folie à plusieurs," the "madness of many." The more people involved, however, the scarcer the condition. This syndrome, known today by its more sterile scientific name, **shared psychotic disorder,** is seen in settings in which two or more persons live in close proximity and often in isolation from others; while the persons can be equally and independently afflicted with the delusional system (e.g., a married couple who believe they are both being followed), more often one person is the primary, and additional persons are the secondaries. Interestingly, in some published cases in which a secondary is removed from the proximity of the primary, the former clears more rapidly, sometimes even without psychotropic medications, raising the unavoidable question of whether the secondary individual was actually ill at all or instead under the environmental influence of a charismatic and delusional Svengali.

Adapted from the *DSM-IV-TR*, the **simplified criteria for shared psychotic disorder** are:

A. One or more delusions develop in an individual in the context of a close relationship with another person(s), who has an already-established delusional system.
B. The delusion is similar in content to that of the person who already has the established delusional system.
C. The disturbance is not better explained by substance use, a general medical condition, or another disorder with psychotic features.

For those old enough to remember, *They Might Be Giants*, the 1971 film starring George C. Scott and Joanne Woodward, illustrates, Hollywood-style, a classic example of a primary-secondary folie à deux.

Take-Home Pearls

- The psychoses and neuroses encompass those *DSM* conditions that today fall mainly under the psychotic disorders, mood disorders, and anxiety disorders.
- In the author's opinion, the descriptor "depression" is used so freely in the vernacular as to have been rendered largely useless for meaningful discourse on the disease of major depression.
- There are no simple lab tests that can diagnose mental disorders, though a thorough organic (physical) evaluation is *always* indicated before a diagnosis is reached.
- Schizophrenia is probably the best known among the public of the psychotic disorders , but by no means is it the only such condition that can produce similarly appearing symptoms.
- As one studies the nosology of mental conditions, the symmetry that exists on paper across the diagnostic spectrum becomes apparent. However, it remains unclear if nature is really this symmetrical, especially given the subjectivity of many of the diagnostic criteria, and that many of the disorders listed are easily visualized as existing at various points along a continuum with grey zones.
- Applying the diagnosis of "not otherwise specified" can be a good idea, but it is probably clinically misused quite a bit.

Chapter 5

The Personality Disorders

> [There are those who exhibit] a tendency to magnify all matters of personal significance, often leading to actions that prove outrageous to society.
> —Najab ud-din Unhammad (A.D. 870–925)[1]
>
> How can you come out [of therapy] any better when the psychiatrist has you pegged even before you open your mouth? If you arrive for your appointment late, he'll say you're hostile. If you're early, you must be anxious, and if you're right on time, you're a compulsive!
> —Robert Mendelsohn[2]

Unhammad described a person who might have suffered from what we today call a personality disorder. There is little doubt that such conditions have been around for a very long time. We do know that one particular subtype of personality disorder, that of the antisocial, was first described in a scientific manner in the early nineteenth century; at that time, alienists (psychiatrists) spoke of patients

---

1. MILLON, THEODORE. MASTERS OF THE MIND: EXPLORING THE STORY OF MENTAL ILLNESS FROM ANCIENT TIMES TO THE NEW MILLENNIUM. New York: John Wiley & Sons (2004), p. 38.
2. MENDELSOHN, ROBERT. CONFESSIONS OF A MEDICAL HERETIC. Chicago: Contemporary Books, Inc. (1979), p. 99.

with moral insanity, a descriptive phrase for those who did not appear floridly psychotic and yet seemingly had no ability to abide by expected principles of societal conduct. By the late nineteenth century, J.L. Koch coined the term "psychopathic inferiority" to describe such persons, and shortly thereafter that descriptor inspired the well-known terms "psychopathy" and "sociopathy" that we use today (more on those shortly).[3]

Otto Kernberg was a pioneer in the study of what he called character pathology; he was one of the first to write extensively on personality disorders in general, and in particular about one of its subtypes, that of the borderline. Kernberg described borderline personality organization as a type of cognitive structure employing primitive stress defenses to bolster a weak sense of identity. Though persons with this borderline personality enjoyed intact reality testing, it was a condition that nevertheless inhabited the "border" between the psychoses and the neuroses.[4] These people were not psychotic in the classic sense, but their perception of the world around them deviated far from that of most others.

So, in plain English, what exactly is a personality disorder? According to Kaplan and Sadock, "[a] personality disorder is an enduring pattern of inner experience and behavior that deviates [substantially] from the expectations of the individual's culture, is pervasive and inflexible, has an onset in adolescence or early adulthood, is [relatively static] over time, and leads to distress or impairment."[5] Personality is the inner quality controlling how we deal with each other and with the stressors, both big and small, of everyday life. It refers to the distinctive set of traits, behavior styles, and coping mechanisms that comprise one's individuality. A personality disorder, then, suggests impairment in healthy coping and interpersonal dynamics. Those with personality disorders have a great deal of difficulty dealing with other people and situations. They tend to be

---

3. Millon, Theodore, et al., *Historical Conceptions of Psychopathy in the United States and Europe*, in PSYCHOPATHY: ANTISOCIAL, CRIMINAL, AND VIOLENT BEHAVIOR. N.Y.: Guilford Press (1998), p. 8.

4. KERNBERG, OTTO. SEVERE PERSONALITY DISORDERS: PSYCHOTHERAPEUTIC STRATEGIES. New Haven: Yale University Press (1993), p. 112.

5. KAPLAN, HAROLD & SADOCK, BENJAMIN. COMPREHENSIVE TEXTBOOK OF PSYCHIATRY, 5th ed. Baltimore: Williams & Wilkins (1989), p. 685.

rigid and unable to successfully respond to many of the challenges of life. Perhaps most surprisingly, despite such impairments, these individuals often feel that their behavior patterns are normal, and that it is instead the external world that is wholly at fault.

While the diagnosis of a personality disorder has an inescapably subjective component, its proper application is reserved for those with a long-standing pattern of dysfunction that is often first detected as early as adolescence and is formally diagnosed only upon the individual reaching adulthood. Excluded from this application are those who have only a single instance of maladaption. While no single etiology of personality disorders is known, researchers have identified certain factors that seem to increase the risk of such pathology, including:

1. suffering verbal or physical abuse or neglect, especially when young;
2. an unstable or chaotic childhood, often involving the loss of parents or primary caretakers through contentious divorce, death, or abandonment;
3. behavioral difficulties as an adolescent;
4. lower socioeconomic status; and
5. a history of mental illnesses in primary relatives or caretakers.[6]

The above red flags appear to be environmentally determined (with the arguable exceptions of the third and fifth factors, which could represent both nature and nurture). There are ongoing studies to determine if the predisposition to development of personality disorders has a genetic component (triggered by environmental stressors if encountered). Some researchers support this idea by noting that not every child who grows up in a chaotic environment and is a victim of abuse or neglect becomes disordered of personality. Studies employing scans of the brain suggest alterations in glucose metabolism and impaired neural connections between the amygdala (the seat of emotions) and the prefrontal cortex (the seat of reason) when normal controls are compared with patients having border-

---

6. Cohen, P., *Child Development and Personality Disorder*, Psychiatric Clinics of North America, vol. 31, no. 477 (2008), p. 43.

line personality disorder. This remains a very fresh line of inquiry, and for now, we can only postulate about genetic and physiological contributions to a group of disorders that have long appeared mainly environmental and psychological in origin.[7]

Personality disorders present a special challenge for non-clinicians because they are relatively common and can be difficult to manage. The National Epidemiologic Survey on Alcohol and Related Conditions suggests that almost 15 percent of American adults meet diagnostic criteria for at least one personality disorder. Individuals with personality disorders can exhibit erratic and seemingly unprovoked behavior, reacting far out of proportion to real and perceived slights. And yet it is the very fact that these (largely subconscious) coping mechanisms are so rigid and maladaptive that creates such serious social impairment for those so afflicted.[8]

Self-injury, unfortunately, is sometimes the only way in which sufferers can express distress. It is not uncommon to see a patient with borderline personality disorder who has multiple railroad-track scars on both forearms from repeated acts of self-laceration over the years. Exasperated family and friends may dismiss these acts as nothing more than attempts at gaining attention. However, it is imperative that the clinician not dismiss these acts of self-harm as purely attention-seeking in nature and therefore unworthy of emergent intervention. Whether or not those with personality disorders do actually want to end their lives, they can sometimes inadvertently succeed at self-termination when they may have been ambivalent about it all along. For a jury later examining the fact pattern leading up to such a death, the failure of the clinician to seriously heed the warnings may appear inexcusable.

Personality disorders command their own section within the *DSMs* (on Axis II along with mental retardation, wholly separate in listing from all other mental states which are coded on Axis I). While

---

7. Moran, Mark, *Neurobiological Secrets*, Psychiatric News, vol. 46, no. 8, April 15, 2011, p. 4.

8. Grant, B.F., et al., *Co-Occurrence of 12-Month Alcohol and Drug Use Disorders and Personality Disorders in the United States: Results from the National Epidemiologic Survey on Alcohol and Related Conditions,* National Institute on Alcohol Abuse and Alcoholism, National Institutes of Health, Archives of General Psychiatry, vol. 61 (April 2004), pp. 361–68.

there is a spectrum of varying degrees of affliction for every mental condition, many posit a significant difference between the "real" disorders of Axis I and the personality disorders of Axis II. However, this difference is difficult to succinctly put into words; one faces the same challenge expressed by Justice Potter Stewart, when he commented in *Jacobellis v. Ohio* that he was unable to define pornography, but he knew it when he saw it.

Perhaps the difference is best reflected in the likelihood of patient insight. I have found that the majority of those diagnosed with conditions of the Axis I spectrum eventually will admit to feeling poorly and will want help to relieve their distress. This is less commonly the case with those suffering from personality disorders. This does not mean that individuals with personality disorders cannot benefit from psychotherapy and come to realize the destructiveness of the conditions with which they grapple. It is simply to note that the individual with an Axis I disorder usually knows that something is wrong in *his* world, while the individual with character pathology cannot understand why *everyone else* is so dysfunctional. Or to (over)simplify by using one pearl from a former professor: "The depressed person or the anxious person or the psychotic person will be just as depressed or anxious or psychotic on a desert island as anywhere else, but the person with a personality disorder, absent other individuals but with supplies of food, water, and shelter, might very well do just fine."

Another facet of the personality disorders that makes diagnosis difficult is the nature of their continuum. There are many people who have never experienced profound biological depression, panic attacks, or intense paranoia. Conversely, the very essence of personality disorders—involving personality, something we all share—indicates that there is hardly a person alive who has not at some point experienced the unhealthy thoughts that are associated with personality disorders *in extremis*. Most everyone has felt lonely, underappreciated, or suspicious without clear reason. So where is the diagnostic line in the sand? Unlike many who suffer from Axis I conditions, it is the frequency and degree to which one experiences Axis II maladaption and not the presence of any one maladaptive thought or act that is the measure of diagnosable pathology. That makes the line between healthy and unhealthy seem very fuzzy indeed. Put another way, lots of persons have the occasional Axis II maladaptive thought, but not everyone has an Axis II diagnosis.

To illustrate this point, consider that coping traits that are perceived as useful in one setting and in moderation can be pathological when taken to excess. A person who is organized, follows rules diligently, and strives for excellence would make a good employee in a competitive workplace, but when mental rigor mortis sets in, that same person might be plagued by obsessive-compulsive personality dysfunction. A fascinating 2005 study, conducted at the University of Surrey in the U.K., sought to interview senior-level business executives in London along with forensic psychiatric patients at Broadmoor Hospital. The researchers found that histrionic, narcissistic, and obsessive-compulsive personality structure was more common in the executives than in the forensic patients. This caused one of the study's authors to suggest that the businessmen were nothing more than successful sociopaths while the patients were the unsuccessful ones![9]

Here is more food for thought: Consider a story that aired on National Public Radio (NPR) in December, 2010, which stated, in part, "It seems you need only flip through a few channels of reality television to feel there's a lot of narcissism in our culture these days." One glaring example would be Nicole Polizzi, a.k.a. Snooki, of the reality TV show "Jersey Shore," who told Barbara Walters, "I think I'm fascinating." Another NPR story that aired four months later drew attention to an article published in *Psychology of Aesthetics, Creativity, and the Arts,* which discussed the proliferation of self-centered lyrics in popular music over the past decade and how this focus reflects increasing narcissism in society in general.[10] But whether Polizzi, other "Jersey Shore" cast members, and pop musicians can be diagnosed as clinically narcissistic is debatable. What is publicly known about an entertainment figure is not necessarily diagnostic of narcissistic personality disorder as much as it is a reflection of P.T. Barnum-esque self-promotion. The December 2010

9. Board, Belinda Jane, Fritzon, Katarina. *Disordered Personalities at Work,* PSYCHOLOGY, CRIME, AND LAW, vol. 17, no. 11 (2005), p. 65.

10. Norris, Michele, "Narcissism on Rise in Pop Lyrics," National Public Radio, April 26, 2011. *Available at* http://www.npr.org/2011/04/26/135745227/study-narcissism-on-rise-in-pop-lyrics (retrieved Dec. 2, 2011).

NPR story further noted, "In most cases there is a difference between a clinical narcissist and one you see on TV. . . . [What] makes it clinical is when you go to an extreme where it [becomes] pervasive [and] where it affects all aspects of your life."[11] As anyone who has endured a reality TV marathon can attest, whatever initial entertainment value may exist regarding narcissistic behavior wears thin quickly because of its constant, unremitting impact affecting every aspect of domestic and social interaction.

Another thing to consider is that the pharmaceutical industry has not succeeded in winning FDA approval for drugs created for the treatment of any of the personality disorders. There are medications that can be employed for related symptoms, but they are all used off-label for Axis II pathology. This is telling, as industry has rarely shied from attempts to market a pharmacological "cure" for anything it could target. And even recognized experts in mental health remain divided about the role of drugs in such treatment. A recent meta-analysis conducted by the National Institute for Health and Clinical Excellence in the United Kingdom stated that there was no convincing evidence that psychotropic medications assist those with borderline personality disorder at all, concluding by instructing clinicians, "Do not use drug treatment specifically for [this condition] or for the individual symptoms or behaviors associated with it." And yet, at almost the same time, a different study of the same clinical evidence recommended numerous drug treatments to target the core symptoms—impulsivity, mood swings—associated with borderline personality disorder.[12]

According to current nosology, personality disorders include those that are paranoid, schizoid, schizotypal, antisocial, borderline, histrionic, narcissistic, avoidant, dependent, obsessive-compulsive, and not otherwise specified. There are many other proposed subcategories of personality disorders that are not in the *DSM-IV-TR* canon but

11. _____, "It's All About Me: But Is Narcissism a Disorder?," NPR, Dec. 11, 2010. *Available at* http://www.npr.org/2010/12/11/131991083/it-s-all-about-me-but-is-narcissism-a-disorder (retrieved Dec. 2, 2011).

12. Jancin, Bruce, *Dueling Borderline Guidelines Spark Debate in U.K.,* CLINICAL PSYCHIATRY NEWS, vol. 38, no. 8, Aug. 2010, p. 15; *see also* Lieb, Klaus, et al., *Pharmacotherapy for Borderline Personality Disorder*, BRITISH JOURNAL OF PSYCHIATRY, vol. 196, Jan. 2010, pp. 4–12.

represent facets of presentation that, if not currently accepted as diagnostic, certainly are of potential clinical import. These include behaviors that are passive-aggressive, sadistic, self-defeating, psychopathic, cyclothymic, and inadequate, among others.

Adapted from the *DSM-IV-TR*, the **simplified criteria for a personality disorder** in general are:

A. An enduring, inflexible, and pervasive pattern of inner experience and behavior, with antecedents in adolescence and early adulthood, that deviates markedly from the expectations of the individual's culture and leads to clinically significant distress or impairment in social or occupational functioning. This pattern is manifested in at least two of the following areas: (1) perception of self, other people, and events; (2) range, intensity, and instability of emotions; (3) interpersonal functioning; (4) impulse control.

B. This enduring pattern is not better explained as a manifestation of another mental disorder, the direct effects of substance abuse, or a general medical condition (e.g., head trauma).

Though clinical laziness sometimes permeates the use of NOS (not otherwise specified) diagnoses in general, within the personality disorders NOS is often more useful. It is not uncommon that a patient falls just short of Axis II diagnostic criteria, but still will be markedly impaired in both social and occupational functioning. Likewise, there will be times in which debilitating symptoms exist that do not conform to currently accepted diagnostic labels (e.g., passive-aggressive, sadistic, self-defeating traits). Also, because various accepted personality disorders share some similarities, they are often grouped into related clusters and labeled "A," "B," and "C." The cluster A disorders are those that exhibit odd or eccentric behaviors: the paranoid, the schizoid, and the schizotypal traits that we will examine shortly. The cluster B disorders are those that tend to be dramatic, emotional, and erratic: the antisocial, borderline, histrionic, and narcissistic traits. The cluster C disorders are those that exhibit anxiety and fearfulness: the avoidant, dependent, and obsessive-compulsive traits. Therefore, if a patient is not fulfilling exactly the elements of any one specific diagnosis, it is clinically useful to describe that person as having "personality disorder NOS with cluster B traits," or "personality disorder NOS with borderline traits." This approach alerts other clinicians that the patient shares symptoms suggestive of borderline, narcissistic, histrionic, and antisocial states without fully meeting the criteria of any one of them.

As noted, the cluster A disorders include those that are primarily odd or eccentric. For example, adapted from the *DSM-IV-TR*, the **simplified criteria for schizoid personality disorder** are:

> A pervasive pattern of detachment from social relationships and a restricted range of expressions of emotion, as indicated by at least four of the following: (1) neither desires nor enjoys close relationships; (2) almost always chooses solitary activities if able; (3) has little if any interest in having sexual experiences; (4) takes pleasure in few if any activities; (5) lacks close friends or confidants; (6) appears indifferent to the praise or criticism of others; (7) demonstrates emotional coldness, or flattened expression.

This is the classic loner, wholly detached from the praise or criticisms of others, and lacking all semblance of interpersonal warmth.

Adapted from the *DSM-IV-TR*, the **simplified criteria for schizotypal personality disorder** are:

> A pervasive pattern of social and interpersonal deficits marked by acute discomfort with, and reduced capacity for, close relationships as well as by cognitive or perceptual distortions and eccentricities of behavior, as indicated by at least five of the following: (1) the belief that innocuous events have special personal significance; (2) odd beliefs and magical thinking that influence behavior and are inconsistent with cultural norms; (3) unusual perceptual experiences, especially illusions; (4) odd and often stereotypical speech patterns; (5) paranoid ideation; (6) inappropriate or constricted facial expressions; (7) behavior that is eccentric or peculiar; (8) lack of close friends or confidants; (9) excessive social

anxiety that does not diminish with familiarity and tends to be associated with paranoid fears.

This is an individual who is remote and indifferent like the schizoid, but who also tends to engage in unusual thinking and superstitious beliefs.

Both schizoid and schizotypal persons have characteristics relating to the schizophrenic spectrum, but they do not meet the criteria for schizophrenia (such as hallucinations); schizoid personality disorder demonstrates more symptoms on the negative end of the spectrum (e.g., withdrawal) while schizotypal personality disorder exhibits more symptoms on the positive end of the spectrum (e.g., unusual perceptions). Either way, persons with these conditions come across socially as idiosyncratic. When they are employed, they often prefer (and sometimes function well at) solitary pursuits, such as those of a night-shift security guard or retail stock clerk. We may find in the future that these disorders are milder versions of the schizophrenic spectrum, but for now they are classified independently.

Turning to the last of the cluster A disorders, adapted from the *DSM-IV-TR*, the **simplified criteria for paranoid personality disorder** are:

An intense and pervasive distrust of others such that motives are interpreted as malevolent, presenting in a variety of contexts, as indicated by at least four of the following: (1) suspects, without sufficient basis, that others are exploiting, harming, or deceiving; (2) is preoccupied with unjustified doubts about the loyalty or trustworthiness of friends or associates; (3) is reluctant to confide in others because of unwarranted fear that the information will be used maliciously; (4) reads hidden or threatening meanings into benign remarks or events; (5) persistently bears grudges for perceived sleights; (6) perceives attacks on his or her character or reputation that are not apparent to others and is quick to react angrily or to counterattack; (7) has recurrent suspicions, without justification, regarding fidelity of spouse or sexual partner.

This is the individual who is constantly on the lookout for trickery, who is cold and humorless, and who tends to blame others for all misfortunes. Again, we see a clinical presentation that may best be described as "Axis I lite," exhibiting many hallmarks of paranoia that interfere with interpersonal relationships but do not meet the criteria for any of the psychotic disorders.

The cluster B disorders include those that are primarily dramatic, emotional, and unpredictable. For example, adapted from the *DSM-IV-TR*, the **simplified criteria for antisocial personality disorder** (ASPD) are:

A pervasive pattern of disregard for and violation of the rights of others occurring since early adolescence, as indicated by at least three of the following: (1) failure to conform to social norms with respect to lawful behaviors; (2) deceitfulness, as indicated by repeated lying, use of aliases, or conning others for personal profit or pleasure; (3) impulsivity; (4) irritability and aggressiveness, as indicated by repeated physical fights or assaults; (5) reckless disregard for safety of self or others; (6) consistent irresponsibility regarding commitments; (7) lack of remorse for actions.

Antisocial persons can sometimes be superficially charming, although this stems not from genuine enjoyment of the human connection but rather from the ability to disarm potential targets. Many successful criminals demonstrate such traits, and this character pathology is among the most common in jails and prisons.

There is often confusion concerning the use of the related terms "sociopath" and "psychopath" and the *DSM-IV-TR* diagnosis of antisocial personality disorder. Laypersons tend to reflexively think of serial killers when confronted with the former two descriptors. Actually, under the current *DSM* construct, there are no separate and distinct sociopathic or psychopathic diagnoses, and while serial killers would easily make the cut for antisocial personality disorder, so too might financial con men. Antisocial personality is thus a large category, as *DSM-IV-TR* has allowed for individuals with very different, albeit undesirable, personality traits and motivations to share the antisocial label. If one thinks in terms of possible further divisions, then sociopaths and psychopaths could at some point become distinct subsets within antisocial personality disorder, but at present they are not.[13]

Adapted from the *DSM-IV-TR*, the **simplified criteria for borderline personality disorder** are:

> A pervasive pattern of instability of interpersonal relationships, self-image, and mood, and marked impulsivity, beginning by early adulthood and indicated by at least five of the following: (1) frantic efforts to avoid real or imagined abandonment; (2) a pattern of unstable and intense interpersonal relationships characterized by alternating between extremes of idealization and devaluation; (3) identity disturbance: markedly and persistently unstable self-image or sense of self; (4) impulsivity in at least two areas that are potentially self-damaging (e.g., spending, sex, substance abuse, reckless driving, binge eating); (5) recurrent suicidal behavior, gestures, or threats, or acts of self-mutilation; (6) mood instability; (7) chronic feelings of intense emptiness; (8) inappropriate, intense anger or difficulty controlling anger (e.g., frequent displays of temper, constant anger, recurrent physical fights); (9) transient, stress-related paranoid ideation or severe dissociative symptoms.

These persons see the world entirely in black and white. For reasons that are not entirely clear, more than two thirds of them are female.[14] The hallmarks of their presentation include erratic emo-

---

13. Hare, Robert, *Psychopathy and Antisocial Personality Disorder: A Case of Diagnostic Confusion*, PSYCHIATRIC TIMES, vol. 13, no. 2, Feb. 1, 1996, p. 6. Psychopathy sometimes confounded the phrenologists. The San Francisco *Daily Evening Bulletin* of Jan. 5, 1869, referenced a story that had appeared two weeks earlier in the *Salt Lake Reporter* under the headline "Dreadful Depravity." Apparently a local thug in his late teens was convicted of murder and robbery, capping a criminal career that had stretched back to wanton vandalism as an adolescent. The news reporter stated prior to the execution of the convict that he demonstrated "perverted moral instinct," but then added that, "strangely enough, the young man has what phrenologists would call 'rather a good head.'" *See* _____, *Chauncey Millard*, EXECUTED TODAY, Jan. 29, 2011. *Available at* http://www.executedtoday.com/ (retrieved Dec. 26, 2011).

14. Moran, Mark, *supra* note 7.

tions, impulsivity with a tendency toward self-depreciation and self-mutilation, and frequent intense yet unstable relationships. Borderlines will often recall past events much differently, albeit subconsciously, than everyone else; the colloquial term "gas-lighting," from the 1944 movie *Gaslight,* refers to this phenomenon.

Adapted from the *DSM-IV-TR,* the **simplified criteria for histrionic personality disorder** are:

> A pervasive pattern of excessive emotionality and attention seeking, beginning by early adulthood and present in a variety of contexts, as indicated by at least five of the following: (1) is uncomfortable in situations in which he or she is not the center of attention; (2) interaction with others is often characterized by inappropriate seductive or provocative behavior; (3) displays rapidly shifting and shallow expression of emotions; (4) consistently uses physical appearance to draw attention to self; (5) has a style of speech that is excessively impressionistic and lacking in detail; (6) shows self-dramatization, theatricality, and exaggerated expression of emotion; (7) is easily influenced by others or circumstances; (8) considers relationships to be more intimate than they are in actuality.

This is the classic drama queen of either gender, notable for being superficial, displaying exaggerated attention-seeking behaviors, and having shallow interpersonal skills.

Adapted from the *DSM-IV-TR,* the **simplified criteria for narcissistic personality disorder** are:

> A pervasive pattern of grandiosity (in fantasy or behavior), need for admiration, and lack of empathy, beginning by early adulthood and present in a variety of contexts, as indicated by at least five of the following: (1) has a grandiose sense of self-importance; (2) is preoccupied with fantasies of unlimited success, power, brilliance, beauty, or ideal love; (3) believes that he or she is special and unique and can only be understood by, or should associate with, other special people; (4) requires excessive admiration; (5) has a sense of entitlement; (6) is interpersonally exploitative; (7) lacks

empathy; (8) is often envious of others or believes that others are envious of him or her; (9) shows arrogant, haughty behaviors or attitudes.

Such persons are extremely grandiose and self-centered, constantly in search of accolades from others, and regularly expressive their belief in being special and privileged. They are the classic prima donnas.

The cluster C disorders include those who are primarily anxious or fearful. For instance, adapted from the *DSM-IV-TR*, the **simplified criteria for avoidant personality disorder** are:

A pervasive pattern of social inhibition, feelings of inadequacy, and hypersensitivity to negative evaluation, beginning by early adulthood and present in a variety of contexts, as indicated by at least four of the following: (1) avoids occupational activities that involve significant interpersonal contact, because of fears of criticism, disapproval, or rejection; (2) is unwilling to get involved with people unless certain of being liked; (3) shows restraint within intimate relationships because of the fear of being shamed or ridiculed; (4) is preoccupied with being criticized or rejected in social situations; (5) is inhibited in new interpersonal situations because of feelings of inadequacy; (6) views self as socially inept, personally unappealing, or inferior to others; (7) is unusually reluctant to take personal risks or to engage in any new activities because they may prove embarrassing.

These individuals suffer from intense feelings of inadequacy and extreme sensitivity to any negative feedback. They avoid social interactions for these reasons, and they are often deemed to have very thin skin.

Adapted from the *DSM-IV-TR*, the **simplified criteria for dependent personality disorder** are:

A pervasive and excessive need to be taken care of that leads to submissive and clinging behavior and fears of separation, beginning by early adulthood and present in a variety of contexts, as indicated by at least five of the following: (1) has difficulty making everyday decisions without an excessive amount of advice and reassurance from others; (2) needs others to assume responsibility for most major areas of his or her life; (3) has difficulty expressing disagreement with others because of fear of loss of support or approval; (4) has difficulty initiating projects or doing things on his or her own; (5) goes to excessive lengths to obtain nurturance and support from others, to the point of volunteering to do things that are unpleasant; (6) feels uncomfortable or helpless when alone because of exaggerated fears of being unable to care for himself or herself; (7) urgently seeks another relationship as a source of care and support when a close relationship ends; (8) is unrealistically preoccupied with fears of being left to take care of himself or herself.

These individuals demonstrate a pathological dependence on others. They are needy to the point of suffocating those around them.

Adapted from the *DSM-IV-TR*, the **simplified criteria for obsessive-compulsive personality disorder** are:

A pervasive pattern of preoccupation with orderliness, perfectionism, and mental and interpersonal control, at the expense of flexibility, openness, and efficiency, beginning by early adulthood and present in a variety of contexts, as indicated by at least four of the following: (1) is preoccupied with details, rules, lists, order, organization, or schedules to the extent that the major point of the activity is lost; (2) shows perfectionism that interferes with task completion; (3) is excessively devoted to work and productivity to the exclusion of leisure activities and friendships; (4) is over-conscientious, scrupulous, and inflexible about matters of morality, ethics, or values; (5) is unable to discard worn-out or worthless objects even when they have no sentimental value; (6) is reluctant to delegate tasks or to work with others unless they submit to exactly his or her way of doing things; (7) adopts a miserly spending style toward both self and others; views money as something to be hoarded for future catastrophes; (8) shows rigidity and stubbornness.

This condition is not to be confused with obsessive-compulsive disorder, but instead is best conceptualized as another lite version of an Axis I condition. Persons with obsessive-compulsive personality disorder demonstrate rigid conformity to the rules and perfectionism. They tend to be workaholics, are usually serious and formal, and have difficulty loosening their ties and relaxing. They also have difficulty experiencing and expressing any genuinely tender emotions toward others. However, they fall short of the diagnostic criteria required for obsessive-compulsive disorder.

~~~~~~~~~~~~~~~~~~~~~~~~

As mentioned before, there are times when affliction with character pathology renders an individual "on the border" between intact and disrupted reality testing. Such disorders can be tremendously disruptive to quality of life and function, but make no mistake: while those with personality disorders may be markedly impaired in their social and occupational abilities, they are not psychotic. If psychosis does exist in sufferers, it is due to an additional and independent disorder. Co-morbidities can and do exist, and when a person with two conditions is treated with medication for an Axis I condition, for example, one is afterward left with the residual personality symptoms underneath.

From the foreword of the fourth edition of the *DSM:*

Although this [work] provides a classification of mental disorders, it must be admitted that no definition adequately specifies precise boundaries for the concept of "mental disorder." The concept of mental disorder . . . lacks a consistent operational definition that covers all situations. . . . Despite these caveats, the definition of "mental disorder" that was included in *DSM-III* and *DSM-III-R* is presented here because it is as useful as any other available definition and has helped to guide decisions regarding which conditions on the boundary between normality and pathology should be included in *DSM-IV*. In *DSM-IV*, each of the mental disorders is conceptualized as a clinically significant behavioral or psychological syndrome or pattern that occurs in an individual and that is associated with present distress or disability or with a significantly increased risk of suffering death, pain, disability, or an important loss of freedom.[15]

The foreword goes on to state that "inclusion here . . . of a diagnostic category . . . does not imply that the condition meets legal or other nonmedical criteria for what constitutes mental disease, mental disorder, or mental disability."[16]

Accordingly, how might courts view personality disorders in the context of legal proceedings? As noted above, a condition can be listed as a diagnostic category within the *DSM*s, but being so diagnosed does not mean that that person will be regarded as having a mental illness for all purposes of adjudication. This is an important point, as our jails and prisons are filled with individuals who meet the criteria for antisocial personality disorder—or at least personality disorder NOS with cluster B traits. But recall that those with personality disorders are usually fully cognizant of their actions and could not mount a defense of presumed insanity or diminished capacity. Some states expressly prohibit personality disorders from consideration if an insanity defense is being pursued (e.g., California, Utah, Oregon).[17] And the criteria for insanity of the Model Penal Code of the American Law Institute expressly state that "the terms mental disease or defect do not include an abnormality that is manifested only by repeated criminal or otherwise antisocial conduct."[18] Thus, those called sociopathic and psychopathic, while perceived as being "insane" by most laypersons, would encounter great difficulty in using aspects of their mental state as a defense in a court of law.

---

15. _____. Diagnostic and Statistical Manual of Mental Disorders, 4th ed., text revision. Washington, D.C.: American Psychiatric Ass'n (2000), p.xxxi.

16. *Id.*, p. xxxvii.

17. *Available at* http://www.justia.com/criminal/docs/calcrim/3400/ 3450.html (retrieved on July 24, 2011).

18. *Available at* http://law.jrank.org (retrieved on May 22, 2011); *see also* http://www.ali.org.

In closing, imagine how a law office happy-hour gathering might appear if many of the attendees had personality disorders. As you read the vignettes, see if you can identify specific facets of presentation that suggest the symptoms of personality disorders instead of those of frank Axis I disorders:

Bill went to the party against his wishes. A senior partner had told him that his attendance was expected. Bill might normally have ignored an invitation, but he was convinced for as long as he had worked there that the firm was plotting for a way to terminate his employment. Given the evil stares he was receiving in every meeting—even those meetings with persons he barely knew or had never met—he was further convinced that his absence this evening would be the excuse for which management was waiting in order to fire him as they had been planning all along. Bill's performance evaluations for his work in the research department were excellent—he did his work quietly and by himself in the stacks and on the computer—and he had received productivity bonuses in each of his past seven years. Words of appreciation for his attention to detail were just veneer, though. Bill knew that all of this was a front to lull him into a sense of complacency before firing him at the most humiliating moment. Before he entered the party, he spent at least 15 minutes watching the guests from a vantage point outside. A few entering the party had attempted to exchange pleasantries as they approached him outside, but he merely nodded as he viewed them with distrust. Even the waitstaff had looked at him with disdain through the window! When he finally did enter, Bill picked up a drink—ginger ale, not wine, since the latter would provide more ammunition for the termination that was being planned—and positioned himself near an exit so that he could slip away as soon as no one appeared to be watching him.

Gwen arrived late, and loudly. Her laugh was high-pitched and seemed forced at times, and before long she was hugging men she barely knew and making suggestive comments to some of the more staid associates. One (married) man particularly caught her eye, and before long she had confessed her deep affection for him, much to his embarrassment. Gwen's dress was bright red, skin-tight, and very low-cut, drawing attention to her recent breast augmentation, and her gestures were expansive and flamboyant. One concerned female associate tried to redirect her, but the helper's efforts were promptly rebuked with a sharp and insulting comment that was heard by many. Predictably, Gwen started drinking, and after a short while, she was so inebriated that she had to be helped to a back room to compose herself. Angered, she threw a glass on the floor, shattering it, and then broke down in tears, pulling at her bleached hair and gushing to anyone within hearing range that she was miserable and had often thought about what it would be like to go to sleep and never wake up. A car was called to drive her home, but halfway there, she told the driver that she had taken a handful of pills, and he diverted to the nearest emergency room.

Ted arrived at the party early because he was anxious to regale the partners with his latest success stories. This was the perfect venue in which to share with his coworkers his myriad accomplishments and the plaudits he had earned since their last time together. Working in the office during the busy day just didn't afford him a proper opportunity to broadcast his victories so that others could properly appreciate his skills and contributions. While at first interesting, Ted's stories soon became monotonous, repetitive, self-focused, and uncomfortable. Once, he had hijacked a conversation among a group of coworkers about a fellow attorney's struggle with chemotherapy. Ted had redirected the topic into a retelling of a high-end art deal that he had single-handedly brokered, while the ill attorney was forced to listen. When not talking at length about courtroom victories, he would elaborate on his recent publications and their glowing reviews, and about the killings he had made in the stock market. He rambled at length about his new BMW and recent trips to Europe and South America. He seemed not to notice the subtle social cues that people were tiring of his tales, and after one person abruptly and unceremoniously left a story mid-sentence, Ted had made insulting comments. He later made an unflattering (and unnecessary) remark about a suit worn by one of his coworkers, obviously embarrassing the man, but rather than apologize when the gaffe became too apparent to ignore, Ted talked around the issue and then made further comments to suggest that it was his coworker's fault for being so upset.

Scott slipped into the party without much notice. He immediately went to the northernmost corner of the room, which he had determined in advance, and situated himself so that his back was next to the wall and he faced in a southerly direction. He did this because he could feel the bad vibes in the room, and he knew from past experience that situating himself in this manner would neutralize any ill effects on his psychic being. A few staff members tried to engage Scott in conversation, but they found him to be "spacey" and made their exit quickly. Scott stayed in that position until exactly 7:14 p.m., the preordained time, at which point he put his untouched drink three inches from the edge of the nearest table and walked briskly to the door.

Mark arrived promptly at 5:00 p.m. He then proceeded to talk to each of the partners, allowing between five and eight minutes per interaction. He glanced at his watch several times during the interactions to make certain that he was not running overtime. It seemed to many that he was checking off each name from an internal mental list as he spoke to them. He didn't smile, and his face showed no signs of enjoyment. His conversation with the partners involved no pleasantries, but instead he focused on talking about the cases to which he had been assigned and the current status of each, even though he was at a social gathering after the workday had ended. One partner attempted to ask him about his family, and Mark quickly deflected the question and returned to his discussion of a recent motion in court. After having spoken to each of the seven partners present, he promptly headed for the door. On his way out he told one of the administrative assistants that he had to go home and work, despite this being the Friday evening of a long holiday weekend.

Take-Home Pearls

- A personality (character) disorder is an enduring, pervasive, and inflexible pattern of perception and behavior that deviates markedly from societal norms, has an onset by adolescence or early adulthood, and leads to considerable distress and impairment in social and occupational functioning. In short, it represents maladaptive and unhealthy stress management and coping mechanisms.
- The symptoms of personality disorders are fairly common in the general population. You will encounter such individuals, whether they are clients, attorneys, judges, or family members.
- While researchers continue to search for a biological explanation, current understanding is that some, but not all, individuals who are exposed in early life to neglect and abuse are at a higher risk of developing the maladaptive coping styles that are the hallmark of personality disorders.
- Treatment and management remain challenging, as there are no medications specifically indicated for use in personality disorders, and those so diagnosed rarely spontaneously accept that the pathology is theirs, and not that of everyone around them. Long-term psychotherapy, the best single management tool, requires a level of motivation and commitment that relatively few with personality disorders exhibit.
- Self-mutilation is one particularly disturbing and dangerous hallmark of disordered coping (seen most often in those with borderline personality disorder). Some may dismiss such acts as "just trying to get attention," but it is imperative that the clinician closely monitor and intervene when indicated, as some individuals can succeed at suicide despite actual ambivalence toward self-termination.

- Everyone has, at one point or another, experienced some of the milder maladaptive thoughts or behaviors that are associated with personality disorders *in extremis*. And yet while everyone has the occasional moment of maladaptive coping, not everyone has an Axis II diagnosis. The gray zone of the continuum makes differentiation of normalcy from pathology all the more challenging.
- Sociopathy and psychopathy, useful descriptive terms, are not freestanding diagnoses, and instead are currently subsumed under the larger umbrella of antisocial personality disorder.
- Symptoms seen among the personality disorders can be grouped into clusters A, B, and C. Cluster A involves those who are odd or eccentric, cluster B involves those who are dramatic and unpredictable, and cluster C involves those who are anxious and fearful.
- Axis I and Axis II disorders can be, and often are, comorbid; treating the former does little or nothing to the latter.
- A condition—such as a personality disorder—can be listed as a diagnostic category within the *DSM,* but that inclusion does not automatically mean someone so diagnosed has a mental disease or defect for purposes of adjudication.
- Attending a law office happy hour with colleagues with diagnosable personality disorders would not be fun.

Chapter 6

Psychotropic Medications and Other Treatment Options

> Physicians pour medicines about which they know little,
> for diseases about which they know less, into human be-
> ings about whom they know nothing.
>   —Voltaire, Eighteenth Century[1]
>
> It is high time that we should cease to search for the herb or
> salt or metal which in homeopathic or allopathic doses will
> cure mania. It will not be found any sooner than one will
> find pills which will make a great artist out of an ignorant
> lout, or a well-behaved child out of a spoiled one.
>   —Neumann, Nineteenth Century[2]
>
> Don't analyze me. . . . It's a deep, dark hole and you don't
> want to go there.
>   —Wednesday Addams, Twenty-First Century[3]

Psychiatry has come a long way in the past century. Available
interventions have evolved from insulin shock and lobotomies to

---

1. *Available at* http://www.ncbi.nlm.nih.gov/pmc/articles/PMC2574219/
pdf/rcgpoccpaper00050-0019.pdf (retrieved Dec. 3, 2011).
2. _____. Chlorpromazine and Mental Health: Proceedings of the Symposium Held by SmithKline and French Labs, June 6, 1955. Phila.: Lea & Febiger,
Inc. (1955), p. 178.
3. "The Addams Family," A New Musical Comedy, 2010 Broadway production.

seemingly more-tailored medications and psychotherapies. Proper and timely interventions for the right conditions alleviate much disability and misery. But somewhere along the way we have collectively come to expect that there is a diagnosis for every feeling and a cure for every diagnosis. This, in my view, is at the root of much of the generalized dissatisfaction with current mental health care.

Perhaps this expectation started with direct-to-consumer pharmaceutical advertising. The Food and Drug Modernization Act of 1997 ended the government's prohibition of such public marketing. Every nonphysician could afterward learn the names and indications of a host of medicines of which they otherwise would not know. Hypochondriacs rejoiced! The numbers of prescriptions shot skyward. In 1996, 13 million Americans were taking antidepressants, and that number more than doubled by 2005. Somewhat shockingly, one in ten Americans older than age six are now taking an antidepressant, and 5 percent of American minors are taking psychostimulants daily. Are we that much sicker? One cannot help but think of the line from the movie *Field of Dreams*: "If you build it, [they] will come."[4]

Before there was Prozac, however, there was "the talking cure," which became widely applied in the late nineteenth century with the advent of the works of Freud and his contemporaries. Granted, not all psychiatric conditions respond equally well to psychotherapy,

---

4. CARLAT, DANIEL. UNHINGED. N.Y.: Free Press (2010), p. 69; *see also* Bernstein, Carol, *Meta-Structure in DSM-5 Process*, PSYCHIATRIC NEWS, March 4, 2011, p. 7, for an op-ed piece suggesting that the entire schema of the *DSM* is nothing more than a template to support the expanded use of psychotropic medications (e.g., "it became necessary in the 1970s to facilitate diagnostic agreement among clinicians, scientists, and regulatory authorities given the need to match patients with newly emerging pharmacologic treatments"). *See also* Sayani, Daniel, *CDC: Antidepressant Use Up 400% in Past Decade*, THE NEW AMERICAN, Oct. 21, 2011. *Available at* http://www.thenewamerican.com/usnews/health-care/item/1937-cdc-antidepressant-use-up-400-in-past-decade (retrieved Dec. 26, 2011).

   From *Field of Dreams*, the correct quote is, "If you build it, he will come" (in reference to the spirit of a baseball great). From *Wayne's World 2*, the ghost of the late Jim Morrison apparently said, "If you book them, they will come." Together, these two quotes morphed into the near-universally stated but incorrect, "If you build it, they will come."

but at last the profession had something of apparent benefit to offer the afflicted.

The Talking Cure

"To my mind, psychotherapy remains the single most helpful technology for the treatment of *minor* depression and anxiety."

—Peter Kramer[5]

Psychotherapy as we know it today started not dissimilarly from the genesis of some religious sects, with a prophet and later disagreement among adherents regarding the correct interpretation of canon. And just as Henry Ford did not invent the automobile but has come to enjoy universal name recognition because of his popularization of the product, Freud arguably did not invent psychotherapy (but if you ask 100 laypersons to name its founder, many would, if not with much familiarity, name him).

In 1900, Freud published his seminal work, *The Interpretation of Dreams*, which sparked a revolution in the field of psychiatry. His psychoanalysis sprang largely from these writings. Not long afterward, however, two of Freud's disciples, Jung and Adler, broke with him and pursued conceptual paths of their own, setting up theoretical schisms that remain to this day.[6]

Psychotherapy, of which psychoanalysis is one flavor, is a technique for exploring problems of living with an eye toward invoking, if not a cure, at least a healthy understanding and acceptance by which a person can cope and develop a sense of well-being. Often this involves delving into the roots of the thoughts or feelings that are causing the difficulties, but other times the approach may be more superficial. Much depends on what the patient wants and can tolerate. While psychiatrists and psychologists are naturally associated with psychotherapy, there are many other practitioners of the art with widely ranging qualifications, including social workers, lay counselors, family and marriage therapists, rehabilitation

---

5. Kramer, Peter, *In Defense of Antidepressants*, N.Y. TIMES, July 9, 2011, p. SR-1, *referencing* LISTENING TO PROZAC (1993).

6. LYONS, A. & PETRUCELLI, R. MEDICINE, AN ILLUSTRATED HISTORY. N.Y.: Abradale Press (1987), p. 445.

specialists, nurses, physician extenders, and clergy (and, in far less formal settings and without training, friends and family).

If one were to gather psychotherapists in a room, there would be considerable agreement about preferred therapies for treatment, and for the most part the group would break down into several large subsets of those devoted to one mainstream approach or another. Cognitive behavioral therapy is currently big. Dialectic behavioral therapy is another oft-used approach for certain presentations. There are approaches employing psychoanalysis, applied behavioral analysis, psychodynamic psychotherapy, existential psychotherapy, humanistic psychotherapy, brief goal-directed psychotherapy, systemic psychotherapy, interpersonal psychotherapy, problem-solving psychotherapy, and the somewhat mysteriously named eclectic psychotherapy. One practitioner, only half in jest, described one of the more frequently used modalities, supportive psychotherapy, as "[a] poor relation of the [other] psychotherapies, a Cinderella stuck at home doing the routine psychiatric chores while her more glamorous psychotherapeutic sisters are away at the ball."[7] There are probably too many approaches to fully list.

But does psychotherapy work? And if so, does any single theoretical avenue rise above the rest? While the answer is far from settled, the opinion of many practitioners is that, when approached with reasonable expectation, sufficient motivation, and the necessary cognitive resources, any flavor of psychotherapy can prove both helpful and enlightening.[8, 9] Each philosophical option has its adherents, but what seems to help most in psychotherapy is the establishment of the therapeutic relationship between the patient and the therapist, and whatever approach fosters and maintains that

---

7. Hellerstein, David, *From Cinderella to Straw Man? Supportive Psychotherapy in the 21st Century,* PSYCHIATRIC TIMES, vol. 28, no. 8, Aug. 11, 2011, p. 7.

8. CARLAT, *supra* note 4, at p. 192; *see also* Shute, Nancy, "Shop for a Psychotherapist to Avoid the Lemons," *Morning Edition,* National Public Radio, May 16, 2011. *Available at* http://www.npr.org/2011/05/16/136283080/shop-for-a-pyschotherapist-to-avoid-the-lemons (retrieved Dec. 3, 2011).

9. Parker, Gordon & Fletcher, Kathryn, *Debate: What's the Evidence for the Evidence-Based Treatments of Depression?,* PSYCHIATRIC TIMES, Sept. 8, 2011, p. 13.

relationship is the "correct one" to use. It is worth noting that a recent meta-analysis of those diagnosed with depression who were treated employing one of seven different psychotherapy models revealed no major differences in outcome between any of them.[10] Further supporting evidence comes from the STAR*D trial, which illustrates that cognitive behavioral psychotherapy and interpersonal psychotherapy were just as effective as antidepressants in treating major depression.[11] Some investigators claim that cognitive behavioral psychotherapy, dialectic behavioral psychotherapy, psychodynamic psychotherapy, and interpersonal psychotherapy all measurably alter brain function, as seen on EEGs in patients suffering from depression, anxiety, and borderline personality disorder.[12] If so, it appears that properly applied psychotherapy is one more potentially powerful arrow in the quiver of treatment options available, usually regardless of the theoretical orientation.

Unfortunately, the success of psychotherapy has led to initially unforeseen outcomes. In the first half of the last century, only psychiatrists and psychologists provided psychotherapy, yielding a virtual lock on the market. Other disciplines eventually moved into psychotherapy despite howls of distress from the progenitors, and increasingly, third-party payers, responding to the law of supply and demand, decreased reimbursement for psychotherapy sessions as the market broadened. Many clinicians then had to choose between continuing to provide psychotherapy or maintaining their previous income levels. This challenge was further compounded

---

10. Hellerstein, *supra* note 7; some would further argue that a human therapeutic relationship is not even a necessity, as therapy animals have long been shown to exert a beneficial effect on those suffering from conditions such as depression and dementia; *see also* Boschert, Sherry, *Computer-Based CBT Brings Immediate Mood Improvement*, CLINICAL PSYCHIATRY NEWS, May 31, 2011, p. 5, for a discussion on one recent study that revealed an improvement in mood, albeit probably a transient one, in hospitalized depressed patients who received a single session of computer-assisted Cognitive Behavioral Psychotherapy on their PCs or smartphones (an effect described by the principal investigator as a "cost-effective and practical adjunct to face-to-face therapeutic approaches and antidepressant pharmacotherapy").

11. Shute, *supra* note 8.

12. Karlsson, Hasse, *Understanding the Mechanisms—How Psychotherapy Changes the Brain*, PSYCHIATRIC TIMES, vol. 28, no. 8, Aug. 11, 2011, p. 14.

by training programs in psychiatry that emphasized medications over psychotherapy, creating a gaping disconnect in treatment resulting from different disciplines providing different non-overlapping services.[13] In clinical situations in which medication is believed necessary, patients may now see a psychiatrist, OB-GYN, or family doctor for their prescription, and then see a different provider, perhaps a psychologist or social worker, for (the less handsomely reimbursed) psychotherapy.[14] This is far from the ideal, but it is the current reality.

A raging debate began in March 2011 when an article on this very topic appeared in the *New York Times*. The reporter described a psychiatrist trained in psychodynamic theory, Donald Levin of Doylestown, Pennsylvania, who had become a "mere pill pusher" and had outsourced his patients' talk therapy because he could not maintain his standard of living on the relatively paltry sums that third-party payers reimburse for psychotherapy alone. Dr. Levin described this medication treatment format as "working in a bus station," though by switching the emphasis of his clinical activity, he saw his caseload expand from fewer than 60 active patients to well over 1,200. He is far from alone in shifting the paradigm of his practice, for only 11 percent of active psychiatrists are estimated to still provide talk therapy to all of their patients.[15] And yet most practitioners acknowledge the benefit of psychotherapy for their patients. As one clinician stated, "Medication is important, but it's the relationship that gets people better."[16]

Of course, without big advertising dollars in direct-to-consumer pitches behind them, the psychotherapies don't have the same marketing power as do new pharmaceuticals. Psychotherapy is not always seen as quick and easy (e.g., once a day with breakfast), as are pills. Many hold that the public is quick to jump on the medication bandwagon merely because it's the only treatment option of

---

13. Weissman, Sidney, *Are We Training Psychiatrists to Provide Only Medication Management?*, PSYCHIATRIC TIMES, June 2011, p. 20.

14. BEITMAN, BERNARD. INTEGRATING PSYCHOTHERAPY AND PHARMACOTHERAPY. N.Y.: W.W. Norton (2003), p. 143.

15. Harris, Gardiner, *Talk Doesn't Pay, So Psychiatry Turns to Drug Therapy*, N.Y. TIMES, March 5, 2011, p. 8.

16. *Id.*

which they've heard—repeatedly and *ad nauseum* through the media—and which is perceived as not requiring much effort on their part.[17]

Other Treatment Modalities

The use of medications does not represent the only somatic attempts to conquer nervous afflictions. In the darkest reaches of clinical practice, sedation was once accomplished by simply knocking a patient unconscious.[18] It is said that the ancient Greeks threw depressed patients into the sea from the cliffs at Lefkas, and those who survived were pulled from the water and deemed cured. The Roman court physician Scribonius Largus is said to have treated Emperor Claudius's vague spells with the application of an electric eel to his scalp.[19] Other treatments for nonspecific fits included abstinence from bathing and sex, and the ingestion of human tissue, weasel and turtle blood, he-goat livers, and stork dung.[20] Smelly detritus from unwashed parts of the body were also applied to the faces of hysterical women in an attempt to repel an offending uterus back to its original position.[21]

More recently, in 1917, Austrian neurologist Julius Wagner-Jauregg started intentionally inoculating psychiatric patients with malaria to evoke a fever-cure for advanced syphilis (he won the Nobel Prize for this 10 years later).[22] The practice of Manfred Sakel at the Lichterfelder Asylum near Berlin also merits comment. Based on the archaic and incorrect belief that those with epilepsy are somehow protected from the ravages of other nervous conditions, Sakel

17. Shute, *supra* note 8.

18. LEGAL ASPECTS OF HEALTH CARE ADMINISTRATION (Pozgar, George ed.). Boston: Jones & Bartlett (2007), p. 2.

19. _____. THE VISITOR, OR MONTHLY INSTRUCTOR FOR 1841. London: The Religious Tract Society (1841), p. 363.

20. Paola, Suzanne, *Up From the Falling Sickness*, HELIX (Winter 1990-91), p. 7.

21. _____, *Do All Men Think All Women Are Like This?*, INSIDE UVA, vol. 20, no. 19, Nov. 15, 1990, p. 12.

22. Brown, E.M., *Why Wagner-Jauregg Won the Nobel Prize for Discovering Malaria Therapy for General Paresis of the Insane*, in HISTORY OF PSYCHIATRY, vol. 11 (Dec. 2000), pp. 371–82.

espoused the use of insulin coma therapy, in which seizures were induced by intentionally lowering a patient's blood sugar to dangerous levels with insulin before they were rescued by a shot of glucose.[23] And other so-called therapeutic seizures were accomplished by practitioners through the administration of camphor, Metrazol, and even toxic levels of vitamin C.[24, 25, 26]

Some clinicians opted instead for dangerous invasive procedures. In 1888, Swiss psychiatrist Gottlieb Burckhardt excised portions of the cerebral cortices of six sufferers "to extract from the brain mechanism the emotional and impulsive element in order to bring back the patient to calm."[27] The Portuguese neurologist Antonio Egas Moniz is then credited with popularizing leucotomy, the invasion of the cranial cavity in an operation that would later be known as a lobotomy. In 1935, he supervised a neurosurgeon in performing what was to be the first pre-frontal lobotomy, a procedure that consisted of drilling holes into the skull and strategically injecting small amounts of ethanol to destroy specific neural connections. Later, more refined lobotomies severed the neural connections to the frontal lobes using a steel probe. This procedure is now in disrepute, but it nevertheless earned Moniz the Nobel Prize for Medicine in 1949.[28]

Variations on the initial techniques were soon developed; the Italian psychiatrist Amarro Fiamberti in 1937 perfected the transorbital lobotomy. Instead of holes being drilled in the cranium, naturally occurring openings in the bony structure of the eye sockets were used to introduce a long metal skewer to sever the offending neurons. This technique was advertised as being an outpatient of-

---

23. Doroshow, Deborah, *Performing a Cure for Schizophrenia: Insulin Coma Therapy on the Wards*, in JOURNAL OF THE HISTORY OF MEDICINE AND ALLIED SCIENCES, vol. 62, no. 2 (2007), pp. 213–43.

24. Pearce, J.M.S., *Leopold Auenbrugger: Camphor-Induced Epilepsy— [A] Remedy for Manic Psychosis*, EUROPEAN NEUROLOGY, vol. 59, nos. 1/2 (2008), pp. 105–07.

25. BELLAK, LEOPOLD. DEMENTIA PRAECOX. N.Y.: Grune & Stratton (1947), p. 343.

26. *Id.*

27. Ford, Mary Ellen. *A History of Lobotomy in the United States*, in THE PHAROS (Summer 1987), p. 7.

28. *Available at* http://www.nobelprize.org (retrieved Dec. 4, 2011).

fice procedure, after which the patient could then leave wearing sunglasses![29] Regardless of whether the operation was pre-frontal or trans-orbital, as his technique evolved and spread in popularity, Moniz is quoted as having said, "Lobotomy is a simple operation, always safe, which may prove to be an effective surgical treatment in certain cases of mental disorder."[30]

Psychiatrist Walter Freeman and neurosurgeon James Watts introduced lobotomies to the United States in 1936. Even in the day, there was considerable controversy; the preface to the second edition of their joint effort, *Psychosurgery*, reads: "The authors regret to announce that they have been unable to reach an agreement on the subject of trans-orbital lobotomy. Freeman believes that he has proved the method to be simple, quick, effective and safe to entrust to the psychiatrist. Watts believes that any procedure involving cutting of brain tissue is a major operation and should remain in the hands of a neurological surgeon. In all other respects the authors are in complete and cordial agreement." At the peak of use in 1950, about 5,000 lobotomies were performed in the United States.[31] *Life* magazine even ran an article that said, in part, "the surgeon's blade, slicing through the connections between the prefrontal area and the rest of the brain, frees the tortured mind from its tyrannical ruler [while] intelligence is not affected."[32]

While long discredited as originally employed, psychosurgery has not entirely gone extinct. Though rare, occasionally procedures such as amygdalotomies, the severing of neural connections involving the brain's amygdala, are still performed in the United States to treat intractable aggression.[33] Additionally, deep-brain stimulation, requiring surgical implantation of an electrical device known

---

29. *Id.*

30. *Id.* Moniz apparently ignored the well-known case of Phineas Gage, a laborer who, in 1848, had a metal rod driven through his skull in a workplace accident and then had marked difficulties with cognition, emotion, and "animal passions."

31. *Id.*

32. _____, *Prefrontal Lobotomies*, LIFE, March 3, 1947, p. 95.

33. *See* Fountas, K., Smith, J. & Lee, G., *Bilateral Stereotactic Amygdalotomy for Self-Mutilation Disorder: A Case Report and Review of The Literature*, STEREOTACTIC AND FUNCTIONAL NEUROSURGERY, vol. 85, nos. 2/3, Jan. 12, 2007, p. 121–28.

as a brain pacemaker, is approved by the Food and Drug Administration (FDA) for the treatment of severe obsessive-compulsive disorder and major depression.[34]

In the 1750s, returning to the belief that epilepsy provided protection from other nervous system afflictions, English physician Richard Lovett and French physician J.B. LeRoy reported success in treating an unspecified mental illness by administering an electrical current, generated by rubbing amber with wool, to the body of a sufferer.[35] It was not until the 1930s, though, that electroconvulsive therapy (ECT) was pioneered by Italians Cerletti and Bini. The idea for ECT came to them while watching pigs being electrically stunned in slaughterhouses before being dispatched by knives. As the shocks merely dazed the pigs and didn't kill them, Cerletti and Bini concluded that the technique must be safe for use in humans. Before long, ECT was on its way to nonspecifically treating a number of different mental illnesses. It was found that patients with major depression benefited from ECT far more than patients with other conditions, so those with mood disorders thereafter became the treatment focus of ECT.[36, 37]

ECT started out barbarically. Electrodes were placed on the patient's temples, and an alternating current was administered to produce a seizure. At first, muscle relaxants were not used, so patients experienced violent muscle contractions during which they often bit their tongues, injured their limbs, and were incontinent. Staff had to hold a patient down, and if not careful, they were shocked as well. The patient would remain unconscious for up to 30 minutes, and this procedure would be repeated four times per week for a month or more.[38] Although the procedure was usually performed in hospitals,

---

34. Thomas, John, *Deep Brain Stimulation Surgery for OCD*, PSYCHIATRIC TIMES, vol. 28, no. 9, Sept. 2011, p. 1.

35. Whether this produced a seizure is unknown; *see* BELLAK, *supra* note 25, at p. 343.

36. KALES, ANTHONY. EVALUATION AND TREATMENT OF INSOMNIA. N.Y.: Oxford Univ. Press (1984), p. 3.

37. Selvin, Beatrice, *Electroconvulsive Therapy - 1987*, ANESTHESIOLOGY, vol. 67, no. 3, Sept. 1987, pp. 367–85.

38. Perryman, Kent, *Shocking Treatment*, SIERRA SACRAMENTO VALLEY MEDICAL SOCIETY NEWSLETTER, vol. 58, no. 1, January/ Feb. 2007, p. 1.

some patients received ECT at home, as psychiatrists were known to carry portable devices on house calls.[39, 40, 41]

The ECT of today, in contrast, is rather anticlimactic. With chemically induced paralysis, often the only way one can tell that a patient is experiencing a seizure is by watching the EEG needle dancing along the graph paper, or by noting slight twitching in the eyelids or fingers of the patient. It is unfortunate that ECT—introduced in the United States at almost the same time as lobotomies and Metrazol seizure therapy—is often associated with these other, far less successful treatments. Despite its antecedents, evidence strongly suggests that ECT can resolve symptoms of what might otherwise be intractable depression. That being said, medical science, as with so much else in psychiatry, still does not understand its mechanism of action. Nevertheless, PubMed currently catalogues more than 9,000 citations of scientific articles on the efficacy and safety of ECT.[42] As Charles Kellner stated in a recent issue of *Psychiatric Times*, "Many articles about electroconvulsive therapy [contain] a statement about ECT's stature as the most effective treatment for serious

39. *Id.*

40. In the author's personal collection is one of these portable ECT machines, the Model B-24, manufactured by Medcraft of Skipjack, Penn., some time prior to 1964. The settings allow for a range of 70–170 volts, in 10-volt increments, with 0.1- to 1.0-second pulses. The machine operates on 115v current, weighs 11.5 pounds, and is 5" x 6" x 11". It in a leatherette carrying case with handle.

41. In the earliest days of ECT, when treatment didn't yield any apparent benefit or the patient worsened, doctors simplistically believed that the patient must have a space-occupying lesion (brain tumor); *see* Reinhart, Melvin & Shafii, Mohammad, *Profound Regression Following Two Electroconvulsive Treatments*, Canadian Psychiatric Ass'n Journal, vol. 12, 1967, p. 426, for an interesting and disturbing case study of a young woman who was given a series of ECTs in the late 1950s and early 1960s for apparent depression, and after brief improvement suffered memory loss, psychotic disorganization, anorexia, incontinence, respiratory distress, and death, despite a normal physical exam and a lack of brain pathology at autopsy.

42. Kellner, Charles, *Electroconvulsive Therapy: The Second Most Controversial Medical Procedure*, Psychiatric Times, vol. 28, no. 1, Feb. 8, 2011, p. 9.

depression; the statement is a reminder to the reader that, yes, ECT is still used and is still a part of mainstream psychiatry."[43]

Not only does ECT often work where other interventions fail, but it can be used safely in certain populations (e.g., cardiac patients) from whom medications can be problematic.[44] While side effects such as memory loss are still possible, modern techniques have been refined to lessen that likelihood.[45, 46] Nevertheless, biases remain, and ECT is still not practiced universally. In an editorial, Kellner further noted that the 1975 film *One Flew Over the Cuckoo's Nest*, which depicted a version of ECT that was by then more than 20 years obsolete, did more damage to the public perception of ECT than probably any other event. He added:

> A vocal minority of people expends substantial effort to discredit ECT and its practitioners, promulgating a view that ECT is some-how morally wrong and should be banned. Education about ECT, although listed among the Psychiatry Residency Review Committee requirements, is mostly given short shrift in residencies, not to mention in medical school curricula. . . . Almost all of the controversy about ECT is anecdotal opinion, unsupported by evidence. The negative opinions are largely driven by organizations that are anti-psychiatry in general, not just anti-ECT.[47]

In the author's opinion, for carefully selected patients with severe and treatment-resistant major depression, there is no medication therapy that can exceed the efficacy of ECT.[48]

---

43. *Id.*; *see also* Kellner, C.H., Knapp, R., Husain, M.M., et al., *Bifrontal, Bitemporal and Right Unilateral Electrode Placement in ECT: A Randomised Trial*, British Journal of Psychiatry, no. 196 (2010), pp. 226–34.

44. Rasmussen, Keith, et al., *Electroconvulsive Therapy in the Medically Ill*, The Psychiatric Clinics of North America, vol. 25, no. 1, March 2002, p. 180.

45. Kellner, *supra* note 43.

46. Selvin, *supra* note 37.

47. Kellner, *supra* note 43.

48. It never takes long before postulated treatment modalities are extrapolated from original intent, only sometimes successfully. A noninvasive brain stimulation technique called transcranial direct current stimulation (TDCS) was applied to 15 subjects for 20 minutes a day over a week in a study conducted at Oxford University. Based on the polarity of the current applied to the brains'

The distaste that many still feel for ECT has resulted in efforts to find additional non-pharmacologic interventions for certain psychiatric conditions. One alternative is transcranial magnetic stimulation, which, as the name suggests, involves applying magnets to the scalp. This technique is said to be best for the negative symptoms of refractory schizophrenia but of only limited benefit to those with major depression. As with much of psychiatry, its mechanism of action is unknown. It is considered safe, however, as it does not require implanted electrodes, and the initial clinical trials administering the magnetic treatment twice daily for five days did not reveal any side effects other than mild headaches.[49, 50]

There is also stimulation of the brain's vagus nerve, first postulated as a potential treatment for mental illness prior to World War II and recently approved by the FDA for control of intractable seizures. In patients treated with this anticonvulsant protocol, an accompanying elevation of emotion was sometimes noted. Researchers have since suggested that vagal stimulation might have the ability

---

parietal lobes, it appears in this small study that electricity can enhance the retention of recently learned numerical material for up to six months. The Oxford team proposed this intervention for those suffering from stroke or degenerative illnesses, but the mainstream media picked it up almost instantly and implied it as a possible treatment for those who don't like math classes and have poor grades. *See* Spiegel, Alix, *Can Electric Shocks to the Brain Improve Math Skills?,* Health Blog, NPR, Nov. 5, 2010. *Available at* http://www.npr.org/blogs/health/2010/11/05/131104148/move-over- math-tutors for a more balanced approach from the lay press (retrieved Dec. 4, 2011). *See also* Kadosh, R., et al., *Modulating Neuronal Activity Produces Specific and Long-Lasting Changes in Numerical Competence,* Current Biology, vol. 20, no. 22, Nov. 4, 2010, pp. 2016–2020.

49. Daban, C., Martinez-Aran, A., Cruz, N., and Vieta, E., *Safety and Efficacy of Vagus Nerve Stimulation in Treatment-Resistant Depression—A Systematic Review,* Journal of Affective Disorders, no. 110 (2008), pp. 1–15; *see also* George, M.S., Lisanby, S.H., Avery, D., et al., *Daily Left Prefrontal Transcranial Magnetic Stimulation Therapy for Major Depressive Disorder— A Sham-Controlled Randomized Trial,* Archives of General Psychiatry, no. 67 (2010), pp. 507–16. TMS is felt to be promising for negative symptoms, but for a contrarian view on its apparent lack of efficacy for positive symptoms, *see* Boschert, Sherry, *Guided TMS Not Effective for Hallucinations,* Clinical Psychiatry News, Oct. 11, 2011, p. 12.

50. Jancin, Bruce, *Theta Burst Stimulation Promising for Refractory Schizophrenia,* Clinical Psychiatry News, April 8, 2011, p. 11.

to alter other brain functions, such as those that mediate mood disorders. Studies are currently ongoing to see if this therapy could be clinically beneficial for the eradication of not only depression but also anxiety, insomnia, and chronic pain.[51]

The World of Psychotropic Medications

This is not to be a dry iteration of pharmacokinetics (how the body acts on drugs) and pharmacodynamics (how drugs act on the body).[52, 53] Instead, this section will be a whirlwind tour through the major classes of psychiatric medications and will provide at least a passing familiarity with available compounds for the non-prescriber.

Medications used for psychiatric purposes, at least in the eighteenth and nineteenth centuries, were discovered by accident and applied in a manner decidedly nonscientific. Benjamin Rush used to employ opium for the nonspecific treatment of lunatics. Samuel Woodward used hemlock for the same purpose. Amariah Brigham used cannabis.[54] Saltpeter and bromides were employed as anti-aphrodisiacs for the chronically institutionalized who exhibited hormonal impulse-control problems. Gold injections were sometimes used as well.[55] Everything was anecdotal, and often these

51. George, Mark, et al., *Vagus Nerve Stimulation: A Potential Therapy for Resistant Depression?*, THE PSYCHIATRIC CLINICS OF NORTH AMERICA, vol. 23, no. 4, Dec. 2000, pp. 758, 767, 777.

52. *See* STAHL, STEPHEN. PSYCHOPHARMACOLOGY OF ANTIDEPRESSANTS. London: Martin Dunitz, Ltd. (1998), p. 101.

53. Beware of the carefully crafted pharmaceutical marketing ploy posing as unbiased scientific literature. For example, there is the *MRP Psychiatrists' Edition Drug Reference Manual*, financed and distributed to psychiatrists for free by AstraZeneca. The author has the 2008 edition, which purports to cover medications for all different mental health and non-mental health indications. Predictably, AstraZeneca products are prominently and repeatedly advertised (e.g., the antipsychotic Seroquel on both front and back covers, plus large, color, multipage ads in the middle). A legal disclaimer states, "It should be understood that in funding this edition, AstraZeneca does not assume, and expressly disclaims, any obligation to obtain and include in this compilation any information about any other manufacturers' products."

54. _____. CHLORPROMAZINE AND MENTAL HEALTH: PROCEEDINGS OF THE SYMPOSIUM HELD BY SMITHKLINE AND FRENCH LABS, JUNE 6, 1955. Phila.: Lea & Febiger, Inc. (1955), p. 178.

55. LARSON, ERIK. THE DEVIL IN THE WHITE CITY. N.Y.: Vintage Press (2004), p. 161.

agents relieved symptoms through nothing more than extreme sedation, and did nothing to actually address the (unknown) root cause
of the underlying disease. There were no blinded clinical trials, as
the concept was then unknown.[56]

By the late nineteenth century, patent medicines had taken the
United States by storm. Interestingly, the term "patent medicine" is
misleading, since the majority of these agents were not patented (so
the inventors would not have to reveal the questionable ingredients). The name stems instead from letters-patent, documents originally issued by the royal houses of Europe for certain favored
products.[57] The name eventually was applied to any similarly appearing potions, even though it is unlikely that many, if any, of
such worthless mixtures ever darkened the doorway at Windsor
Castle. These compounds were marketed under an array of colorful
names and fanciful claims—including the ability to cure mental illnesses—in the days before FDA oversight. This was the era that
coined the descriptor "snake oil," since essence-of-reptile was often listed as an ingredient in more than one useless suspension
hawked at traveling medicine shows.[58]

The first modern psychiatric drugs were discovered by sheer
happenstance. Thorazine [chlorpromazine] was found to have antipsychotic properties only during the hunt for a better antihista-
mine. Tofranil [imipramine], an antidepressant, came about after
random tweaking of the molecular structure of Thorazine. One of
the first postulated clinical uses of the antidepressant Prozac

---

56. Chlorpromazine and Mental Health, *supra* note 54, at p. 388; *see also*
Oliver, John. Sexual Hygiene and Pathology: A Manual for Physicians. Phila.:
J.B. Lippincott Co. (1955), p. 22.

57. *Available at* http://www.hagley.lib.de.us/library/exhibits/patentmed
(retrieved on Sept. 9, 2011).

58. Once FDA regulations squeezed the industry, patent medicine makers
segued into other lines of production, often toiletries that were not ingested
and required minimal or no oversight. One surviving descendent of patent
medicine is modern herbal shampoos, which claim to contain all manner of
fruits and vegetables, and almost certainly do nothing extra for one's hair
other than make it smell like the ingredients in question. Nutritional supplements—with required disclaimers that they haven't been clinically tested
and are not intended to diagnose or treat any disease—are also descendents
of the patent medicine era.

[fluoxetine] was actually as a diet pill. The antimanic lithium was, quite by accident, noted to sedate guinea pigs in the lab.[59] Medications were discovered marketed, and they began to dominate the psychiatric landscape; deinstitutionalization of the chronically hospitalized quickly followed. Starting in the late 1950s when psychotropic pills were first employed widely, for better or worse, available hospital beds for the mentally ill in the United States shrunk from more than half a million to less than one-tenth of that number by the turn of the twenty-first century.[60] Medications were to render psychiatric facilities obsolete.

~~~~~~~~~~~~~~~~~~~~~~~~~

Given the purported complexities of psychopharmacology, who actually does all of this prescribing? For the coming decade, there is a projected shortfall of more than 45,000 psychiatrists in the United States.[61] Because of this, a large number of psychotropic medications are already prescribed and monitored by nonpsychiatric physicians, or by extenders such as physician assistants or nurse practitioners.[62] Physician assistants can prescribe in all states under the supervision of a licensed physician, though differences among states do exist regarding the ability to prescribe controlled substances. State laws vary more widely concerning nurse practitioners, though a supervising physician is still needed. Either way, a specific familiarity with mental health issues is not required for these extenders or their supervisors to prescribe psychiatric agents. Thus, a physician extender can prescribe all noncontrolled psychotropic medications the same as she would be able to prescribe antihypertensives or anti-

---

59. CARLAT, at p. 87–90.

60. Mojtabai, Ramin & Olfson, Mark, *Proportion of Antidepressants Prescribed Without a Psychiatric Diagnosis Is Growing*, HEALTH AFFAIRS, vol. 30, no. 8, Aug. 2011, pp. 1434–42; *see also* Hayes, Emily, *Non-Psychiatric Prescribing Fuels Rise in Antidepressant Use*, CLINICAL PSYCHIATRY NEWS, Aug. 5, 2011, p. 8.

61. Geppert, Cynthia & Taylor, Peter, *Should Psychiatrists Prescribe Neuroenhancers for Mentally Healthy Patients?*, PSYCHIATRIC TIMES, vol. 28, no. 3, April 1, 2011, p. 5.

62. *See* Rutkow, Lainie, et al., *Prescribing Authority During Emergencies*, JOURNAL OF LEGAL MEDICINE, no. 32, July 2011, pp. 249–60; *see also* Yates, Deanna, et al., *Should Psychologists Have Prescribing Authority?*, PSYCHIATRIC SERVICES, no. 55 (2004), p. 1420; Mojtabai & Olfson, *supra* note 60; Hayes, *supra* note 60.

biotics. Also, licensed general practitioners—physicians without any specific expertise in the use of psychotropics—can prescribe whatever they so choose without any specialty-specific supervision.

In addition to rankling many psychiatrists, who see others prescribing psychotropic medications as impinging on their exclusive domain, generalists and extenders who prescribe have also raised hackles among some doctoral-level psychologists.[63] At present, only Louisiana and New Mexico confer specially trained psychologists with psychotropic prescribing privileges.[64] Many psychologists have argued that because their knowledge of mental health issues is far above that of most family doctors and physician extenders, they too could prescribe at least as effectively as the current crop of nonpsychiatrists doing the very same thing, provided they received proper training in psychopharmacology.[65]

While there may be some strong arguments against such privileges for nonphysicians, their lack of understanding about drug mechanisms of action has not been one of the more convincing objections. Neuroscientists and psychiatrists have attempted to understand psychotropic mechanisms for years, but with little success.[66] However, that has not stopped psychiatrists from prescribing. Theories abound as to the neurotransmitters that are responsible for central nervous system dysfunctions: norephinephrine, serotonin, dopamine, oxytocin, and multiple combinations.[67, 68] Stephen Stahl posits the existence of no fewer than 63 discreet neurotransmitters. Doubtless there are others; he further postulates that there could be

---

63. Keep in mind that psychiatrists also argued in the past against letting anyone outside the profession perform psychotherapy, and there are now many excellent nonpsychiatrist therapists out there.

64. Rutkow, *supra* note 62; *see also* Stambor, Zak, *Psychology's Prescribing Pioneers*, MONITOR ON PSYCHOLOGY, vol. 37 (2006), pp. 30–33; *see also* _____, *Prescribing Bills Proliferate Despite Numerous Defeats*, PSYCHIATRIC NEWS, vol. 44, no. 14, July 17, 2009, p. 13. The U.S. Dep't of Defense had a pilot program for prescribing psychologists that was allowed to expire.

65. *Prescribing Bills Proliferate, id.*

66. STAHL, ANTIDEPRESSANTS, *supra* note 52, at p. 1.

67. *Id.*

68. Hamilton, Jon, *What Do Women Really Want? Oxytocin*, "Health Blog," National Public Radio, Nov. 15, 2010. *Available at* http://www.npr.org/blogs/health/ 2010/11/15/131336097/what-do-women-really-want-oxytocin (retrieved Jan. 3, 2011).

several thousand unique brain chemicals.[69] Medical science actually knows far more about the mechanisms of adverse effects—constipation, dry mouth, tremors—than about the mechanisms of the beneficial effects.[70]

Daniel Carlat, a psychiatrist in Boston and author of the bestselling *Unhinged*, does not believe that our current psycho-pharmacopeia is particularly complicated to use, let alone precise, although the public is led to believe that it is:

> Patients often view psychiatrists as wizards of neurotransmitters who can choose just the right medication for whatever chemical imbalance is at play. This exaggerated conception of our capabilities has been encouraged by drug companies, by psychiatrists ourselves, and by our patients' understandable hopes for cures.[71]

Dr. Levin, whom we met earlier, stated it even more bluntly:

> I'm good at [prescribing psychiatric medications], but there's not a lot to master in medications. It's like *2001: A Space Odyssey*, where you had Hal the supercomputer juxtaposed with the ape with the bone. I feel like I'm the ape with the bone now.[72]

If the neurotransmitters-are-too-complicated argument does not stand up to scrutiny, there are those who allege that an explosion in off-label prescribing—using drugs for conditions not approved by the FDA—is driven by prescribers who are not familiar with the subtleties of psychopharmacology.[73] But is this allegation any more accurate than the last?

---

69. STAHL, STEPHEN. ESSENTIAL PSYCHOPHARMACOLOGY. N.Y.: Cambridge University Press (2000), pp. 18–19.

70. PSYCHOSIS AND SCHIZOPHRENIA: THINKING IT THROUGH (Stahl, Stephen, ed.). Carlsbad: Neuroscience Education Inst. (2010); *see also* Frances, Allen, *Psychiatry Should Stay Comfortable in Its Own Skin: No Good Comes from Overselling Our Science Base*, PSYCHIATRIC TIMES, May 13, 2011, p. 9; *see also* STAHL, ANTIDEPRESSANTS, *supra* note 52, at p. 83.

71. CARLAT, *supra* note 4, at p.140.

72. Harris, *supra* note 15.

73. Hayes, *supra* note 60.

Medications today are carefully regulated by the Food and Drug Administration through a system that has evolved over the past half century; it is predicated on rigorously controlled and monitored protocols at each step of the development process. If a drug is eventually approved and marketed in the United States, it comes with a detailed medico-legal regulatory document known as the package insert, which includes indications and prescribing information. Any usage of the drug that deviates from the indications and guidelines written in the package insert is accordingly considered off-label.[74, 75]

How prevalent is off-label prescribing? Very. Psychiatric medications are always at the top of the off-label list; a number of studies suggest that nearly half of psychotropic prescriptions nationwide are off-label.[76, 77, 78] Despite the tremendous logistical efforts involved in government vetting, the use of off-label prescriptions, paradoxically, has been explicitly sanctioned, not condemned, by the FDA, professional medical organizations, and the courts. For example, the statement from the FDA that has been printed in the foreword of the *Physicians' Desk Reference* since at least 1981 says, "[w]e recognize[] that [federal statute] does not limit the manner in which a physician may use an approved drug. Once a product has been approved for marketing, a physician may choose to prescribe it for uses or in treatment regimens or patient populations not included in approved labeling. The FDA also observes that accepted medical practice includes drug use that is not reflected in approved drug labeling."[79] And from the courts, this is representative: "[a prescriber]

---

74. *Available at* http://www.archive.org/stream foodsfoodadulter01unituoft #page/n7/mode/2up (retrieved May 23, 2011).

75. *Available at* http://www.fda.gov/regulatoryinformation/legislation/ ucm148690.htm (retrieved May 23, 2011).

76. *Available at* http://www.fda.gov/AboutFDA/WhatWeDo/History/ ProductRegulation/ucm132818.htm (retrieved June 1, 2011).

77. *Available at* http://www.fda.gov/AboutFDA/WhatWeDo/History/ ThisWeek/ucm117831.htm (retrieved May 23, 2011).

78. Edersheim, Judith, *Off-Label Prescribing*, PSYCHIATRIC TIMES, vol. 26, no. 4, April 14, 2009, p. 12.

79. _____. *Foreword*, PHYSICIANS' DESK REFERENCE, 57th ed. Montvale, N.J.: Thomson Medical Economics (2003); *see also* http://www.ncbi.nlm.nih.gov/ pmc/articles/PMC1214572/#B12 (retrieved May 3, 2011).

may prescribe an approved drug for any medical condition, irre-
spective of whether the FDA has determined that the drug is safe
and effective with respect to that illness."[80] The rationale proffered
is that the FDA works to regulate pharmaceutical manufacturers,
and thus it was never intended to regulate the actual practice of
medicine.[81, 82]

In the absence of a better understanding of neurotransmitters
and mental illness, or definitive studies that lay the blame for dangerous off-label prescribing practices squarely at the feet of

---

80. Washington Legal Found. v. Friedman, 13 F. Supp. 2d, 51, 55 (D.D.C. 1998).

81. _____, "Patient Access to Treatments Prescribed by Their Physicians," position statement of the Board of Trustees of the American Psychiatric Association, July 2007. And while no one suggests that off-label prescribing should be prohibited, some studies question how much benefit the practice actually affords patients. For an interesting discussion on this topic, *see* Moran, Mark, *Using Antipsychotics Off Label Often Brings Little Benefit*, PSYCHIATRIC NEWS, vol. 46, no. 20, Oct. 21, 2011, pp. 15–26. *See also* Moon, Mary Ann, *Off Label Use of Atypical Antipsychotics Minimally Effective*, CLINICAL PSYCHIATRY NEWS, Sept. 27, 2011, pp. 9–11.

82. In 2009, the Ethics, Law and Humanities Committee of the American Academy of Neurology (AAN) issued guidelines on patient requests for neuroenhancers. The AAN report defines this term as "prescribing medications to normal adults for the purpose of augmenting their normal cognitive or affective function," the most controversial aspect being the underlying assumption that a valid goal of medicine is to improve the functioning of individuals who have no "diagnosable mental health or medical condition." Off-label prescribing such as this can predictably shift the burden of proof from the patient-plaintiff to the prescriber-defendant. *See* Geppert, Cynthia & Taylor, Peter, *Should Psychiatrists Prescribe Neuroenhancers for Mentally Healthy Patients?*, PSYCHIATRIC TIMES, vol. 28, no. 3, April 1, 2011, p. 11. And even following FDA-approved instructions is not wholly protective. In 1995, the U.S. Supreme Court stated that in general, unless a statute contains clear language that compliance with regulatory standards preempts state tort actions, compliance with such regulations may be considered as evidence by the trier of fact but should not act as a bar to tort liability. *See* Freightliner Corp. v. Myrick, 514 U.S. 280, 115 S. Ct. 1485. Thus, the quality of informed consent documentation becomes even more important. *See* Lansdale, Edward, *Used as Directed? How Prosecutors Are Expanding the False Claims Act to Police Pharmaceutical Off-Label Marketing*, NEW ENG. L. REV., vol. 41, no. 159, pp. 165–66.

nonpsychiatrists, it appears that much of the hype surrounding the complexities of the so-called chemical imbalance theory of psychiatric illness and treatment is magnified by some providers who wish to protect turf and others who may be less than unbiased in the discussion.

~~~~~~~~~~~~~~~~~~~~~~~~~~~~~

Most psychotropic medications can be divided into four main groupings: the antipsychotics, the antidepressants, the anxiolytics, and the mood stabilizers. The lines of delineation among these groups are not as clear as one might think, as there is considerable overlap; antidepressants are often used to combat anxiety, antipsychotics can be used as mood stabilizers, and all of them have numerous off-label uses.[83]

In the early 1950s, the chemical compound chlorpromazine, later widely known as Thorazine, was discovered. The excitement, as reflected in the welcoming words of the president of Smith Kline & French Pharmaceuticals at an industry symposium in 1955, is still evident more than half a century later:

> Ladies and gentlemen: the fact that you are here—attending a conference on mental illness, a conference centered around a new drug and sponsored by a pharmaceutical house—shows that there is today a new climate surrounding the treatment of the mentally ill. . . . In a remarkably short time you have stimulated interest in chemotherapy in hundreds of mental hospitals. . . . [and] just as we accepted the responsibility for making a good drug, so we accepted this role of information center and the responsibility of disseminating information as it develop[s].[84]

Thorazine is a blocker of the neurotransmitter dopamine. It was found to exert considerable antipsychotic effect in psychotic patients. Naturally, these two observations led researchers to the conclusion that it is an excess of dopamine in the central nervous system

---

83. KAPLAN, HAROLD & SADOCK, BENJAMIN. POCKET HANDBOOK OF PSYCHIATRIC DRUG TREATMENT. Baltimore: Williams & Wilkins (1993), p. 15.

84. CHLORPROMAZINE AND MENTAL HEALTH: PROCEEDINGS OF THE SYMPOSIUM HELD BY SMITHKLINE AND FRENCH LABS, JUNE 6, 1955. Phila.: Lea & Febiger, Inc. (1955), p. 9.

that leads to psychosis, and thus it must be a blockade of that same excess dopamine that alleviates symptoms. The problem with this theory is that some medications that block dopamine (e.g., Reglan, used for gastric reflux) do not have measurable antipsychotic effect, so something besides basic dopamine blockade must produce a clinical benefit. Actually, we now know that there are many different subtypes of dopamine receptors, and in addition, it is postulated that other neurochemical receptors are also involved in the genesis of psychosis, including those specific for serotonin, acetylcholine, and glutamate.[85]

Before this was fully appreciated, however, other dopamine-blocking compounds were isolated, and many were found to have antipsychotic effects similar to Thorazine. These included Haldol [haloperidol], Loxitane [loxapine], Mellaril [thioridazine], Navane [thiothixene], Stelazine [trifluoperazine], Trilafon [perphenazine], Moban [molindone], Prolixin [fluphenazine], and a number of other compounds.

Over years of clinical use, these antipsychotics (which would later come to be known as first generation, conventional, traditional, or typical agents) had an unfortunate tendency in some individuals to cause neurological side effects (i.e., tremors and stiffness acutely, and parkinsonism in the long term). Additionally, these drugs were seemingly much better at alleviating what psychiatrists call positive symptoms of psychosis (e.g., hallucinations) than they were at ridding a patient of so-called negative symptoms (e.g., apathy and social withdrawal).[86] The search was on, then, for medications that would lessen neurological side effects and increase efficacy in regard to both positive and negative symptoms.

In 1989 Clozaril [clozapine], an antipsychotic compound originally studied and shelved in the 1970s, was reintroduced. It worked very well, even in many cases of psychotic patients thought to be untreatable. Here at last was a drug, chemically different from the conventional antipsychotics, that appeared to alleviate entrenched symptoms that other agents sometimes did not touch.[87] Even more

---

85. Stahl, *supra* note 52, at p. 3.
86. *Id.*, p. 35.
87. *Id.*, p. 49.

surprising, this compound seemed to work as well, if not better, for negative symptoms as it did for positive ones.

Clozaril was the first marketed of what would come to be known as second-generation or atypical antipsychotics. The atypicals were believed to act upon both dopamine and serotonin receptors in the brain, unlike the older conventional antipsychotics that were then thought to strictly target dopamine.[88] These atypicals include Abilify [aripiprazole], Zyprexa [olanzapine], Invega [paliperidone], Seroquel [quetiapine], Risperdal [risperidone], Fanapt [iloperidone], Saphris [asenapine], Latuda [lurasidone], and Geodon [ziprasidone]. Clozaril remains to this day in a class by itself, and for reasons beyond its often superior efficacy. Clozaril also has a known risk of causing agranulocytosis, a precipitous drop in a certain type of white blood cell; approximately 1 percent of patients who take Clozaril will develop this potentially fatal complication, which is not even dose-dependent, as it can happen at low dosing. Though some other drugs are known to cause agranulocytosis, no other antipsychotic has the same degree of risk as Clozaril. Because of this, Clozaril must be accompanied by weekly blood draws—something that no other psychotropic medication of any class mandates—to check that the number of white blood cells hasn't markedly decreased since the last check. If white blood cells do decrease, the frequency of lab monitoring increases, but the medication may need to be stopped altogether.[89] Clozaril is a great antipsychotic, but this heavy baggage has markedly impacted its breadth of use.

The longer these two broad groups of antipsychotics have been prescribed in the United States, however, the fewer substantive differences are noted. The multi-site, double-blind Clinical Antipsychotic Trials of Intervention Effectiveness (CATIE) study, sponsored by the National Institute of Mental Health, led many clinicians to question the accepted wisdom of employing the newer atypicals before the older conventional agents, and this question remains unsettled.[90]

88. *Id.*, p. 2.

89. Package Insert *available at* http://www.pharma.us.novartis.com/product/pi/pdf/Clozaril.pdf (retrieved Aug. 3, 2011).

90. Owens, David, *How CATIE Brought Us Back to Kansas: A Critical Re-Evaluation of the Concept of Atypical Antipsychotics and Their Place in the Treatment of Schizophrenia*, ADVANCES IN PSYCHIATRIC TREATMENT, no. 14 (2008), pp. 17–28.

Originally marketed as safer than the conventional antipsychotics because they were thought to have no risk of neurological side effects, the atypicals have instead been found to present a substantial risk of weight gain, glucose intolerance, and elevated lipids in the blood.[91] Also, although infrequently, sudden cardiac death can occur when taking conventional and atypical antipsychotics.[92] Studies of both classes regarding the risk of birth defects in pregnant women under treatment remain uncertain. Other commonly encountered side effects of the antipsychotics in general can include, but are not limited to, sedation, breast milk production in both genders, anticholinergic side effects (e.g., dry mouth, constipation, urinary retention, low blood pressure, blurred vision, erectile dysfunction), and seizures. It is likewise possible for any of the antipsychotics to cause neuroleptic malignant syndrome, a medical emergency in which a patient becomes stiff and feverish and must be taken to a hospital immediately for supportive intervention.

~~~~~~~~~~~~~~~~~~~~~~~

Just as the discovery of Thorazine was serendipitous, the same can be said of the discovery of antidepressants. Prior to 1950, amphetamines were often used to treat depression; they exerted some antidepressant effect but at the risk of potential addiction and all of the side effects associated with stimulant use. In the early 1950s, several drugs were being investigated as possible advances in the treatment of tuberculosis. Two of them—isoniazid and iproniazid— are known inhibitors of monoamine oxidase (a chemical in the body that breaks down monoamine neurotransmitters such as dopamine, serotonin, and norepinephrine).[93] Patients who received either of the proposed tuberculosis treatment drugs were noted to "perk up"

91. See STAHL, *supra* note 52, at p. 36; *see also* Lieberman, J.A. & Tasman, Allan, *The Mood Stabilizers*, *in* HANDBOOK OF PSYCHIATRIC DRUGS. Chichester: Wiley & Sons, Ltd. (2006), p. 27; *see also* STAHL, PSYCHOSIS AND SCHIZOPHRENIA, *supra* note 70, at p. 19.

92. _____, *New Data Blur Typical-Atypical Drug Distinctions*, CLINICAL PSYCHIATRY NEWS, vol. 38, no. 8, Aug. 2010, p. 22.

93. While there may or may not be an absolute systemic deficit in monoamines, active metabolites, or related receptors, there is strong and growing evidence that these systems do not respond normally in certain psychiatric conditions; *see* STAHL, *supra* note 52, at p. 187.

emotionally. This beneficial effect was attributed to an increase in monoamines caused by decreased breakdown in the body. This led Joseph Schildkraut to publish his paper *The Catecholamine Hypothesis of Affective Disorders* in 1965. And the hunt for other antidepressants was on.

The monoamine oxidase inhibitors (MAOIs) included Parnate [tranylcypromine], Marplan [isocarboxazid], Nardil [phenelzine], and Emsam [selegiline]. The problem with MAOIs, though, is not their apparent efficacy, but rather the strict dietary parameters that patients have to follow. Eating certain foods or supplements that are high in the amino acid tyramine can trigger a potentially serious and, in some cases, fatal hypertensive reaction.[94]

The tricyclic antidepressants (TCAs) came next (so-named because of their molecular structure). This class of drugs targets norepinephrine; the first of the class, Tofranil [imipramine], arrived in the late 1950s; others include Elavil [amitriptyline], Anafranil [clomipramine], Sinequan [doxepin], Surmontil [trimipramine], Vivactil [protriptyline], Norpramin [desipramine], and Pamelor [nortriptyline]. While the TCAs did not immediately replace the MAOIs (the latter are still on rare occasions used today), the TCAs were initially deemed easier for patients to use because they had no dietary restrictions. Further adjusting the molecular structure of the TCAs resulted in their first cousins, the tetracyclics, of which Desyrel [trazodone] and Asendin [amoxapine] are the most commonly seen.[95] However, chemically and physiologically, the tetracyclics bear considerable similarity to their three-ringed forebears.

Unpleasant side effects of the TCAs can include those of an anticholinergic nature, such as sexual dysfunction, sedation, weight gain, and rebound insomnia if abruptly discontinued. These medications can cause the elderly to become unsteady and confused and at times delirious. Drug concentrations have to be monitored by blood draws, since in overdose TCAs can result in abnormal

---

94. *See* http://www.mayoclinic.com/health/maois/HQ01575 (retrieved Dec. 8, 2011); *see also* Shulman, K.I. & Walker, S.E., *Refining the MAOI Diet*, J. OF CLINICAL PSYCHIATRY, vol. 60, no. 3, March 1999, pp. 191–93, for an interesting discussion of chain- versus family-restaurant pizzas and the MAOI diet.

95. From where do brand names come? "Desyrel" is said to be an amalgamation of the words "depression," "symptom," and "relief."

cardiac rhythms and death. Also, it is posited that in some younger patients (i.e., those younger than age 24), antidepressants of all classes, these included, can exacerbate suicidal ideation, requiring that these patients be carefully monitored throughout treatment.[96]

With the chemical imbalance theory of depression by now firmly in the collective consciousness, other antidepressants were churned out with regularity, each purporting to address a different receptor combination and thus yield results somehow superior to those of the competition. The selective serotonin reuptake inhibitors (SSRIs) were next and include now-famous names such as Celexa [citalopram], Lexapro [escitalopram], Prozac [fluoxetine], Luvox [fluvoxamine], Paxil [paroxetine], and Zoloft [sertraline]. These drugs target serotonin, another of the monoamine neurotransmitters suspected of being involved in the genesis of depression. Selective serotonin and norepinephrine reuptake inhibitors (SNRIs) followed and include Pristiq [desvenlafaxine], Cymbalta [duloxetine], and Effexor [venlafaxine]; as their name suggests, they target two monoamines instead of merely one. Remeron [mirtazapine] is a drug said to increase norepinephrine while only partially attaching to serotonin receptors. Wellbutrin [bupropion] is one that inhibits the uptake of dopamine and norepinephrine. Serzone [nefazodone] is a serotonin-norepinephrine-dopamine reuptake inhibitor, and so on.[97]

The newer antidepressants are not necessarily any more effective than the older ones for treating mood symptoms; differences largely involve potential side effects. SSRIs and SNRIs have much better safety and tolerability profiles than the MAOIs or TCAs. There is much less risk of any cardiac problems with SSRIs and SNRIs, and no blood draws are required.[98] Side effects that are seen with SSRIs and SNRIs can include a discontinuation syndrome if stopped

---

96. *See* http://www.nimh.nih.gov/health/topics/child-and-adolescent-mental-health/antidepressant-medications-for-children-and-adolescents-information-for-parents-and-caregivers.shtml (retrieved Aug. 22, 2011).

97. Serzone was pulled off the U.S. market by the FDA due to risk of liver toxicity. And the SSRIs are not entirely without risk themselves. *See* Smith, Jennie, *SSRIs May Not Be Safer Than Tricyclics in Elderly*, Clinical Psychiatry News, Aug. 2, 2011, p. 8.

98. Stahl, *supra* note 52.

abruptly (flu-like symptoms, lightheadedness, restlessness, headaches, and insomnia).[99] Also, during use of the SSRIs and SNRIs, one can see sexual problems, including loss of libido and inability to climax, gastrointestinal disturbances, weight changes, sensitivity to light, and in some cases serotonin syndrome (caused by an excess of serotonin from taking too much of a serotonin-enhancing drug or combining a serotonin-enhancing drug with other medicines that magnify the effect).[100, 101]

~~~~~~~~~~~~~~~~~~~~~

Bromides were commonly employed sedatives of the nineteenth century. As with most medicines of the age, the basis for their use was wholly anecdotal, and without any form of monitoring, it didn't take long before patients were becoming toxic. Barbiturates were first isolated in the 1860s, although no medicinal applications were discovered for them until the early twentieth century with the advent of Veronal.[102] Even then, as barbiturates gradually replaced bromides in clinical medicine, the latter remained in various preparations (e.g., Bromo-Seltzer, once popularly used as a hangover remedy) until the mid-twentieth century.

Barbiturates are central nervous system depressants and, depending on dose, can produce effects ranging from mild sedation to unconsciousness. When first marketed, they were often used to control anxiety and also as sleep aids. Unfortunately, they have considerable addictive potential, but this wasn't fully appreciated until decades after their first clinical use.

Benzodiazepines were isolated in the 1950s, with the advent of Librium [chlordiazepoxide]. Benzodiazepines influence GABA receptors in the brain, an inhibitory neurotransmitter. Others of the class include Klonopin [clonazepam], Tranxene [clorazepate], Valium [diazepam], Ativan [lorazepam], Xanax [alprazolam], Serax

---

99. Preskorn, Sheldon, *Avoiding SRI Discontinuation Syndrome*, PSYCHIATRIC TIMES, June 2011, p. 64.

100. STAHL, *supra* note 52, at p. 40.

101. *See* http://www.ncbi.nlm.nih.gov/pubmedhealth/PMH0004531 (retrieved Dec. 8, 2011).

102. It is claimed that Joseph von Mering, one of the two German chemists who initially isolated barbital, said that Verona, Italy, was the most tranquil place he had ever visited, resulting in the compound's trade name of Veronal.

[oxazepam], Restoril [temazepam], Halcion [triazolam], and Versed [midazolam]. They have largely replaced barbiturates in routine clinical application, in no small part because the benzodiazepines are not as dangerous in overdose when taken as single agents (they can still be lethal, however, when combined with alcohol or other drugs). Unfortunately, they can be addictive, as are barbiturates, and like barbiturates, they can precipitate seizures if stopped abruptly. Benzodiazepines can result in sedation, decreased coordination, confusion, memory deficits, and a drop in blood pressure. The benzodiazepines are known to increase the risk of birth defects and have been associated with cleft palate.[103] They can also yield paradoxical agitation and disinhibition in the elderly, and this is why they should be used carefully and sparingly in older patients. Of note, the benzodiazepines all act similarly but come in short-acting varieties (used for anesthesia induction), intermediate-acting varieties (used for sleep), and longer-acting varieties (used for control of anxiety and seizures, as well as for alcohol detoxification).

Other anxiolytics exist, some of which are employed off-label, but none really packs the punch of the benzodiazepines, which explains why the latter are mainstays of anxiety treatment half a century after they were first isolated. Vistaril and Atarax [both preparations of hydroxyzine] are two antihistamines that are used to treat mild degrees of anxiety; they are not habit-forming, and their only real side effects are those of the anticholinergic variety (such as dry mouth and constipation). Beta blockers such as Inderal [propranolol] are antihypertensive agents, but can assist with symptoms of anxiety, especially the racing heart of those fearful of public speaking. And antipsychotics are used off-label to address anxiety, as are many antidepressants.

Buspar [buspirone] is indicated for the treatment of generalized anxiety disorder but, unlike the benzodiazepines, has no known associated addictive or birth defect risks, nor physiologic withdrawal upon cessation. Despite industry assurances to the contrary, most clinicians feel that Buspar has a much slower onset of action than do the benzodiazepines and therefore is not always ideally suited

---

103. Laegreid, L., Olegard, R., Walstrom, J. & Conradi, N., *Teratogenic Effects of Benzodiazepine Use During Pregnancy*, J. OF PEDIATRICS, vol. 114, no. 1, Jan. 1989, pp. 126–31.

for those who are in the midst of intense anxiety and cannot wait.[104] For this reason too, Buspar is seemingly best suited for patients who are benzodiazepine-naïve, since persons who have taken benzodiazepines in the past and know of the immediate relief afforded by those agents will rarely be pleased with the delayed onset of action seen with Buspar. Buspar does have some very positive features: it is usually well-tolerated in patients, and most of the side effects seen, if any, fall into the mild category (i.e., upset stomach, headache, drowsiness).

~~~~~~~~~~~~~~~~~~~~~

In the 1920s, an entrepreneur from St. Louis named C.L. Grigg was experimenting with various concoctions that he wanted to market as hangover cures. After two years of unsuccessful attempts, he found a formula that he thought would be successful: a caramel-colored beverage with seven natural flavors. However, his timing couldn't have been worse—he unveiled the new creation in October 1929, two weeks before the stock market crash—and the name of the potion was unwieldy: Bib-Label Lithiated Lemon-Lime Soda. Despite the economy and the name, the soda sold well, and Grigg decided to call it instead 7UP.[105]

Lithium has been an element of the periodic table since that chart was created. However, in the early days of psychiatry, its benefits and potential risks were poorly understood (numerous now-extinct beverages once contained lithium, and 7UP stopped using lithium in its formula in 1950). People historically took to the spa waters to treat a variety of ailments, and, as many natural springs contain lithium, those people were, without knowing it, self-medicating—and probably at times becoming toxic as well.[106] It wasn't until 1949, 20 years after 7UP started quenching thirst, that an Australian psychiatrist, J.F.J. Cade, suggested using lithium specifically to treat psychiatric afflictions.[107] While successful for management

---

104. Manual of Clinical Psychopharmacology, 6th ed. (Schatzberg et al. eds.). Washington, D.C.: American Psychiatric Press (2007), p. 373.

105. *Available at* http://www.mariettasodamuseum.com/7up_facts.htm (retrieved March 8, 2011).

106. Arehart-Treichel, Joan, *Higher Levels of Lithium Linked to Lower Suicide Rates*, Psychiatric News, vol. 46, no. 12, June 17, 2011, p. 31.

107. Cade, J.F., *Lithium Salts in the Treatment of Psychotic Excitement*, Medical J. of Australia, no. 2, 1949, pp. 349–52.

of emotional disorders, lithium and its mechanism of action are poorly understood. Paradoxically, despite being widely used for the treatment of mood instability today, lithium was only approved for that indication by the FDA in 1970.[108]

Lithium, which goes by brand names Eskalith and Lithobid, among others, is considered by many to be the gold standard for the treatment of clinically significant mood swings, also known as cyclical mood disorders.[109] Other products in that category, however, are anticonvulsant medications that were randomly discovered to have mood-stabilizing properties as well (lithium exerts no clinical anticonvulsant effects). Those other anticonvulsant mood stabilizers included Depakene [valproic acid], Depakote [divalproex sodium], Lamictal [lamotrigine], and Tegretol [carbamazepine], and to a lesser degree Neurontin [gabapentin] and Topamax [topiramate]. More recently, some antipsychotics— notably Seroquel—have won FDA approval for treatment of various stages of the bipolar cycle as well.

With lithium, it is crucial to check blood levels, thyroid and kidney function, and blood chemistry, and an electrocardiogram should be ordered as well. The use of lithium in conjunction with diuretics, as well as with some antihypertensives and pain medications, needs to be monitored carefully to avoid toxicity. Patients can experience a fine tremor, weight gain, upset stomach, and diarrhea when using lithium. Additionally, lithium is associated with an increased risk of heart defects in fetuses. As lithium chemically acts like salt, patients will often experience increased thirst and urination, and those taking lithium can get toxic quickly if they do not consume adequate fluids to remain hydrated.[110] Increasing tremors and unsteadiness when standing or walking can be warning signs of elevated lithium blood levels. Lithium works wonderfully in the right patient, but the person prescribed lithium needs to be edu-

---

108. Lieberman and Tasman, *supra* note 91, at 65.

109. Though myriad demographic factors are known to influence the incidence of suicide, a recent meta-analysis showed that regions in which lithium is found in drinking water in greater concentrations (e.g., Japan, Austria, Texas) have lower baseline rates of suicide than areas with less lithium in the water. *See* Arehart-Treichel, *supra* note 106.

110. *See* http://www.drugs.com/lithium.html.

cated on the risks and benefits, motivated, reliable when keeping appointments, and able to follow instructions. It is not a drug therapy for everyone.

Concerning the anticonvulsant mood stabilizers, there are some medications that do not mix well with them, and as anticonvulsants can alter the rate of the body's metabolism and clearance of drugs in general, the monitoring of blood levels becomes all the more vital (Tegretol is particularly one to watch). Lamictal can also cause serious side effects, such as Stevens-Johnson syndrome (a rare but potentially fatal skin reaction).[111] There are varying degrees of risk of birth defects associated with the use of seizure medications. Weight gain, nausea, pancreatitis, dizziness, and sedation are all possible to varying degrees within this class. If toxic, some anticonvulsants can affect the liver and kidneys, and thus blood chemistry analyses, white blood counts, and liver enzyme measurements are usually drawn before treatment begins and then regularly repeated along with drug levels. As with lithium, this sort of therapy requires an informed and motivated patient.

~~~~~~~~~~~~~~~~~~~~

A question yet begs asking: Do psychiatric medications actually work as claimed? A number of polemics have been published—*The Emperor's New Drugs, Talking Back to Prozac, Anatomy of an Epidemic,* and *Mad in America* are just a few—that question the value of psychotropics in general.

It seems that this query is most often leveled at the antidepressants. After a period of jubilation when these agents were first refined and marketed, some recent studies have thrown doubt on the class, claiming that these drugs yield a surprisingly small clinical effect overall and that statistical significance is attained only in cases of treatment of patients with the most severe depression.[112] This

---

111. Package insert *available at* http://us.gsk.com/products/assets/us_lamictal.pdf.

112. Parker, Gordon & Fletcher, Kathryn, *What's the Evidence for the Evidence-Based Treatments of Depression?,* Psychiatric Times, Sept. 8, 2011, p. 16; *see* Whitaker, Robert, *The New York Times' Defense of Antidepressants,* Psychology Today, July 10, 2011, p. 117; *see also* Kinon, B.J., Potts, A.J. & Watson, Susan, *Placebo Response in Clinical Trials with Schizophrenia Patients,* Current Opinion in Psychiatry, vol. 24, no. 2, 2011, pp. 107–13; *see also*

doubt is reinforced by the observation that, despite numerous advances over recent decades, psychiatric treatment outcomes are not substantially better today than they were a quarter-century ago.[113] Even *USA Today* and *Newsweek* ran headline stories questioning the efficacy of some psychotropics (antidepressants in particular) in 2011.

A recent publication went further, suggesting that the healthcare industry collectively overprescribes psychotropics relative to any objective clinical benefit. In the study, a group of patients being treated for psychosis with two or more antipsychotic agents were instead switched to single-agent therapy. Of those who switched, two-thirds experienced no worsening of symptoms on the streamlined regimen.[114] If accurate, then the addition of the second (or third) antipsychotic to each patient's treatment protocol was largely irrelevant in the majority of cases.

Then a bombshell was dropped by Marcia Angell, M.D., the former editor-in-chief of *The New England Journal of Medicine*, who suggested in *The New York Review of Books* that antidepressants are essentially high-priced placebos with side effects.[115] She went on to say:

> [Mental health practitioners] are simply wrong in asserting that psychiatry, in using drugs to treat signs and symptoms of illness without understanding the cause of the illness or how the drugs work, is no different from other medical specialties. First, mental illness is diagnosed on the basis of [subjective] symptoms and behaviors, not [objective] signs. Most diseases in other specialties produce physical signs

---

Frances, Allen, *Are College Students Getting Sicker? No, Diagnoses Change Faster Than People*, PSYCHIATRIC TIMES, Jan. 11, 2011, p. 14; *see also* Walsh B.T., Seidman, S.N., Sysko, R., Gould, M., *Placebo Response in Major Studies of Depression*, JAMA, vol. 287, no. 14, 2002, pp. 1840–47.

113. Mintz, Daniel, *Psychodynamic Psychopharmacology*, PSYCHIATRIC TIMES, Sept. 9, 2011, p. 19; *see also* Kessler, R.C. et al., *The Epidemiology of Major Depressive Disorder: Results from the National Comorbidity Survey Replication*, JAMA, vol. 289 (2003), pp. 3095–3105.

114. Moran, Mark, *Monotherapy after Polypharmacy Effective for Some Patients*, PSYCHIATRIC NEWS, vol. 46, no. 11, June 3, 2011, p. 15.

115. Kramer, *supra* note 5.

and abnormal lab tests or radiologic findings, in addition to symptoms. Moreover, even if the underlying causes of other diseases are unknown, the mechanisms by which they produce illness usually are, and the treatments usually target those mechanisms.[116]

Of course, proponents of current modalities of mental health treatment immediately countered that there are objective findings to support psychiatric diagnoses, such as weight loss in major depression, psychomotor agitation and distractibility in bipolar disorder, catatonia and stereotyped movements in schizophrenia, and so on.[117] The battle lines remain drawn nonetheless.

One challenge to obtaining convincing drug-efficacy data involves overcoming some of the inherent loose and subjective *DSM* parameters for diagnosing conditions. Regarding antidepressants, the widespread use of the word "depression" in the modern vernacular further complicates matters. I would personally offer, based on decades of clinical practice, that some individuals who are included in "mildly to moderately depressed" cohorts are, in fact, not biologically depressed at all and therefore will benefit little from any biochemical intervention; put another way, if everyday problems become falsely labeled as mental illness, then "response" to medications might be nothing more than a robust placebo effect.[118] Plus, it's rather difficult to design a true double-blind placebo controlled drug study, since most psychotropics have discernible, if not incapacitating, side effects, and therefore both patient and investigator might easily guess who is taking inert pills and who is not.[119] Also, unless one is willing to cloister study participants for

116. Pies, Ronald, *Misunderstanding Psychiatry (and Philosophy) at the Highest Level*, PSYCHIATRIC TIMES, vol. 28, no. 9, Sept. 2011, p. 1.

117. *Id.*

118. Frances, Allen, *Biomarkers Oversold in Medicine: Implications for Psychiatry*, PSYCHIATRIC TIMES, June 8, 2011, p. 9; *see also* Miller, F.G. & Colloca, L., *The Legitimacy of Placebo Treatments in Clinical Practice*, AMERICAN J. OF BIOETHICS, vol. 12, no. 9, 2009, pp. 39–47, for an interesting and counterintuitive discussion on one study cohort of 14 anxious and depressed patients who were given open-label inert placebo capsules ("sugar pills . . . with no medication at all") and yet who all reported symptomatic improvement after one week.

119. KIRSCH, IRVING. THE EMPEROR'S NEW DRUGS. New York: Basic Books (2010), p. 33.

months on end, there is the issue of medication noncompliance. One recent study illustrated that nearly a third of patients in a given cohort did not take their antidepressants as prescribed over a six-month period, resulting in prescribers changing the dosing based on nonresponse when in fact such changes might not actually have been necessary.[120]

Back to the original question: Do psychiatric medications actually work as purported? Certainly this chapter cannot hope to analyze all that has been exchanged between psychiatry's polemicists and apologists. Clinical evidence strongly indicates—I would dare say proves—that in carefully diagnosed and properly managed patients with mental illness, many available psychotropic medications are tremendously helpful in improving quality of life and level of functioning. That being offered, weaknesses in our current diagnostic schema, the harried nature of some psychiatric evaluations, and the difficulties (and conflicted interests?) in designing, performing, and digesting drug studies equally suggest that not all available medications are wholly effective, and not all patients necessarily need them.

Take-Home Pearls

- If attaining a healthy equilibrium regarding stress management and a sense of well-being is the goal, then psychotherapy is a valuable modus of treatment, either by itself or in conjunction with other interventions. Whether one form of psychotherapy is better than any other remains far from settled.
- Many clinicians have held the unfortunate view that psychotherapy is a treatment for "psychologically based" disorders, while medication is for "biologically based" disorders. The best management of mental illness involves both approaches and a multidisciplinary effort.

---

120. Mahoney, Diana, *Poor Adherence Boosts Antidepressant Dosing*, Clinical Psychiatry News, vol. 38, no. 11, Nov. 2010, p. 13.

- A number of invasive non-pharmacologic interventions, most bordering on quackery, have been attempted in the past. The most effective of these, electroconvulsive therapy (ECT), is often clumped with the others, which is unfortunate given that, for those with severe and intractable major depression, ECT appears to be the best and sometimes last hope for meaningful improvement.
- Do psychotropic medications work? To answer this question, we have to consider: 1. chemical compounds that are not fully understood by mechanism of action, 2. diseases the etiologies of which remain far from settled, 3. evidence of a strong placebo effect, 4. many agents that are currently used off-label and therefore may have only anecdotal evidence to support their benefits, and 5. considerable prescribing by providers who are not necessarily trained in aspects of mental health. However, clinical evidence strongly illustrates that in carefully diagnosed and properly managed patients with mental illnesses, many available psychotropic medications are tremendously helpful in improving quality of life and level of functioning.

Chapter 7

Things Are Not Necessarily as They Appear

> Lord, Lord, how this world is given to lying!
> —Falstaff, *Henry IV*, Part I[1]
>
> A good poker player probably knows better than a mental health professional whether a person is lying. A psychiatrist is a doctor, not a lie detector.
> —Slovenko[2]

Here are five brief vignettes. Can you tell the differences diagnostically?

1. A 36-year-old divorced white female appeared at the local urgent-care facility for the eleventh time in the last year. She manifested unusual skin infections. She seemed oddly undisturbed by the frequency of her trips to the doctor or by the lesions themselves, which are large, raised red pustules covering the front of both thighs. She said she has no idea how she has acquired these infections. When outpatient antibiotics were prescribed, she asked to be hospital-

---

1. Shakespeare, William, *Henry IV*, part I, act V, scene IV.
2. SLOVENKO, R. PSYCHIATRY IN LAW/LAW IN PSYCHIATRY. N.Y.: Brunner-Routledge (2002), p. 122.

ized "just to be on the safe side." She denied any pending disability applications or problems at her job as a night stock clerk. She was not known to have any legal charges. Cultures of the skin revealed *B. fragilis*, a pathogenic bacterium found in human waste. It was strongly suspected that she had been injecting feces under her skin and then waiting for infections to develop before repeatedly presenting for medical evaluation and treatment.

2. An 81-year-old right-handed widowed Hispanic female came to the attention of the physician who covers the residential facility at which the widow lives. She was fully alert and oriented and was housed on the skilled care unit because of unsteadiness on her feet and concerns that she might fall if not receiving assistance. Though the patient did not complain of any debilitation, staff members noticed paralysis of the right arm of several weeks' duration. Fearing a stroke, the physician ordered a CT scan of the head; that study was unremarkable. Other neurological testing and a physical examination failed to reveal any causation. Family informed staff, however, that the patient had become incensed at her favorite daughter while discussing estate planning recently and had lashed out at her, striking the daughter's cheek in anger. The inability to use the right arm was noted thereafter.

3. A 37-year-old married white male had an 11-year history of numerous ill-defined and seemingly unrelated physical symptoms that came and went without apparent pattern and that caused him intense subjective discomfort and debilitation when present. These complaints included sharp, shooting pains in his back, chest, rectum, and head. They were usually accompanied by instances of nausea and bloating, difficulty achieving and maintaining erections during intercourse, and double vision. Extensive outpatient testing and physical examinations, plus two hospitalizations, failed to uncover the cause of any of the symptoms. The patient then left each doctor in frustration, "so I can find someone who knows what's going on!"

4. A 47-year-old single black male made monthly appointments at his primary care physician's office. His complaints were always the same. He stated that when he ate any food, he became nauseated and felt like throwing up (although he rarely if ever actually vomited, and he had not lost weight). He was convinced that he had stomach cancer and would die shortly. The symptoms were ongoing for more than six years, according to available records. He had every blood test and radiographic study of which his physician could think, as well as two endoscopic exams to analyze the lining of his stomach, all of which were unremarkable. He did not respond to the gentle redirection of his physician, who attempted to reassure him at every visit of his overall good health. At a recent noontime appointment, the patient heard his stomach growling while on the examination table and exclaimed, "See? That's the tumor making that sound!"

5. A 19-year-old single white male was arrested and charged with assault with a deadly weapon. Following the incident, he exhibited no apparent thought disorganization, according to police, but was calm and conversant. However, once in jail awaiting arraignment, he said that he was hearing the voice of Satan telling him to attack people, and at the same time he claimed to be seeing little green men running around his cell carrying hatchets and truncheons. He then reported having been visited by Satan and his demons every night since he was a child. He also said that he could read minds. There was no known psychiatric history. The patient did spend some time in a foster home as an adolescent because of parental neglect. However, he graduated high school on time and with average grades. When asked orientation questions, he replied that the year was 1776 and he was in China. He claimed not to be able to identify primary colors shown to him. However, when observed surreptitiously by jail staff, he appeared at ease in his cell, spending time reading novels.

Malingering is likely occurring in the fifth and final vignette above (we will later return to the others). Malingering is not considered to be a mental disorder. It is included in the *DSM* as a "v code," meaning it is a condition, not an illness, that may be a focus of clinical attention.[3] *DSM-IV-TR* describes it thus:

> V65.2: The essential feature of malingering is the intentional production of false or grossly exaggerated physical or psychological symptoms, motivated by external incentives such as avoiding military duty, avoiding work, obtaining financial compensation, evading criminal prosecution, or obtaining drugs or a warm place to stay during inclement weather. Under some circumstances, malingering may represent adaptive behavior—for example, feigning illness while a captive of the enemy during wartime. Malingering should be strongly suspected if any combination of the following is noted: a medico-legal context of presentation (e.g., the person is referred by an attorney); a marked discrepancy between the subject's claimed stress or disability and the objective findings; a lack of cooperation during the diagnostic evaluation and in complying with the prescribed treatment regime; or the presence of antisocial personality disorder.[4]

In all likelihood, fabrication has been around since mankind learned to communicate. According to Homeric lore, Ulysses pretended to be insane, plowing his fields with mismatched beasts and sowing salt instead of seeds in order to avoid having to join the force sailing for Troy.[5] In the Bible, David, fearful of the wrath of King Saul, "changed his behavior before them, and feigned himself mad in their hands, and scrabbled on the doors of the gate, and let his spittle fall down upon his beard."[6] In Elizabethan England,

---

3. _____. DIAGNOSTIC AND STATISTICAL MANUAL OF MENTAL DISORDERS, 4th ed., text rev. Washington, D.C.: American Psychiatric Ass'n (2000).

4. *Id.*

5. *Available at* http://www.pantheon.org/articles/o/odysseus.html (retrieved Dec. 4, 2011).

6. 1 Samuel 21:13, KING JAMES BIBLE.

Hamlet said he would "put an antic disposition on" and directed Horatio and Marcellus not to give him away no matter "how strange or odd . . . I bear myself."[7, 8]

Moral issues of deception aside, not all symptom fabrication is of equal gravity. The tired spouse who tells the partner, "not tonight, dear, I have a headache," may indeed be faking for secondary gain, but the spouse has only to answer to the dearly beloved. The child who conjures a bellyache to avoid going to school, and the employee who calls in sick to enjoy a gorgeous autumn day, arguably have little impact on the greater scheme of things. Taken to extremes, though, lying of this nature can have far more severe consequences. First, it can reduce productivity of the workforce through absenteeism, which then impacts the morale of the employees who have to shoulder the added burden and then feel embittered. Those who engage in false-hoods often deplete government coffers to the detriment of those truly in need. Additionally, such actors abuse finite health-care resources through inappropriate and unnecessary usage.[9] Such fabrications can pervert the administration of justice. Also, as there appears to be an increase in certain psychiatric disorders that are difficult to objectively diagnose, many fake having such a disorder to manipulate the system and easily get a psychiatric diagnosis and medication. Once a person has these authenticators, disability benefits may only be a mailed application away.[10]

How often do individuals misrepresent or minimize symptoms in a clinical setting? One recent article suggests that this might be a

7. Shakespeare, William, *Hamlet*, act I, scene V.

8. Wendling, Patrice, *Most Depressed Patients Admit to Lying to Their Doctors*, CLINICAL PSYCHIATRY NEWS, Oct. 2011, p. 16; *see also* Kashy, D. A. & DePaulo, B. M., *Who Lies?*, J. PERSONALITY & SOCIAL PSYCHOLOGY, no. 70 (1996), pp. 1037–51; *see also* Kashy, D.A. & DePaulo, B.M., *Everyday Lies in Close and Casual Relationships*, J. PERSONALITY & SOCIAL PSYCHOLOGY, no. 74 (1998), pp. 63–79.

9. Wen, Patricia, *The Other Welfare: A Legacy of Unintended Side Effects*, BOSTON GLOBE, Dec. 12, 2010. *Available at* http://www.boston.com/news/local/massachusetts/articles/2010/12/12/with_ssi_program_a_legacy_of_unintended_side_effects/ (retrieved Dec. 2, 2011).

10. Carlat, Daniel, *Robert Whitaker's 'Anatomy of an Epidemic'—the Carlat Take*, CARLAT PSYCHIATRY BLOG, Jan. 21, 2011. *Available at* http://carlatpsychiatry.blogspot.com/2011/01/robert-whitakers-anatomy-of-epidemic.html (retrieved Dec. 9, 2011).

common practice. A study earlier this year revealed that 43 percent of respondents admitted to not disclosing symptoms of depression to their primary care physicians. The reasons for this reportedly stemmed mostly from patients' fears that an antidepressant would be prescribed or a referral to a psychiatrist would be initiated if the truth and magnitude of depression were revealed. While one cannot discern from this single study what other motivations might have been at play, the large numbers of individuals who freely admitted to having misled the very clinicians tasked with their recovery should raise more than a few concerns.[11]

To further investigate the occurrence of deception in a clinical setting, one can turn to the forensic realm, a demographic that would have much to gain from "developing" or manipulating a mental illness. A recent article in the *Washington Post* stated that every year in the United States there are as many as 12,000 criminal defendants who have their court dates delayed because of a perceived need for mental evaluation and, when necessary, restoration of mental capacity to proceed to trial. Studies have shown that approximately three-quarters of those requiring such stabilization are successfully restored to capacity to proceed within six months. Left unaddressed are the many others who are not restored in that time frame. Some, certainly, have intractable mental illnesses, but some also are probably resisting restoration by magnifying or fabricating symptoms. A landmark study from the late 1980s revealed that up to 40 percent of defendants who claimed insanity were found on later psychological testing to be malingering.[12] These guileful de-

---

11. Fink, Paul, *Have You Been Misled by Patients?*, CLINICAL PSYCHIATRY NEWS DIGITAL NETWORK, Oct. 4, 2011. ttp://www.clinicalpsychiatrynews.com/views/fink-still-at-large-by-dr-paul-j-fink/blog/have-you-been-misled-by-patients/30873df9bc7f9b2ab4efaf647b4a4774.html?tx_ttnews[sViewPointer]=2 (retrieved Dec. 9, 2011); *see also* Wendling, *Most Depressed Patients Admit to Lying. See also* Bell, Robert, et al., *Suffering in Silence: Reasons for Not Disclosing Depression in Primary Care*, ANNALS OF FAMILY MEDICINE, vol. 9, no. 5 (Sept./Oct. 2011), pp. 439–46.

12. Nakamura, David, *Loughner Ruling Creates Potential Obstacles on Path to Trial in Arizona Shootings*, WASH. POST, May 27, 2011, p. A-7. *See also* Grossman, Linda, and Wasyliw, Orest, *A Psychometric Study of Stereotypes: Assessment of Malingering in a Criminal Forensic Group*, J. OF PERSONALITY ASSESSMENT, vol. 52, no. 3 (1988), pp. 549–63.

fendants provide a challenge that can be every bit as complex as that of the genuinely afflicted, but for entirely different reasons.

The past 30 years have seen the establishment of strict parameters regarding the use of forced medication for the restoration of mental capacity to proceed to trial. There has also been considerable tightening, and in some jurisdictions elimination, of the applicable statutes regarding the use of the insanity defense.[13, 14] Neither of these developments, though, had any impact on what is among the most notorious demonstrations of pretrial malingering of the recent past, a particularly egregious episode that made national headlines in the 1990s, but with roots going back many years.

Vincent "The Chin" Gigante served as a Mafia capo in the 1950s before he assumed the reins of New York's Genovese crime family. Starting in the early 1970s, Gigante began to feign dementia, turning the act into a full-time job to avoid prosecution and deflect attention from his role in running what was then the largest organized crime family in the country.[15] Known to the media as the Oddfather, he was often seen shuffling around Greenwich Village in pajamas and slippers and mumbling incoherently to himself, and occasionally falling to the ground and praying, all the while being followed by a bodyguard. The act sometimes extended indoors; once when being served with a subpoena, Gigante was found standing naked in a running shower holding an umbrella over his head.[16]

After years of such acting, Gigante was finally arrested in 1990 and charged with racketeering and conspiracy. However, the trial

---

13. Sell v. United States, 539 U.S. 166.
14. 18 U.S.C. § 17. The federal act provides:

> It is an affirmative defense to a prosecution under any Federal statute that, at the time of the commission of the acts constituting the offense, the defendant, as a result of a severe mental disease or defect, was unable to appreciate the nature and quality of the wrongfulness of his acts. Mental disease or defect does not otherwise constitute a defense.

This statute eliminated the Irresistible Impulse Test from an insanity defense under federal law, and it also provided that "the defendant has the burden of proving the defense of insanity by clear and convincing evidence."

15. Raab, Selwyn, *Vincent Gigante, Mafia Leader Who Feigned Insanity, Dies at 77*, N.Y. TIMES, Dec. 19, 2005, p. A-7.
16. *Id.*

on those charges did not take place for over seven years because of wrangling between mental health experts for the defense and prosecution. Gigante's family maintained that he had both paranoid schizophrenia and dementia. Interestingly, a number of prominent mental health clinicians also held that Gigante suffered from mental illness and that he was not competent to stand trial or to be sentenced; this group included some of the most respected names in forensic psychiatry and neuropsychology, including the prominent Harvard psychiatrist Thomas Gutheil, five past presidents of the American Academy of Psychiatry and the Law, and the researcher who had developed the standardized test for malingering.[17] Other clinicians, primary among them psychiatrist Jonathan Brodie of New York University School of Medicine, steadfastly held that Gigante was fully cognizant of his surroundings and able to run the Genovese family's daily business using trusted intermediaries. The prosecution's hand was later bolstered when a number of Mafia turncoats began to cooperate with the government, saying that they saw Gigante regularly in the community and that he exhibited no evidence of confusion or cognitive impairment at any of those meetings.[18]

Gigante was convicted in 1997 on the racketeering and conspiracy charges and was given a 12-year sentence. Six years later, before the U.S. District Court in Brooklyn, he pleaded guilty to the additional charge of obstruction of justice, admitting to having malingered for all those years. Thirty-six months were added to the previous sentence.[19]

Granted, the clinicians testifying for the defense had been lulled into error in part by Gigante's brain scans that showed abnormalities of blood flow that were suggestive, though not diagnostic, of vascular dementia. After Gigante's admission of malingering, in a face-saving attempt, one of the mistaken experts suggested—cor-

---

17. Newman, Andy, *Analyze This: Vincent Gigante, Not Crazy After All Those Years*, N.Y. Times, April 13, 2003, p. A-9.

18. McShane, Larry, *Oddfather Ends Insanity Ruse*, CBS News Online, Feb. 11, 2009, *available at* http://www.cbsnews.com/stories/2003/04/07/national/main548132.shtml (retrieved Dec. 8, 2011); *see also* Raab, *supra* note 15.

19. *Id.*

rectly, in theory—that Gigante could have been both mentally ill and malingering at the same time.[20] Regardless, the criminal mastermind with a ninth-grade education had succeeded in flummoxing some of the brightest minds in clinical and academic psychiatry and psychology for years.

Gigante died in prison in 2005.

The Gigante case was attention-grabbing, but it is not alone in illustrating that psychiatric practice can be flawed at detecting malingering, or as one author posited, "experience teaches me that an ounce of fact is worth a pound of expertise."[21] The reader should rest comfortably, though: successful malingering of symptoms is far more difficult than it appears, the Gigante case notwithstanding. Most lay people learn about mental illness from Hollywood, and real-world attempts at faking are usually easy to discern. Yet paradoxically, it appears that many practitioners in non-forensic settings are reluctant to tag a patient as a malingerer, even in the face of strong supporting evidence. This might be because of a clinician's trusting nature; giving a patient the benefit of the doubt; a desire not to stigmatize; going the path of least resistance when busy; or concerns over liability should the determination of malingering later be found incorrect.

Nevertheless, when reviewing clinical data and conducting interviews with persons for whom malingering remains in the differential diagnosis, the presence of any known or suspected secondary gain should raise suspicion and at least put the clinician on guard. Additionally, one must be cognizant of the following red flags:

> ➤ The presence of rare, absurd, overly inclusive, or contradictory symptoms that do not correlate with any recognized mental or neurological conditions. A lay malingerer, not familiar with the subtleties of presentation, might endorse psychosis, amnesia, mental retardation, depression, and anxiety all at the same time, a rather rare constellation indeed. This is especially true if the endorsements are accompanied with silly wrong answers to simple questions. Beware

---

20. Newman, *supra* note 17.
21. Nakamura, *supra* note 12.

if previously average- to higher-functioning subjects have trouble recalling, even with cues, nearly universally familiar material (e.g., the colors of the American flag). In short, when individuals with established cognitive abilities suddenly appear "both crazy *and* stupid," such decline might suggest an overplaying of the role.

It is worth noting that this tendency to miss the subtleties of presentation was noted in the first American text on (what was to become) forensic psychiatry, in 1838. In this work, Isaac Ray, M.D., presciently wrote:

> [T]he grand fault committed by imposters is that in their anxiety to produce an imitation [of mental illness] that shall deceive, they overdo the character they assume, and present nothing but a clumsy caricature.[22]

Or, to paraphrase psychiatrist Phil Resnick at the annual meeting of the American Psychiatric Association in 2011, "monster hallucinations are for the movies."[23]

➤ Conversely, malingerers might follow a more understated route, such as the "schizophrenic" individual who exhibits nothing more than the isolated symptom of hearing voices, or the "cognitively impaired" person who reports amnesia solely for alleged misdeeds.

➤ Those employed in the medical field, with at least a basic knowledge of mental illness and terminology, are also sometimes given further scrutiny when the presentation is unusual and not supported by known history.

➤ Persons who eagerly endorse any symptoms proffered by the clinician. Some fellow residents used to inquire, at the end of a long list of symptoms to which a subject had answered affirmatively, if that person's teeth also itched. The reader might be surprised to learn just how many individuals endorse this finding without a second thought.

---

22. Ray, Isaac. A Treatise on the Medical Jurisprudence of Insanity. Boston: Charles Little & James Brown (1838), p. 341.

23. Resnick, Phil, *Detecting Malingered Mental Illness*, presentation to the American Psychiatric Ass'n Annual Conference, Honolulu, Haw. (May 2011).

➢ Those who seem overly eager to draw attention to their symptoms, especially if they've already endorsed those same symptoms over and over, and lack any signs of distress.

➢ Those who manifest varying appearances on an inpatient ward depending on who they think is observing them and then become evasive when the seeming inconsistencies are noted. The person appears unstable only when she is aware that she is being watched by staff members. A fluctuating clinical course, including rapid development of complications or a new pathology if the initial work-up findings prove negative, is also suspicious.

➢ Subjects who endorse nonstop hallucinations (even those with treatment-resistant schizophrenia will almost always be able to endorse the waxing and waning of symptoms over time). Subjects whose hallucinations have no delusional amplification (i.e., auditory hallucinations of threatening voices, but without any evidence of anxiety or paranoia).

➢ Individuals who complain of terrible symptoms but are reluctant to accept referrals to psychiatrists.

➢ Those who malinger rarely fake the negative symptoms of psychosis and likewise rarely fake perseveration; seeing either of these facets of presentation suggests a lower likelihood of fabrication. Likewise, malingerers usually do not endorse command hallucinations of a demeaning nature. Endorsements of insulting gender-based auditory hallucinations are not nearly as common for fakers as for those truly suffering.

➢ Those who claim to have disturbed thought content without any evidence of disorganized thought process. This disconnect is often manifested when one can articulately describe psychotic symptoms using medical jargon correctly or knowing textbook descriptions thoroughly. Such incongruity is also sometimes seen in those whose speech illustrates a degree of disorganization not seen in their written communications, or in those who can delineate in great detail the times during which they have experienced memory lapses.

➤ There are certain buzz phrases that should put an astute clinician on guard: "I've never told anyone this before . . ." and "You don't believe me!?" are particularly commonplace.

➤ Fatigue sets in over time. It's hard to act mentally unbalanced forever. Accordingly, many malingerers appear more normal with the passage of time.

➤ The endorsement of symptoms that are plausible on the surface but are vague and amorphous when further detail is sought.

➤ The presence of extensive medical records from multiple providers, many times in different geographic locations, always raises the question of whether the person is trying to cover her tracks. Be especially wary when a person refuses to allow current providers to contact past providers, usually explained as "that doctor didn't know what he was doing," or "we didn't agree on treatment."

➤ Be suspicious of those who endorse that their auditory and visual hallucinations include invisible friends or pets with names; those whose visual hallucinations change appearance when the subject opens or closes his eyes; those who state that all command hallucinations are always obeyed; those who claim that auditory hallucinations emanate from inside their heads (most genuine hallucinations are perceived as being external in origin); or those who claim that their visual hallucinations are in black and white (most genuine hallucinations are said to appear just as they would in normal vision).

➤ Presentation in the emergency department during times when obtaining old medical records is hampered or when an experienced staff is less likely to be present (e.g., holidays, late Friday evenings). This will occur most often when involving persons with a known or suspected history of substance abuse, especially of prescription medications.[24]

---

24. *See* Resnick, *id.*; *see also* Vance, Charles, *Malingering in a Forensic Context*, presentation to the Forensic Fellowship Conference, Dorothea Dix Hospital, Raleigh, N.C., Nov. 17, 2009; *see also* Clinical Assessment of Malingering and Deception, 2d ed. (Rogers, R., ed.). New York: Guilford Press (1997), p. 45.

In addition to obtaining as much collateral information, both from observation and review of available records, what else can a clinician do in the hopes of identifying the untruthful? Psychological testing can be a tremendous resource, especially when applied in the context of contradictory or seemingly illogical facets of presentation. Numerous tests are available to help determine the fine line between poor performance and deliberate underperformance.[25] Many of these tests can be administered quickly in an office setting, but they do require the services of a psychologist trained in the scoring and interpretation of psychometrics.

The Minnesota Multiphasic Personality Inventory (MMPI), second edition, or MMPI-2, is one of the most frequently employed psychological tests. Its predecessor, the MMPI, was first developed in 1939 using clinical scales derived from selected answers from adult patients known to have certain pathological conditions. It is a 567-item questionnaire in a true-false format. It usually requires at least two hours to complete, depending on the reading level of the person taking the test. Answers are tallied into scores on different scales, such as depression, anxiety, control issues, gender roles, paranoia, introversion, and so on. In addition, the MMPI-2 contains validity scales that can reveal exaggeration of symptoms, downplaying of symptoms, or inconsistent responding, all of which are useful in determining the "fake good" and "fake bad" presentations seen in those who wish to mislead. Rather than diagnose, MMPI scores illustrate trends toward certain personality structures that can be helpful in making or refuting a diagnosis. Said another way, fake good and fake bad profiles are not insignificant problems depending on the population being tested; one study from 1997 illustrated that more than 16 percent of male inmates freely admitted to lying on the MMPI-2 at the time of incarceration.[26]

---

25. Vance, *id.*

26. Butcher, J.N., et al. The Minnesota Multiphasic Personality Inventory-2 (MMPI-2): Manual for Administration and Scoring. Minneapolis: Univ. of Minn. Press (1989); *see also* Clinical Assessment of Malingering and Deception (Rogers, R., ed.). New York: Guilford Press (1997), p. 33. *See also* Gallagher, Robert, Ben-Povath, Yossef & Briggs, Sylvester, *Inmate Views About the Purpose and Use of the MMPI-2 at the Time of Correctional Intake*, Criminal Justice and Behavior, vol. 24, no. 3, Sept. 1997, pp. 360–69.

The Miller Forensic Assessment of Symptoms Test, or MFAST, is a quick screening tool that is used to discern fabrication of psychotic symptoms.[27] The Structured Interview of Reported Symptoms, SIRS and SIRS-2, can be administered in an hour or less; the SIRS is used to suggest the fabrication of symptoms, whereas the SIRS-2 is used to uncover evidence of exaggeration of symptoms.[28] The Test of Memory Malingering, or TOMM, is a visual recognition instrument that is designed to help clinicians recognize feigned memory impairment.[29] The Rey 15-Item Test is a measure of short-term memory that also can uncover those who are purposefully underperforming on the task.[30, 31, 32] There are many other instruments available to examine a wide range of purported diagnoses

27.   *See* Clinical Assessment, *id.*; *see also* Jackson, R.L., Rogers, R. & Sewell, K.W., *Forensic Applications of the Miller Forensic Assessment of Symptoms Test (MFAST),* Law and Human Behavior, vol. 29, no. 2 (April 2005), pp. 199–210.

28.   Rogers, R., et al. Structured Interview of Reported Symptoms. Odessa: Psychological Assessment Resources (1992), p. 228; *see also* Rogers, R., et al., *Faking Specific Disorders: A Study of the Structured Interview of Reported Symptoms,* J. Clinical Psychology, vol. 48, no. 5 (Sept. 1992), pp. 643–48.

29.   Tombaugh, T.N., *The Test of Memory Malingering (TOMM): Normative Data from Cognitively Intact and Cognitively Impaired Individuals,* Psychological Assessment, vol. 9, no. 3 (Sept. 1997), pp. 260–68.

30.   *See* Clinical Assessment, *supra* note 26; *see also* Schretien, David, et al., *Some Caveats in Using the Rey 15-Item Memory Test to Detect Malingered Amnesia,* Psychological Assessment, vol. 3, no. 4, Dec. 1991, pp. 667–72.

31.   Heinze, Michaela, *Developing Sensitivity to Distortion: Utility of Psychological Tests in Differentiating Malingering and Psychopathology in Criminal Defendants,* J. Forensic Psychiatry & Psychology, vol. 14, no. 1 (April 2003), pp. 151–77.

32.   Kim, Michelle, et al., *The Warrington Recognition Memory Test for Words as a Measure of Response Bias: Total Score and Response Times Cutoffs Developed on 'Real World' Credible and Non-Credible Subjects,* Archives of Clinical Neuropsychology, vol. 25, no. 1 (2010), pp. 60–70; *see also* Prigatano, G.P., et al., *Digit Memory Test: Unequivocal Cerebral Dysfunction and Suspected Malingering,* J. Clinical Neuro-psychology, vol. 15, no. 4 (July 1993), pp. 537–46; *see also* Millis, S.R., *The Recognition Memory Test in the Detection of Malingered and Exaggerated Memory Deficits,* Clinical Neuropsychologist, no. 6 (1992), pp. 405–13; *see also* Hiscock, M. & Hiscock, C.K., *Refining the Forced-Choice Method for the Detection of Malingering,* J. Clinical & Experimental Neuropsychology, no. 11, no. 6 (1989), pp. 967–74.

and clinical presentations. The reader must again keep in mind that none of these tests is diagnostic in itself, but instead can be used to provide the examiner with additional compelling information.

The Rorschach Inkblot Test was developed in 1921 by its namesake, Swiss psychologist Hermann Rorschach. At one time it was the most widely used projective personality test, though its popularity has diminished as charges of pseudoscience have increasingly been leveled against it. In the past it was employed extensively as a tool to discern malingering. However, more recent studies have shown that while malingerers give responses that tend toward the dramatic on the Rorschach, no specific malingering pattern has been found that replicates across all studies, and thus even those practitioners professing expertise in interpretation can be misled.[33] For this reason, many hold that it is only when the Rorschach is used in conjunction with another instrument, such as the MMPI, that the combination has good validity regarding the detection of over-endorsement of symptoms.[34]

~~~~~~~~~~~~~~~~~~~~

Though faking can be seen in any clinical setting, malingerers are most often successful when fabricating conditions that have a significant subjective component (or said another way, it's hard to malinger a broken bone once an X-ray has been obtained). Because of ongoing professional controversies and a lack of objectively verifying tests, the following diagnoses represent the author's three favorite examples of conditions in which subjectivity and a desire to fabricate often collide (note, too, that all three come with trendy acronyms).

---

33. Perry, G.G. & Kinder, B.N., *The Susceptibility of the Rorschach to Malingering: A Critical Review*, J. PERSONALITY ASSESSMENT, vol. 54, no. 1/2 (1990), p. 47; *see also* Albert, S., et al., *Faking Psychosis on the Rorschach: Can Expert Judges Detect Malingering?*, J. PERSONALITY ASSESSMENT, vol. 44, no. 2 (April 1980), pp. 115–19.

34. Ganellen, R.J., et al., *Can Psychosis Be Malingered on the Rorschach? An Empirical Study*, J. PERSONALITY ASSESSMENT, vol. 66, no. 1, Feb. 1996, pp. 65–80; *see also* Frueh, B.C. & Kinder, B.N., *The Susceptibility of the Rorschach Inkblot Test to Malingering of Combat-Related PTSD*, J. PERSONALITY ASSESSMENT, vol. 62, no. 2 (April 1994), pp. 280–98.

Multiple Personality Disorder (MPD)

The first-known documented case of MPD comes from 1817.
In that year, the case of a Mary Reynolds, who was noted to
have "strange fits" that started when she was 18 years old,
was published in the *Medical Repository*. These episodes
involved periods of deep sleep during the day, and upon
awakening, exhibiting marked discrepancies in memory,
style of penmanship, and temperament. When further questioned, Reynolds is said to have acknowledged two different states of being that alternated inside her.[35] Since these
events occurred two centuries ago, it is impossible to know
what, if any, genuine condition caused Reynolds's suffering. Aside from the nonspecific and unscientific descriptors
"spell" or "fit," such a presentation has additionally been
called hysteria, hysterical neurosis, and the current, though
decidedly less catchy, term from the *DSM-IV-TR*, dissociative identity disorder. In the vernacular, though, such a presentation remains that of multiple personalities.

But is it even real? Literary and Hollywood treatments
aside—those seen in *The Strange Case of Dr Jekyll and
Mr Hyde* (Robert Louis Stevenson, 1886), *The Three Faces
of Eve* (Thigpen and Cleckley, 1957), and *Sybil* (Schreiber,
1973)—those who purport that such a condition is genuine point to studies that "alter states" exhibit different EEG
brainwave tracings, something they say cannot be faked.[36]
These apologists maintain that the development of alters
is a defense mechanism stemming from severe childhood
abuse that can extend into adulthood. Those who doubt
the authenticity of MPD hold that the condition is largely
culture-bound in highly suggestible individuals, as it is sub-

35.   Rogers, Rayna, *Multiple Personality and Channeling*, JEFFERSON J. OF
PSYCHIATRY, vol. 9, no. 1 (1991), p. 3.
36.   Coons, P.M., Milstein, V. & Marley, C., *EEG Studies of Two Multiple
Personalities and a Control*, ARCHIVES OF GENERAL PSYCHIATRY, vol. 39, no. 7
(July 1982), pp. 823–25.

jective for both the patient and the clinician.[37] EEG changes between alters, they maintain, are due to varying degrees of concentration, mood, and muscle tension, and not due to intrinsic differences in the brain's electrical activity pattern.[38] They additionally point to the anecdotal evidence that a small number of clinicians make a large number of these diagnostic finds. Many polemicists hold that MPD more likely represents a histrionic manifestation of other conditions, such as anxiety states, thought disorders, cyclical mood disorders, severe personality disorders, or downright malingering.

Is it that easy to fake MPD? How subjective is the diagnosis? According to the *DSM-IV-TR*, to fulfill the criteria, one must manifest (*commentary added*):

- The presence of two or more distinct identities or personality states (each with its own relatively enduring pattern of perceiving, relating to, and thinking about the environment and self) (*entirely subjective by this criterion*);
- At least two identities or personality states that recurrently take control of the person's behavior (*again, entirely subjective*);
- The inability to recall important personal information that is too extensive to be explained by ordinary forgetfulness (*once more, subjective*);
- That the disturbance is not due to the direct physiological effects of a substance (e.g., blackouts during alcohol intoxication) or a general medical condition (e.g., complex partial seizures). (*Depending on sensitivity, toxicology screens can miss certain substances, and de-*

37. Piper, A. & Merskey, H., *The Persistence of Folly: Critical Examination of Dissociative Identity Disorder, part II – The Defense and Decline of Multiple Personality or Dissociative Identity Disorder*, CANADIAN J. OF PSYCHIATRY, vol. 49, no. 10 (2004), pp. 678–83.

38. Coons et al., *supra* note 36.

pending on timing, EEGs can likewise fail to detect intermittent electrophysiologic changes in the brain.)[39]

Claims of Multiple Personality Disorder must therefore be met with a large dollop of skepticism directed at both the subject and the clinician. In the author's opinion, that this condition remains in the *DSM-IV-TR* is an embarrassment to the profession.

Post-traumatic Stress Disorder (PTSD)

Unlike MPD, where serious controversy exists as to whether the condition is even genuine, there is little doubt in professional circles that PTSD is real. While the disorder may be of situational etiology, a genetic or biochemical predisposition in some individuals has been postulated but is as yet undiscovered.

The issue instead is the loose nature of diagnostic application. One respected reference on the subject claims that PTSD is the fourth most common psychiatric disorder in the United States, afflicting more than 10 percent of men and 18 percent of women at some point in their lives.[40] To me, this seems exaggerated, especially because not all who are exposed to trauma develop PTSD; there are many purporting to suffer from PTSD who seemingly have not been exposed to extraordinary and overwhelming events that yield the degree of trauma required: think violent sexual assaults, kidnappings, combat, terrorism, torture, catastrophic motor vehicle accidents, etc.[41] To make this diagnosis meaning-

39. _____. DIAGNOSTIC AND STATISTICAL MANUAL OF MENTAL DISORDERS, 4th edition, text rev. Wash., D.C.: American Psychiatric Association (2000).

40. YEHUDA, RACHEL & DAVIDSON, JONATHAN. CLINICIAN'S MANUAL ON POSTTRAUMATIC STRESS DISORDER. London: Science Press (2000), p. 1.

41. *See* Levin, Aaron, *Campus Shooting Follow-Up Shows New Approach Needed*, PSYCHIATRIC NEWS, vol. 46, no. 19, Oct. 7, 2011, p. 14, for an interesting discussion of how some Virginia Tech students who were not directly exposed to the shooting later displayed symptoms of PTSD, and how those directly and personally exposed to the shooting made up only a small fraction of those claiming PTSD symptoms; *see also* Jancin, Bruce, *PTSD 'Not a Given' After Mass Catastrophes*, CLINICAL PSYCHIATRY NEWS, May 2011, p. 16.

ful, one must separate the traumatic from the merely stress-ful and unfortunate.[42] Increasingly, this seems not to be the case in the clinical world.

Additionally, many with genuine PTSD may try to hide or deny symptoms because they want to avoid addressing the trigger event, they want to appear stoic, or both. Those who seek disability benefits or monetary damages, how-ever, can behave quite oppositely. Because there is no way indpendent of patient report to rule the diagnosis in or out, the potential for abuse of this diagnosis is rife.[43] As Allen Frances presciently noted, "PTSD is probably one of the most under-diagnosed and also one of the most over-diag-nosed of DSM disorders."[44]

Malingering is motivated by potential secondary gain, often monetary or legal. A survey of more than 300 foren-sic psychologists in the 1990s yielded estimates of more than 15 percent malingering of PTSD symptoms in a foren-sic setting and 7.4 percent in a non-forensic setting.[45] A sepa-rate study by the same research team suggested a frequency of more than 20 percent malingering of PTSD symptoms among defendants undergoing insanity evaluations.[46] Also, a rate of up to 30 percent malingering among veterans seek-ing PTSD compensation has been postulated by another group of researchers.[47] Certainly not all of these patients

42. YEHUDA & DAVIDSON, *supra* note 40, at p. 3.

43. Frances, Allen, *PTSD, DSM-5, and Forensic Misuse*, PSYCHIATRIC TIMES, Sept. 30, 2011, p. 10; *see also* Vedantam, Shankar, *A Political Debate on Stress Disorder: As Claims Rise, VA Takes Stock*, WASH. POST, Dec. 27, 2005, p. A-16, *available at* http://www.washingtonpost.com/wp-dyn/content/article/2005/12/26/AR2005122600792.html (retrieved Nov. 3, 2011); *see also* Frueh, B. C. et al., *Apparent Symptom Over-Reporting Among Combat Veterans Evalu-ated for PTSD*, CLINICAL PSYCHOLOGY REV., vol. 20, no. 7 (2000), pp. 853–85.

44. Frances, *Forensic Misuse, id.*

45. SIMON, ROBERT & GOLD, LIZA. TEXTBOOK OF FORENSIC PSYCHIATRY. Wash., D.C.: American Psychiatry Publishing, Inc. (2010), p. 455.

46. *Id.*

47. *Id.*

were faking, but in the same breath, it is also likely that not all were genuinely afflicted.

Furthermore, it's not always merely the doing of the patients. A study from an Australian university compared diagnostic agreement between a group of mental health experts who were retained by defense teams with those from a group retained by plaintiffs, or the prosecution, in court cases. The study showed that agreement occurred more often in certain diagnostic categories, and less so in others. For example, there was a greater degree of agreement between the experts involving patients with primary thought disorders, such as schizophrenia. Personality and mood disorders had less overall agreement between the two groups of health experts. The least agreement was found regarding PTSD! The study authors held that it is difficult, given the subjectivity of diagnosis, to ascertain the presence of PTSD "in a reliable way in legal settings."[48] Some would argue that teasing out objectivity regarding PTSD can be almost as difficult in any clinical setting.

Is it that easy to fake PTSD? How subjective is the diagnosis? Adapted from the *DSM-IV-TR*, to fulfill the criteria, one must (*commentary added*):

- Experience, witness, or be confronted with an event(s) that involves actual or threatened death or serious injury to self or others (*"confronted with" renders this element rather easy to fulfill*); and
- React with fear, helplessness, or horror (*entirely subjective*); and
- For at least one month, re-experience the trauma through recurrent and distressing recollections (images, thoughts, or perceptions); through distressing dreams; through feelings (flashbacks) that the traumatic event is recurring; or through exposure to cues that symbol-

---

48. Arehart-Treichel, Joan, *Surprising Accord Found in Psychiatric Testimony*, PSYCHIATRIC NEWS, vol. 46, no. 3 (Feb. 4, 2011), p. 9.

ize or resemble the traumatic event; with resulting psychological distress or physiologic reactivity, and resulting in clinically significant distress or impairment in social, occupational, or other important areas of functioning (*still subjective*); and

- For at least one month, avoid stimuli associated with the traumatic event by means of at least three of the following: avoiding thoughts, feelings, or conversations; avoiding activities, places, or people; being unable to recall an important aspect of the trauma; manifesting a diminished interest in significant activities; feeling estranged from others; demonstrating a restricted range of emotions and expressions; or sensing a foreshortened future,; all of which resulting in clinically significant distress or impairment in social, occupational, or other important areas of functioning (*remains subjective*); and

- For at least one month, exhibit hyperarousal by at least two of the following: having difficulty with sleep; demonstrating outbursts of anger; experiencing difficulty with concentration; manifesting hypervigilance; or illustrating an exaggerated startle response, all of which resulting in clinically significant distress or impairment in social, occupational, or other important areas of functioning (*yes, subjective*).[49]

Claims of PTSD should be investigated, as much as possible, by looking for any objective collateral evidence to support the claims. Admittedly, this task won't be easy, as most endorsements cannot be corroborated by anything objective.

49. _____. DIAGNOSTIC AND STATISTICAL MANUAL OF MENTAL DISORDERS, 4th ed., text rev. Wash., D.C.: American Psychiatric Association (2000).

Attention Deficit Disorder (ADD) and
Attention Deficit Hyperactivity Disorder (ADHD)

This is another diagnostic category that started out with a good clinical foundation, at least in children, but now suffers from diagnostic creep (wherein a disorder is identified and suddenly found everywhere). Some in the profession doubt its existence, but most believe the conditions are multi-factorial and derive from as-yet-undetermined genetic and physiologic roots along with environment.[50] It is interesting to note that in 2002, almost one out of 10 readers of the *British Medical Journal* who responded to an online survey listed ADD as one of the "top ten non-diseases" in common use.[51]

Here the question is less "Do some children suffer from ADD?" and more "Do children who suffer from ADD segue into adults who still suffer from ADD?" Most clinicians would likely agree that there is nothing magical about one's 18th birthday; it is an artificial societal construct that indicates attaining adulthood, but not one that suggests any condition present on that day suddenly disappears. Are there 18-year-olds who still suffer ADD symptoms that began in their younger years? Almost certainly that is true. But having so noted, there are also adults who are likely to have a self-serving desire to intentionally develop or continue to experience such symptoms.

The ease of purporting to suffer from attention deficit is compounded because most adults endorse the less objective inattentive variant (ADD) ahead of the impulsive hyperactive variant (ADHD). The diagnosis of ADD is entirely subjective in adults, with no confirmatory laboratory tests available. Rates of diagnosis vary across cultures and coun-

50. _____. Treatment of Attention Deficit/ Hyperactivity Disorder. U.S. Dep't of Health and Human Services (Dec. 1999). *Available at* http://archive.ahrq.gov/clinic/epcarch.htm (retrieved Dec. 1, 2011).

51. Smith, R., *In Search of 'Non-Disease,'* British Medical J., vol. 324, no. 7342 (April 2002), pp. 883–85.

tries. Aside from self-report, the diagnosis is one of exclusion (where the condition is determined by eliminating other possibilities) and only requires the retrospective determination of whether symptoms were present in childhood (even if not previously formally diagnosed). This is not a high bar to reach, especially if biased family, intentionally or not, lend a hand.

If we focus on the inattentive variant of the condition, think of the adjectives that can be used to describe those so afflicted: distractible, procrastinative, unmotivated, disorganized, and apathetic. These are many of the same descriptors that could be used for those with depression or anxiety, perhaps a thought or personality disorder, or even a learning disability or dead-end job. The difference, of course, is that those other states are not trendy and are not being treated with abusable stimulants.

Is it that easy to fake adult ADD? How subjective is the diagnosis? Adapted from the *DSM-IV-TR*, to fulfill the criteria, one must manifest (*commentary added*):

- At least six of the following symptoms have lasted for at least six months and are not attributable to another Axis I or Axis II condition: failure to give close attention to detail, or make careless mistakes; often has difficulty sustaining attention; often does not seem to listen when addressed; often does not follow instructions and fails to finish duties in the workplace; often has difficulty organizing tasks and activities; often avoids, dislikes, or is reluctant to engage in tasks that require sustained mental effort; often loses tools and resources necessary for tasks and activities; often is easily distracted by extraneous stimuli; often is forgetful in daily activities (*the use of the word "often" makes these criteria laughably subjective and vague*); and
- Some symptoms of inattention that cause impairment were present before the patient was age 7 (*"some symptoms"?*); and

> - Some impairment from the symptoms is present in school, workplace, and home settings *(some impairment?)*; and
> - There must be clear evidence of clinically significant impairment in social, academic, or occupational functioning. *(This is the closest that this diagnostic schema comes to objectivity, but unfortunately, "clear evidence" is often the report of the subject or family, which waters down the objectivity.)*[52]
>
> Claims of ADD in an adult should be investigated as much as possible by searching for any truly objective collateral evidence to support the claims. As with MPD and PTSD, this isn't easy and is often not pursued adequately in a busy clinical setting.

And what of the other four earlier vignettes? Any of them might at first raise the specter of malingering, but actually they all represent recognized mental illnesses within the *DSM-IV-TR* canon, falling under the umbrella term "somatiform disorders."

The first fact pattern, involving the 36-year-old female, is suggestive of factitious disorder. Also known as Munchausen syndrome and related to *pseudologia fantastica,* or pathological lying, factitious disorder involves the intentional feigning of symptoms for the subconscious purpose of assuming the sick role (remember that malingering is intentional and effected for conscious secondary gain). Factitious disorder does not involve any monetary or legal goals— just being a patient is enough.[53] A fine distinction needs to be drawn between those subjects who feign symptoms for the purpose of obtaining drugs (malingering) and those who feign symptoms to fulfill the subconscious desire to become a patient (factitious disorder), though these two presentations may at first appear identical. A subtype of factitious disorder is Munchausen syndrome by proxy,

---

52. _____. DIAGNOSTIC AND STATISTICAL MANUAL OF MENTAL DISORDERS, 4th ed., text rev. Wash., D.C.: American Psychiatric Association (2000).

53. Purcell, T.B., *Factitious Disorders and Malingering*, EMERGENCY MEDICINE: CONCEPTS AND CLINICAL PRACTICE, 5th ed. St Louis: Mosby (2002), p. 390.

which, although not currently a separate entity in *DSM-IV-TR*, is widely recognized as a condition in which a third party, such as a child or a debilitated elder, is the template for the feigned illness fostered by the mentally afflicted caretaker.[54]

Individuals afflicted by factitious disorder often exhibit numerous surgical scars, especially of the abdomen. They display an evasive manner, provide dramatic and dubious medical histories, and attempt to cover up information about past evaluations, treatments, and insurance claims whenever possible. The challenge for clinicians is not only in the diagnosis, but in the knowledge that true physical conditions can coexist in the subject with factitious disorder.[55] Individuals with factitious disorder can greatly annoy and instill resentment in health-care providers, as they frustrate harried clinicians by wasting precious time and resources through unnecessary hospital admissions and expensive investigatory tests.

The second vignette, involving the 81-year-old female, is suggestive of conversion disorder. Here there is no feigning. Instead, a loss of motor or sensory function similar in appearance to a neurological or general medical condition is instead precipitated by emotional stress and is subconscious. The loss of function is often related to the triggering psychic stressor (e.g., guilt over striking another person results in perceived paralysis of the arm). The medical evaluation will be entirely noncontributory, or if pathology is found, it will be too minimal to explain the loss of function. Conversion disorder is seen more often in young women but can occur in either gender and at any age. Common examples of conversion symptoms include blindness or double vision, paralysis, numbness, amnesia, tics, and difficulties with swallowing or walking. As with factitious disorder, true physical conditions can coexist in patients with conversion disorder, making the evaluation and management of these individuals all the more challenging.[56]

54. Othmer, E. & Othmer, S., *The Clinical Interview Using DSM-IV-TR, in* THE DIFFICULT PATIENT, vol. 2. Wash., D.C.: American Psychiatric Publishing, Inc., 2002, p. 59.

55. Folks, D.G. & Freeman, A.M., *Munchausen's Syndrome and Other Factitious Illness, in* PSYCHIATRIC CLINICS OF NORTH AMERICA, no. 8 (1985), pp. 263–78.

56. *Id.*

The third vignette, involving the 37-year-old male, points to another diagnosis of exclusion, somatization disorder. As with conversion disorder, there is no feigning. However, unlike conversion disorder, the symptoms of somatization are not related to a specific emotional trigger. Persons with somatization disorder present with multiple symptoms without underlying disease (or physical findings that are too minimal to explain the presentation). The symptoms involve combinations of chronic pain, gastrointestinal distress, sexual dysfunction, and neurological impairment. The resulting debilitation is not from actual pathology, but rather from the patient's subconscious perception of impairment. The symptoms tend to wax and wane in severity, often over years, and the onset is always prior to age 30.[57]

A clinical finding that can be seen in both conversion and somatization disorders is that of the psychogenic non-epileptic seizure, or what used to be called the hysterical seizure or pseudoseizure. Psychogenic seizures involve motor activity that appears to be epileptic in nature but is not accompanied by EEG discharges that would indicate the presence of a physiologic process. Clues that such motor activity might not be physiologic include bursts of stop-go motion, irregular progression of the motor activity, distractibility of the subject during the event, generalized motor activity but without loss of consciousness, abrupt cessation, pelvic thrusting, post-episode breathing that is normal or fast, out-of-phase motor activity (e.g., legs moving as if riding a bicycle), side-to-side head or limb shaking, near-absence of post-event confusion, and eyes and mouth that are shut tightly throughout.[58] One researcher (So, 2010) estimated that such events are seen in 10 percent of neurology outpatients and in up to half of all neurology inpatients. Another researcher (Meierkord, 1991) posited that more than 50 percent of those who demonstrate such motor activity have an underlying psychiatric disorder (an estimate that I believe is low).

---

57. _____. DIAGNOSTIC AND STATISTICAL MANUAL OF MENTAL DISORDERS, 4th ed., text rev.

58. Benbadis, S.R., *Psychogenic Non-Epileptic Seizures, in* THE TREATMENT OF EPILEPSY: PRINCIPLES AND PRACTICE, 4th ed.. Phila.: Lippincott, Williams & Wilkins (2005), pp. 623–30.

The fourth vignette, involving the 47-year-old male, is suggestive of hypochondriasis. Again, no intentional feigning of symptoms occurs in this condition. Instead, the sufferer has an abnormally intense preoccupation with physical health and fears of having a serious hidden illness based on the misperception of bodily signs and symptoms.[59] Despite extensive medical work-up revealing no cause for concern, the hypochondriac remains convinced that occult pathology remains, if only an astute practitioner would uncover it. Hypochondriasis can exhaust not only the subject and family, but also the medical providers upon whom the subject calls to produce the long-sought diagnosis and cure.

Take-home Pearls

- Discrepancies between claimed symptoms, reported history, and clinical observations by the practitioner should raise suspicion of malingering, especially in the presence of possible secondary gain.
- Malingering costs society in financial terms, in the expenditure of resources, in lost productivity, in decreased morale, and in the corruption of the legal system.
- Despite the unusual case of Vinny Gigante, successful malingering is not easily performed, and there are a number of simple red flags that should alert the attorney and the health-care provider that fabrication may be at hand.
- In addition to observable clinical red flags, psychological tests can yield additional corroborating information on possible symptom fabrication. Some instruments that are commonly employed for this purpose include the MMPI-2, the MFAST, the SIRS, and the TOMM.

---

59. _____. DIAGNOSTIC AND STATISTICAL MANUAL OF MENTAL DISORDERS, 4th ed., text rev. Wash., D.C.: American Psychiatric Association (2000).

- Malingering should be present in the differential diagnosis of any condition if red flags are present. However, those purporting conditions with considerable subjectivity of the diagnostic elements—including but not limited to multiple personality disorder, post-traumatic stress disorder, and attention deficit disorder in adults—should receive additional scrutiny. On the other hand, the somatiform disorders, which are genuine mental illnesses listed in the *DSM-IV-TR*, can sometimes be mistaken for malingering, given that their clinical presentations are unusual and appear to have considerable overlap with malingering.

Chapter 8

The Divination of Future Dangerousness

> There are three kinds of lies: lies, damned lies, and statistics.
>
> —Mark Twain[1]
>
> While the individual man is an insoluble puzzle, in the aggregate he becomes a mathematical certainty. You can, for example, never foretell what any one man will do, but you can say with precision what an average number will be up to. Individuals vary, but percentages remain constant.
>
> —Sherlock Holmes[2]

Niels Bohr is quoted as once saying, "Prediction is very difficult, especially if it's about the future."[3] Nowhere is this more true than in the fields of psychiatry and psychology. Guesswork on future dangerous behavior is fraught with uncertainties. Unfortunately, divining it is a skill that newly minted mental health clinicians are often called to demonstrate early in their careers, and without the

---

1. Mark Twain, incorrectly attributing to Benjamin Disraeli, *available at* http://www.twainquotes.com/Statistics.html.
2. Doyle, Arthur Conan, *The Sign of Four, in* THE COMPLETE SHERLOCK HOLMES, vol. 2. New York: Barnes & Noble Classics (2003), p. 160.
3. *Available at* http://www.duke.edu/~rnau/411quote.htm.

171

experience to qualify their opinions in context, too many exceed what is appropriate to offer. Or as one author suggested, "the notion that a (mental health) risk assessment (of future dangerousness) will provide an accurate estimate over an unlimited time frame and across an unspecified range of environments seems logically implausible. Yet this is often what is asked of practitioners and implied in, or inferred from, risk assessments. Practitioners, therefore, have a professional responsibility to make such limitations explicit."[4]

There can be serious repercussions when expert opinions are offered without solid scientific founding. The legal safeguards enshrined in our Bill of Rights are effectively neutered should decisions on state-imposed detention be rendered on legally and scientifically shaky grounds.[5] Psychiatric diagnoses, as we have seen, can exist within considerable areas of grey.[6] Add to this the observation that the mentally ill are the only demographic group that can be legally involuntarily detained before a crime has even been committed, and one begins to appreciate the laws of unintended consequences and constitutional erosions.[7] When science is massaged to fit a pre-conceived societal goal—no matter how seemingly worthy—we encounter what the late author and doctor Michael Crichton referred to as "bad science tricked out for public policy ends."[8]

How does it happen that we as a profession overreach? Trainees in the field of mental health usually spend a good amount of time on inpatient psychiatric wards, which are the bread and butter of most academic programs. Needless to say, many patients on those

---

4. CRIGHTON, DAVID. PSYCHOLOGY IN PRISONS. Chapel Hill, N.C.: BPS Blackwell Publishing (2008), pp. 108–09.

5. U.S. CONSTITUTION, amendments IV, V, and VI.

6. *See* Frances, Allen, *Rape, Psychiatry, and Constitutional Rights—Hard Cases Make for Very Bad Law*, PSYCHIATRIC TIMES, vol. 27, no. 9, Sept. 1, 2010, for a valuable discussion of how rape is sometimes labeled "paraphilia not otherwise specified, non-consenting" when in fact no evidence of an Axis I mental illness in the perpetrator exists.

7. MENTAL DISORDER AND CRIME (Hodgins, Sheilagh, ed.). Newbury Park: Sage Publications (1993), p. 39.

8. Knoll, James, *The Political Diagnosis: Psychiatry in the Service of the Law*, PSYCHIATRIC TIMES, May 13, 2010, p. 11.

wards do not want to be hospitalized, so holding commitment hearings, usually on-site, is something to which trainees are exposed from the very beginning. And those hearings often revolve around the question of whether the patients present a danger to themselves or to others.

Predictions of future dangerousness fall loosely into two varieties: long-term and short-term (no black letter definitions exist of these two terms, but the reader will appreciate the difference before long). Evidence strongly suggests that the further into the future that a clinician attempts to project a prediction, the less will be its accuracy. This is not rocket science.

Ponder the essence of these two quotes:

Recent studies report that involuntarily hospitalized patients have a high degree of violence immediately before and [just] after [admission], and that professional judgments about these patients' dangerousness have a relatively high degree of ***short-term predictive validity*** (emphasis added).[9]

Although psychiatric assessments ***may permit short-term predictions*** of violent or assaultive behavior, medical knowledge has simply not advanced to the point where long-term predictions . . . may be made with even reasonable accuracy (emphasis added).[10]

We will return to discuss what is meant by "short-term" later. It will all make more sense once predictions of a longer nature are addressed.

Imagine you are a clinician examining a defendant who has been convicted of assault and first-degree murder, and psychiatric testimony is requested for purposes of sentencing. The defendant murdered a young mother in the presence of her children, inflicting more

---

9. Mossman, Douglas, *Dangerousness Decisions: An Essay on the Mathematics of Clinical Violence Prediction and Involuntary Hospitalization*, University of Chicago Law School Roundtable (1995).

10. Regnier, Thomas, *Barefoot in Quicksand: The Future of 'Future Dangerousness' Predictions in Death Penalty Sentencing in the World of* Daubert *and* Kumho, Akron L. Rev., no. 37 (2003), p. 482.

than 40 stab wounds to her with a butcher knife. He then turned his rage on the children. The little girl was also killed, but the boy miraculously survived, despite having several knife wounds that penetrated his entire torso from front to back. Given the heinous nature of the crimes and the defendant's apparent total lack of remorse, what would most people think? Would they want this individual eventually released into their community after supposed rehabilitation? Would they trust this individual to develop a conscience? Might one hold that this individual is dangerous, is likely to remain so for the foreseeable future, and probably will be forever? Would it be wrong for a mental health professional, empowered by the courts to offer opinions as an expert, to evaluate this individual and then state a position on his future dangerousness given the above?

The U.S. Supreme Court heard this case in 1991 in *Payne v. Tennessee*. The Court allowed for the admission of expert testimony on future dangerousness, despite misgivings about the reliability of such testimony. In justifying the admission of this evidence, the Court stated, "as we explained in rejecting the contention that expert testimony on future dangerousness should be excluded from capital trials, the rules of evidence generally extant at the federal and state levels anticipate that relevant, unprivileged evidence should be admitted and its weight left to the fact-finder, who would then have the benefit of cross-examination and contrary evidence by the opposing party."[11] This sounds reasonable, doesn't it? Give the jury all of the information, and then let the jury decide.

Here is another scenario: a psychiatric patient had killed a state trooper more than two decades earlier during the commission of a suspected drug offense, but he was subsequently acquitted of murder, as his attorney had successfully argued self-defense. Fifteen years later, this patient began to write intimidating letters with violent themes to local policemen and judges; found capable of standing trial, he was convicted of multiple counts of communicating threats. At sentencing, the district court judge deviated from guidelines that called for a sentence of 30 to 37 months and instead handed down the maximum statutory sentence of 120 months. The judge

---

11.   501 U.S. 808, 823.

said in part that the defendant's history of homicide, when taken into account along with his additional recent acts, made it more likely that he would commit further violent offenses in the future.

The Seventh Circuit in Illinois heard this case in 1990 in *United States v. Fonner*. That appellate court remanded for resentencing based on a determination that the district court judge had not clearly articulated his reasons for deviation from usual parameters. However, the circuit court did not specifically disapprove of the lower court judge's analysis of mental state and future dangerousness.[12] An assumption that the defendant was likely to commit more violent acts, perhaps because of mental problems and the known history of homicide, was seemingly felt to be an acceptable basis for extending the sentence, at least had it been more clearly articulated. In other words, the circuit court permitted a determination of future dangerousness to be grounded at least on some actions for which the defendant had not been held criminally culpable, but which were deemed germane to the assessment of violent predisposition nevertheless.

This too sounds reasonable, right? Commission of a homicide, followed by the communication of threats to others, certainly suggests that the individual in question presents a danger to those whom he may encounter.

However, what if the information given to the finder of fact in either of the above cases was faulty? What if the information had shadings of truth that could not be readily determined? What if the information was true but presented in a misleading manner? Would it be correct then to ask a fact-finder to decide a case on the basis of that information? Should there be more stringently enforced standards regarding what is admissible, regardless of whether it comes from a "reliable professional source"?

Over the years, countless attempts have been made to devise protocols wherein those who might present a danger to themselves or others through faulty impulse control could be treated or contained before they become destructive. The nineteenth-century phrenologists believed that the contours of one's skull made discerning personality and behavioral proclivities as easy as a physical exami-

---

12. 920 F.2d. 1330.

nation. More recently, the advent of nuclear medicine held forth the promise that internal anatomic and physiologic markers—especially in the frontal and temporal lobes of the brain—might reveal what had eluded the phrenologists.[13, 14] Numerous studies of male children of alcoholic biological parents in nondrinking adoptive homes showed that, as they grew, those children had a higher incidence of substance abuse than the population baseline. Many proffered the genetics of substance abuse as a potential marker for other dysfunctions.[15] But nothing genetic, physiologic, or anatomic proved to have the requisite predictive value across the board.

Something else had to be found. Psychological testing and its bastard child, the risk assessment, then enjoyed a renaissance that continues to this day.

The Elements of Admissibility

It may seem difficult at first, but everything is difficult at first.
—Miyamoto Musashi[16]

Recall that in 1923, from the Circuit Court of the District of Columbia, came *Frye v. United States*. In this case, it was held by the circuit court that expert scientific opinion was admissible only if the principles on which the opinions were based had gained general acceptance in the relevant scientific community.[17] This was an attempt by the *Frye* court to exclude the testimony of charlatans. However, for those courts that adopted it—and there were many— the common law *Frye* test also succeeded in preventing the factfinder from hearing expert opinions from accomplished scientists who were intellectually credible and yet novel or cutting-edge (i.e., their theories had not yet gained general acceptance within the es-

13. Mills, Shari & Raine, Adrian, *Neuroimaging and Aggression, in* THE PSYCHOBIOLOGY OF AGGRESSION. New York: The Haworth Press (1994), p. 145.

14. MENTAL DISORDER AND CRIME, *supra* note 7, at p. 227, *citing* Coccaro (1989).

15. MILLER, NORMAN, THE PRINCIPLES AND PRACTICE OF ADDICTIONS IN PSYCHIATRY. Phila.: W.B. Saunders Co. (1997), p. 21.

16. TOKITSU, K., MIYAMOTO MUSASHI: HIS LIFE AND WRITINGS. Boston: Weatherhill (2004), p. 2.

17. Frye v. United States, 293 F. 1013 (1923).

tablished scientific community). Many felt that the *Frye* test was thus unduly restrictive.

By the time that the U.S. Supreme Court case of *Daubert v. Merrell Dow* came along in 1993, lower federal courts wanted clarification if the *Frye* test, established seven decades earlier, had been supplanted by the more recent adoption of the Federal Rules of Evidence at 28 U.S.C.A. §702. In lieu of the "general acceptance" stipulation for expert opinion found in *Frye*, §702 simply provides that, "if scientific, technical, or other specialized knowledge will assist the [finder] of fact to understand the evidence or to determine a fact in issue, a witness qualified as an expert by knowledge, skill, experience, training, or education, may testify thereto in the form of an opinion or otherwise."[18] In its *Daubert* ruling, the Court did indeed hold that §702 had supplanted the evidentiary standard of *Frye* as it pertained to actions in federal courts.[19]

A careful reading of §702 will discern three elements pertaining to admissibility. First, there must be "scientific, technical, or other specialized knowledge" involved. *Daubert* describes such knowledge as that which "applies to any body of known facts or to any body of ideas inferred from such facts or accepted as truths on good grounds." *Daubert* goes on to identify four facets that bear on the inquiry into scientific, technical, or other specialized knowledge: 1. Have the theories been tested on which the expert opinions are based? 2. Have the theories been published in professional journals and subjected to peer review? 3. When the scientific theories are applied, is there a known error rate? and, as a residual nod to *Frye*, 4. Do the theories enjoy acceptance within the relevant scientific community? Later, in *Kumho Tire Company v. Carmichael*, the U.S. Supreme Court held that this list is neither exhaustive nor necessarily wholly applicable in every case. Flexibility within these guidelines, the Court held, is imperative.[20]

A second requirement as articulated in §702 is that the proposed expert scientific opinion must "assist the finder of fact to

---

18. 509 U.S. 579, 590.
19. Daubert v. Merrell Dow, 509 U.S. 579.
20. Kumho Tire Co. v. Carmichael, 526 U.S. 137.

understand the evidence or to determine a fact in issue." In short, it must be relevant and helpful to be admissible.

Third, §702 holds that the expert himself must have "superior knowledge, skill, experience, training, or education." He must be qualified to offer his opinion on the matter at hand.

Of the three elements above, the relevance of the testimony and the qualification of the expert are probably the least controversial, if for no reason other than that courts have been ruling on relevance and qualification for years prior to §702. Thus it is the first element—that of scientific knowledge—that potentially causes the most debate in federal actions. (Obviously, state courts are not governed by 28 U.S.C.A. §702 and may still employ variations of the *Frye* test if they so desire.)

Peruse the following commentary—merely the tip of the proverbial iceberg of what has been written and said in some academic and professional legal circles about the application of psychological tests and risk assessments—while keeping *Daubert*, *Frye*, and the Federal Rules of Evidence in mind:

> There are a number of statistical studies which amply demonstrate that the predictions of dangerousness by psychiatrists are unreliable. . . . The findings so consistently demonstrate that psychiatrists over-predict dangerousness by huge amounts that the reports must be taken seriously.[21]

> Studies show that psychiatric predictions of dangerousness were as likely to produce false positives as to correctly predict future dangerousness.[22]

> In general, mental health professionals . . . [w]hen predicting violence, dangerousness, and suicide . . . are far more likely to be wrong than right.[23]

21. Diamond, Bernard, *The Psychiatric Prediction of Dangerousness*, U. PA L. REV., vol. 123, no. 2 (1975), p. 440.

22. Cocozza, J. & Steadman, H., *The Failure of Psychiatric Predictions of Dangerousness*, RUTGERS L. REV., no. 29 (1976), pp. 1096–99.

23. Morse, Stephen, *Crazy Behavior, Morals, and Science: An Analysis of Mental Health Law*, S. CAL. L. REV., no. 51 (1978), p. 600.

Reliance by the courts on testimony by psychotherapists may be misplaced, since the ability to accurately predict dangerousness has not been demonstrated.[24]

A large literature indicates that neither actuarial nor clinical modes of predicting the dangerousness of mental patients released from maximum security have fared very well.[25]

Predictions of violence have been the subject of extensive literature that consistently criticizes psychiatrists' ability to gauge individuals' long-term future dangerousness.[26]

The courts have increasingly relied upon the psychiatrists' and psychologists' predictions in determining an offender's potential for future dangerousness, even though the psychiatric literature stresses the unreliability of these expert predictions.[27]

Although psychiatric assessments may permit short-term predictions of violent or assaultive behavior, medical knowledge has simply not advanced to the point where long-term predictions—the type of testimony at issue in this case—may be made with even reasonable accuracy.[28]

Although the testimony of clinicians about future dangerousness offers little more than that of an astrologer, such clinical testimony is pervasive, and courts persist in circumventing any inquiry into the scientific validity of expert future dangerousness predictions. This is an important

---

24. Hammond, Marilyn, *Predictions of Dangerousness in Texas*, St. Mary's L. J., no. 12 (1980), pp. 141–42.

25. Long, Leonard, *Rethinking Selective Incapacitation: More at Stake Than Controlling Violent Crime*, Univ. of Miss.–K.C. L. Rev., no. 62 (autumn 1993), p. 110.

26. Mossman, *supra* note 9.

27. Skaggs, Clayton, *Kansas' Sexual Predator Act and the Impact of Expert Predictions: Psyched Out by the* Daubert *Test*, Washburn L. J., no. 34 (Spring 1995), p. 327.

28. Regnier, *supra* note 10.

concern because giving the imprimatur of science to chicanery undermines our justice system.[29]

Given their notorious unreliability and divisiveness in the professional community, we might predict that no court would admit predictive opinions either under *Daubert* or *Frye*. Yet no appellate court has ever excluded expert psychiatric testimony about danger in a civil commitment case, either before or after *Daubert*.[30]

If courts applied *Daubert* standards to the kinds of clinical predictions currently offered in our courts, they would not admit the predictions because they do not meet any of the criteria for scientific validity.[31]

Research over the past 30 years has shown a significant degree of inaccuracy in clinicians' predictions of dangerousness, especially with false positives.[32]

Even with relatively sensitive tests for dangerousness, a substantial number of false positives occur because of the low base rate of dangerousness among the patient population.[33]

[Predictions of future dangerousness] are hocus pocus.[34]

29. Beecher-Monas, Erica & Garcia-Rill, Edgar, *Danger at the Edge of Chaos: Predicting Violent Behavior in a Post-*Daubert *World*, CARDOZO L. REV., no. 24 (2003), p. 1855.

30. Scherr, Alexander, Daubert & *Danger: The 'Fit' of Expert Predictions in Civil Commitments*, HASTINGS L. J., no. 55 (2003), pp. 2–3.

31. Beecher-Monas, Erica, *The Epistemology of Prediction: Future Dangerousness Testimony and Intellectual Due Process*, WASH. & LEE L. REV. , no. 60 (Spring 2003), p. 353.

32. _____, *Proof of Qualification for Commitment as a Mentally Disordered Sex Offender*, AMERICAN JURISPRUDENCE PROOF OF FACTS, 3d ed., vol. 51 (Sept. 2005), p. 299.

33. _____, *Liability for Physical Harm, Affirmative Duties, Duty to Third Persons Based on Special Relationship with Person Posing Risk*, § 41, RESTATEMENT (THIRD) OF TORTS, tentative draft. St Paul: American Law Inst. Publishers (2005).

34. Interview with criminal defense attorney Mark Geragos, American College of Legal Medicine Annual Conference, Las Vegas, Nev., Feb. 26, 2011.

Making Sense of Confusion

An unsophisticated forecaster uses statistics as a drunken man uses lamp posts: for support rather than for illumination.

—Andrew Lang[35]

Attempts at divination have been among the Holy Grails of the behavioral sciences for decades, but efforts to employ approaches deemed scientific produced poor results. For example, in the first half of the twentieth century, alcohol, anesthetics, opiates, cocaine, mescaline, hashish, scopolamine, and chloral hydrate were all used in some quarters as "truth serums" to interview patients and ascertain both their past transgressions and their future intentions; unfortunately, such drug cocktails often left subjects too obtunded to be accurately evaluated by anyone.[36] A different method of ascertaining potential dangerousness had to be developed. This was especially pressing as deinstitutionalization took hold and communities worried about potentially dangerous patients being released into the population.[37]

Civil commitment can be justified on the basis of two compelling societal demands: the state's legitimate interest to provide care for citizens who are unable to care for themselves, and the state's authority under its police powers to protect the community from the dangerous tendencies of unstable individuals. Related to both but more to +the latter, and due to the lack of viable alternatives, those who provided mental health care found themselves increasingly in demand for predictive services that were rarely requested in the days of unquestioned lifelong institutionalization. However, as with attempts at employing truth serums, all did not go easily at first. As recently as the mid-1950s, at the dawn of the Age of Deinstitutionalization, there are documented cases in which judges dismissed testifying psychologists from court, not because their credentials

35. *Available at* http://www.quotations.net/author-quotes/8410/Andrew%20Lang.

36. HORSLEY, J.S. NARCOANALYSIS. New York: Oxford University Press (1943), p. 2.

37. PRINCIPLES OF INPATIENT PSYCHIATRY (Ovsiew, Fred & Munich, Richard, eds.). New York: Wolters Kluwer (2009), p. 236; *see also* Grob, G.N., *Deinstitutionalization of the Mentally Ill: Policy Triumph or Tragedy?*, N.J. MED., vol. 101, no. 12 (2004), pp. 19–30.

within the field of psychology were lacking, but because of the court's perception of the discipline itself![38]

In the early 1970s, *Lessard v. Schmidt* sparked a reassessment of mental health law.[39] In deciding *Lessard*, the federal district court for eastern Wisconsin struck down that state's commitment law as being unconstitutionally broad. Instead, that court set far narrower parameters for the determination of dangerousness required before one could be involuntarily hospitalized or detained, and it further mandated that commitment proceedings afford the mentally ill all of the procedural protections accorded to criminal suspects, the foremost being the requirement of a higher standard of proof for the state. The trend appeared unmistakable.

In 1979 the U.S. Supreme Court decision in *Addington v. Texas* raised the necessary burden of proof for civil commitments based on dangerousness from the previously employed "preponderance of the evidence" to the higher "clear and convincing" standard.[40] The Court felt that this was necessary to ensure that the restriction of freedom inherent in commitment was not undertaken lightly. States were thereafter free to employ more-stringent commitment standards, but the new baseline had been set, and proffered predictive mental health testimony had to adapt accordingly.

The trend against easy confinement might have been apparent at the same time that *Lessard* and *Addington* were wending their way through the courts, had anyone studied the matter. In 1974, Steadman and Cocozza published an analysis of the *Baxstrom* cohort. Plaintiff Baxstrom and more than 960 other criminal offenders had been court-ordered for transfer from highly restrictive forensic settings to nonforensic inpatient mental health facilities throughout New York in the late 1960s. Havoc was predicted by mental health professionals, but Steadman and Cocozza documented that relatively few incidences of chaos actually occurred. The offenders had a low rate of re-offending in the less-restrictive settings, despite numerous professional opinions to the contrary. In the ensuing five years, more than half of the cohort patients were

---

38. BLAU, THEODORE. THE PSYCHOLOGIST AS EXPERT WITNESS. New York: Wiley & Sons (1984), p. 3.

39. 414 U.S. 473.

40. 441 U.S. 418.

discharged entirely from their respective facilities and re-entered the community. Moreover, less than 3 percent of this criminal population were reincarcerated due to violence.[41, 42, 43] Might it be that many clinicians, when basing their long-term opinions on unsubstantiated gut feelings, lean toward more dire predictions than eventual outcomes actually support?

One such gut feeling is the oft-repeated perceived association between violence and mental illness itself; as recently as 1999, the U.S. Surgeon General's Report on Mental Health posited that continuing stigmatization of the mentally ill was largely due to the public's fear of violence. Shortly thereafter, John Monahan, one of the nation's foremost academic researchers in the field of violence prediction, observed: "[t]he presumed link between mental disorders and violence has been the driving force behind mental health law and policy for centuries."[44] In 2009, in the most extensive meta-analysis to that date concerning the links between violence and mental illness, an Oxford University team in the United Kingdom revealed that substance use, and not the presence of other Axis I mental disorders, was the single best indicator of potential violence. The mentally ill, now as before, were unfairly being maligned in the court of public opinion, and many testifying experts were inadvertently fanning the flames.[45]

Thus, within half a century's span, mental health experts evolved from suspicious charlatans to mavens of prognostication, largely driven by public policy needs and not science. The assumption pro-

41. HANDBOOK OF PSYCHIATRIC MEASURES (Rush, John ed.). Wash., D.C.: American Psychiatric Publishing (2000), p. 6; *see also* CSERNANSKY, J.G., SCHIZOPHRENIA—A NEW GUIDE FOR CLINICIANS. New York: Marcel Dekker, Inc. (2002), p. 72.

42. HANDBOOK OF PSYCHIATRIC MEASURES, *id.,* at p. 7.

43. Baxstrom v. Herold, 383 U.S. 107; *see also* QUINSEY, VERNON ET AL. VIOLENT OFFENDERS: APPRAISING AND MANAGING RISK. Wash., D.C.: American Psychological Ass'n Press (1998), p. 31.

44. MONAHAN, JOHN, STEADMAN, HENRY, ET AL. RETHINKING RISK ASSESSMENT: THE MACARTHUR STUDY OF MENTAL DISORDER AND VIOLENCE. New York: Oxford University Press (2001), p. 2; *see also* Monahan, John, *Mental Disorder and Violent Behavior: Perceptions and Evidence*, AMERICAN PSYCHOLOGY, vol. 47 no. 4 (1992), p. 511.

45. Bell, Vaughan, *Crazy Talk: We Are Too Quick to Use 'Mental Illness' as an Explanation for Violence*, STATE OF THE UNIVERSE, Jan. 9, 2011, *available at* http://www.slate.com/articles/health_and_science/science/2011/01/crazy_talk.html (retrieved Dec. 10, 2011).

liferated that behavior can be predicted. None of this was at first empirically tested on a large-scale basis, and no one initially seems to have disputed it, especially since it so nicely served the purpose.

Some doubts eventually arose. To quote one research team, the Quinsey group: "people often think that they have more information than they actually have, [and they] are therefore willing to make more extreme judgments than are necessary."[46] A 2003 legal text by Garrison and Schneider observed that "there are [numerous] . . . flaws and limitations in human information processing, such as the propensity of decision makers to be distracted by irrelevant aspects of the alternatives . . . the tendency of decision makers to be swayed by the form in which the information about risks is packaged and presented . . . [and the] reliance on faulty categories and stereotypes."[47] Commenting on the subjective nature of risk assessments, an article in the *American Bar Association Journal* from 2011 observed that "clinicians will weigh the factors, unfortunately, often due to their personal bias: Freudian psychologists might consider the [offender's] relationship with the mother as paramount, while a cognitive psychologist might consider the offender's thoughts and perceptions as more important" in determining and predicting the risk of dangerousness.[48] Additional studies have made clear that predictions of long-term dangerousness are not being made with anything approaching the accuracy needed to meet a judicial standard of proof. Yet the *National Benchbook on Psychiatric and Psychological Evidence and Testimony* of the American Bar Association, in admitting as much in 1998, stated that such predictions of future

---

46. QUINSEY ET AL., *supra* note 43, at p. 56.

47. GARRISON, MARTHA & SCHNEIDER, CARL. THE LAW OF BIOETHICS: INDIVIDUAL AUTONOMY AND SOCIAL REGULATION. St. Paul: Thomson-West (2003), p. 121.

48. There will always be subjectivity. For example, to date there has been little agreement on what makes a crime particularly depraved, but now there is an effort to create a "depravity scale" ranking crimes along a continuum based on society's perceptions. Starting in 1998, those creating the scale, including thought leaders from mental health, law enforcement, and academia, have attempted to eliminate bias and minimize arbitrariness in sentencing. The team has reviewed court decisions and solicited input from the public in order to weight various crimes along a continuum. Their stated hope is that the final product will guide judges and juries, "not [] do their thinking for them." Hansen, Mark, *Depravity Scale May Help Judges and Juries During Sentencing*, A.B.A. J., July 1, 2011, p. 22.

dangerousness, although imperfect, remain the best information that courts have available to them. Imperfect and flawed somehow became good enough.

So how *do* clinicians arrive at their opinions? One study on the subject delineated six usual methods by which mental health professionals go about making determinations of future dangerousness. We have already encountered the first example, that of unguided clinical judgment, which has been called by some nothing more than an (inaccurate) likeability test.[49] Along the continuum there are four intermediate methods that involve forming judgments by relying on combinations of checklists, focused record reviews, and actuarial red flags, though all of these approaches allow, to varying degrees, for adjustments based on an examiner's clinical opinion.[50, 51] Finally, there is that of pure actuarial procedure, in which the clinician essentially has no personal input other than collecting the data and crunching the numbers.[52] Retrospective studies of outcomes suggest that a purely actuarial approach is superior to anything that contains a clinician's personal input, even taking into account those instances in which the clinician reports a very high degree of certainty in the opinion.

Before further commenting on actuarial instruments, one must turn to John Monahan's 2001 monograph on this subject, reputed to have been the largest analysis of its kind then undertaken. The Monahan group focused on data from the MacArthur Violence Risk Assessment Study, research that had been conducted using almost 1,000 persons who had been released from inpatient psychiatric settings and then followed for one year post-discharge.[53] Of those

49. Turney, Brent, *Dangerousness: Predicting Recidivism in Violent Sex Offenders*, KNOWLEDGE SOLUTIONS LIBRARY (March 1996), *available at* http://www.corpus-delicti.com/danger.html (retrieved Dec. 1, 2011).

50. MONAHAN, STEADMAN, ET AL., RETHINKING, *supra* note 44, at p. 6.

51. STONE, ALAN. MENTAL HEALTH AND THE LAW: A SYSTEM IN TRANSITION. Washington, D.C.: U.S. Gov't Printing Office (1976), p. 30.

52. DOREN, DENNIS. EVALUATING SEX OFFENDERS: A MANUAL FOR CIVIL COMMITMENT AND BEYOND. New York: Sage (2002), p. 43; *see also* HANDBOOK OF CORRECTIONAL MENTAL HEALTH (Scott, Charles & Gerbasi, Joan, eds.). Washington, D.C.: American Psychiatric Publishing (2005), p. 60.

53. MONAHAN, STEADMAN, ET AL., RETHINKING, *supra* note 44, at p. 43.

MacArthur patients diagnosed with schizophrenia, 14.8 percent were violent at some point during the follow-up period. Of those diagnosed with depression, the number was 28.5 percent. Of those diagnosed with bipolar disorder, the number was 22 percent. Of those having dual-diagnoses, of which one condition was substance abuse, the number jumped to 31 percent. Overall, 18.7 percent of the patients followed in the MacArthur study were violent at some point post-discharge.

The MacArthur study went on to state:

> "People discharged from psychiatric hospitals" is not a homogeneous category regarding violence. People with a major mental disorder . . . and without a substance abuse diagnosis are involved in significantly less community violence than people with a co-occurring substance abuse diagnosis. The prevalence of violence amongst people who have been discharged from a hospital and who *do not* have symptoms of substance abuse is about the same as the prevalence of violence among other people living in their communities who do not have symptoms of substance abuse.[54]

Substance abuse was involved in fully 75 percent of the violent episodes documented in the MacArthur data.[55]

The MacArthur study noted other trends. Childhood exposure to violence was a strong actuarial predictor for similar future behavior. Not having lived with either biological parent while young, the presence of violent behavior on the part of either parent in the home, and past physical abuse were also associated with later tendencies toward aggressive acts.[56] The presence of command hallucinations and delusions of threats to self or control by others were also related to a higher likelihood of violence.[57, 58] Interestingly, the

---

54. *Available at* http://www.macarthur.virginia.edu/violence.html (retrieved Dec. 1, 2011).

55. MONAHAN, STEADMAN, ET AL., RETHINKING, *supra* note 44, at p. 44; *see also* JOHNSON, SALLY. DEAD RIGHT, DEAD WRONG, OR THE JURY IS STILL OUT: THE COMPLEX WORLDS OF VIOLENCE AND MENTAL ILLNESS. Dep't of Psychiatry Grand Rounds, Univ. of Md. Med. Center (Dec. 2, 2010).

56. *Id.* at 77.

57. *Id.* at 80.

58. *Id.* at 86.

presence of subjective anger was not seen to be a statistically significant risk factor for violence, as the researchers confirmed that not all violence has an anger component.[59, 60]

In reviewing the MacArthur study data, the Monahan group contended that a few variables could be reasonably predictive of a violent predisposition, whereas many others, often counter-intuitively, lacked any predictive value. Even in those cases in which predictive variables were found, there was a complex relationship between competing variables that initially was not readily evident. The Monahan group held that unaided professional opinions are inarguably no better than chance, and then stated, "the complexity of the findings reported here underscores the difficulty of identifying . . . predictors of violence, [those] variables that are across-the-board risk factors for violence in all populations. *This complexity is no doubt one of the principle reasons why clinicians relying on a fixed set of individual risk factors have had such difficulty making accurate risk assessments*" (emphasis added).[61] Or as one of my psychologist colleagues at work recently offered, "there are only a limited number of significant variables that consistently have predictive value, but the research gurus keep putting them together in varying combinations looking for the golden goose. I am oversimplifying, of course, but I'm not too far off. Shhhh, don't tell anyone I said that."[62]

The most potentially troubling evidence, refuting even actuarial attempts to correctly predict the risk of future dangerousness for legal purposes, though, is found between pages 117 and 127 of the 2001 Monahan monograph: "that different predictions [of future dangerousness] may be obtained for the same individual from risk assessment models that have comparable levels of predictive accuracy . . . is a general property of actuarial prediction models." Even after all of the statistics have been discussed, the data collated, and the numbers analyzed, the outcomes can still depend on

---

59. *Id.* at 44.

60. JOHNSON, DEAD RIGHT, *supra* note 55.

61. MONAHAN, STEADMAN, ET AL., RETHINKING, *supra* note 44, at p. 130.

62. Interview with psychologist Charles Messer, N.C. Dep't of Corr. (May 3, 2011) (unpublished).

which elements are included, which questions are asked, what data are even available, and what instruments are used. While the Monahan group purports that employing several concurrent statistical tools is superior to using only one, such complex analytic protocols essentially take the procedure out of the hands of harried clinicians and render them all but useless, in practical terms, to anyone but researchers. Or as the MacArthur study admitted, "it would clearly be impossible for a clinician to commit the multiple models and their scoring to memory, since different risk factors are to be assessed for different patients. . . ."[63]

While not wholly actuarial (as it allows for a flexible semi-structured interview), the Hare Psychopathy Checklist is as close to an accepted gold standard for psychological testing as exists. It is used internationally in forensic settings and has been the subject of countless peer-reviewed articles since its inception in 1991. Interestingly, the creator of the checklist, renowned Canadian psychologist Robert Hare, has recently expressed concern that his instrument, at first designed for research purposes, might be misapplied by clinicians and the criminal justice system. "I feel ambivalent about it [being thus used]," Hare offered. His concerns may be justified; a study performed by a Hare protégé, Dr. Daniel Murphy, compared psychopathy checklists completed in legal settings by prosecution teams with those completed by defense teams, and he often found different scores for the same subject![64]

There are a number of other potential stumbling blocks that might blunt accuracy and compromise an analytic outcome. Here are two such examples:

- There is no universal agreement on the definitions of "violence" and "dangerousness," and thus what is actually being measured. Do they reference attempted bodily harm? Actual bodily harm? If harm does occur, does it have to be

63. *Available at* http://www.macarthur.virginia.edu/risk.html.

64. Spiegel, Alix, *Creator of Psychopathology Test Worries About Its Use*, "All Things Considered," National Public Radio, May 27, 2011. *Available at* http://www.npr.org/2011/05/27/136723357/creator-of-psychopathy-test-worries-about-its-use (retrieved Dec. 10, 2011).

serious to be included, or minimal? Does an arrest or official report have to be completed for the act to count, or does self-report by the subject, or the unofficial reports of others, allow for inclusion? Analytic instruments will be difficult to compare—or even use —unless there is a widely held consensus as to what is being measured. From a 1994 book edited by Monahan, "it is unusual in this field to find two studies that have even defined . . . predictor variables in the same manner. Given the retrospective nature of much of the research, investigators often have had to rely for predictor variables upon whatever information happened to be in the patient's records."[65]

- What are the cutoffs for high-risk and low-risk? What becomes of the gray zone in the middle? The more tightly defined are the boundaries of the high- and low-risk groupings, the more possible it may be that some meaningful data can be extracted based on the smaller and more homogenous cohorts at each extreme, but at the same time, the nebulous middle ground becomes larger. The Monahan group admitted that "in practice, the choice of cutoffs for high- and low-risk must be made on substantive grounds by a decision maker *legally empowered* to do so" (emphasis added), Note the use of the word "legally." Just because one is *legally* empowered to do something—in this case, make a decision on high- and low-risk parameters—is no guarantee that the end result will be based on anything scientific.[66]

The data collected for inclusion in any prediction instrument or protocol are only as good, or as useful, as the collector. The actuarial camp in particular promotes that, by using actuarial tools, the imperfections and biases of human examiners can be eliminated; when definitions and parameters have not been universally defined, though, the very biases that were supposedly removed can be reintroduced. The weak link from the legal perspective will always be

65. Monahan, John & Steadman, Henry, *Toward a Rejuvenation of Risk Assessment Research, in* VIOLENCE AND MENTAL DISORDER. Chicago: University of Chicago Press (1994), p. 12.

66. MONAHAN, STEADMAN, ET AL., RETHINKING, *supra* note 44, at p. 98.

the fallible human who is collecting the data, deciding what to include in which category, and determining what merits clinical significance and what does not.

What Do Courts Say?

It is my opinion that such future-telling is admissible under no theory of law and [is] prejudicial beyond belief.
—Justice Wendell Odom[67]

Those who look to the courts to clarify matters may be sorely disappointed. Take, for example, the following two cases. From within the First Circuit Court in 2005 is found *United States v. Naparst.* In this case, the federal district court was asked to rule on a motion by a convicted sex offender to terminate his supervised release four months earlier than scheduled, a move that was opposed by the U.S. attorney. In granting the motion, the district court acknowledged that the offense in question was serious, but at the same time, the petitioner was noted to have engaged in therapy on a regular basis and to have incurred not even minor infractions since his arrest and incarceration. The district court went on to note that the Massachusetts Sex Offender Registration Board rated the convict at the lowest of three levels with respect to his risk of future dangerousness, and his therapist had written to the board, "looking into the future, I can say that [he] . . . places in the top one percent of individuals . . . who are at a very low risk of recidivism, and who therefore present very little risk to the community."[68]

From 2004, within the Fifth Circuit Court is found *Willis v. Cockrell.* In this case, when weighing predictions by mental health providers on the risk of future dangerousness, the federal district court held that "overall, the theory that scientific reliability underlies predictions of future dangerousness has been uniformly rejected by the scientific community, absent those individuals who routinely testify to, and profit from, predictions of dangerousness."[69]

---

67. State v. Smith, 534 S.W.2d 900, 905.
68. 2005 WL 1868173 at 1 (D.N.H., Aug. 2, 2005).
69. Willis v. Cockrell, 2004 WL 1812698 at 34.

The *Naparst* court had no qualms about relying on the predictions of a mental health provider concerning future dangerousness; the *Willis* court soundly rejected the veracity of such predictions, even calling into question the monetary-based conflicts of interest of those who proffered such opinions.

Confused? Here's a third example: from within the Fourth Circuit Court in 2006 is found *United States v. Thomas*. In this case, the federal district court was asked to rule on supervised pre-trial release of an alleged sex offender into the community. The experts were diametrically opposed in their opinions, with the defense's psychiatrist opining a low risk of harm to the community, and the prosecution's law enforcement expert opining a much higher risk. Though allowing for the release, the court stated that "it must be acknowledged . . . that although the law recognizes the relevance and admissibility of psychiatric evaluation and opinion for the purpose of assessing future dangerousness, the use of such evidence has long been criticized as lacking reliability."[70]

Three federal district courts within a 24-month span, respectively: 1. freely allowed for predictions of future dangerousness, 2. criticized such predictions, and 3. allowed for the admission of such predictions though with a skeptical caveat. Given the volumes of written material in scholarly journals covering this very topic, and especially in light of *Daubert, Frye,* and §702, how can there remain such an incongruity of views?

Returning for a moment to the three disparate examples cited above—*Naparst, Willis,* and *Thomas*—one might ask, which of these is the exception? That is difficult to answer. Prior to *Daubert* and §702, disagreements between courts certainly existed, but those courts that allowed for the admission of expert opinions on future dangerousness would at least be able to point to the conventional wisdom that doctors are best able to predict the potential dangerousness of their patients. That same conventional wisdom would certainly then have passed the *Frye* test, though today we recognize it as arguably invalid.

From California in the mid-1970s, before *Daubert,* came arguably the most widely known and influential of cases that would

---

70. 2006 WL 140558 at 10. (D. Md., Jan. 13, 2006).

hinge on the ability to predict, that of *Tarasoff v. Regents of the University of California.* In 1969, Prosenjit Poddar killed Tatiana Tarasoff, a fellow student whom Poddar perceived as having spurned his romantic overtures. Two months prior to Tarasoff's death, Poddar had confided his intention to kill her, though not by name, to a psychologist employed at the university. The campus police briefly detained Poddar, but released him, as he then appeared rational and voiced no threats. No one warned the Tarasoffs of the possible danger, and the decedent's parents later sued the university based on this apparent oversight.

The trial court dismissed, and the appellate court upheld the dismissal for lack of cause of action. The California Supreme Court overturned the lower courts in 1974, however, holding that mental health professionals have a duty to warn an identifiable and threatened third party, regardless of concerns of confidentiality.[71] A rehearing in 1976 broadened the terminology by mandating a duty to protect, which could be discharged in several ways, including warning the threatened individual, notifying the police, or taking other reasonable (but seemingly ambiguous) steps to prevent harm. The state supreme court added that "[o]nce a therapist does in fact determine, or under applicable professional standards reasonably should have determined, that a patient poses a serious danger of violence to others, he bears a duty to exercise reasonable care to protect the foreseeable victim of that danger," adding that "professional inaccuracy in predicting violence cannot negate the therapist's duty to protect the threatened victim."[72]

The *Tarasoff* court justified this seeming contradiction—duty to warn/protect despite the very real possibility of professional inaccuracy regarding predictions—by contending that any uncertainty over dangerousness, and the concomitant risk of over-predicting the risk of violence, was outweighed by the public's interest in safety from those who would possibly do harm. This suggests what is known as "hindsight bias," the erroneous belief that once an outcome is known, it was in fact predictable all along.[73] Of little seem-

---

71. Judge Mathew Tobriner famously stated in the majority opinion, "The protective privilege ends where the public peril begins."

72. 17 Cal. 3d 425, 439.

73. Quinsey et al., Violent Offenders, *supra* note 43, at p. 4.

ing comfort to practitioners and potential victims, the *Tarasoff* majority offered that clinicians need only satisfy ordinary standards of (nonnegligent) practice using best judgment. "Proof, aided by hindsight, that [a therapist] judged wrongly is insufficient to establish negligence," the state supreme court stated.[74, 75]

There are a number of other pre-*Daubert* decisions that address predictions of future dangerousness in both federal and state courts. One of note is *Barefoot v. Estelle* (1983), in which U.S. Supreme Court Justice Harry Blackmun's dissent is notable because he referenced disclaimers of the psychiatric profession itself. The American Psychiatric Association's amicus brief in that case stated once again that psychiatric predictions of long-term future dangerousness are deemed unreliable by the profession. The APA's best estimate was that two out of three predictions of long-term future violence made by psychiatrists are eventually proven to be wrong, even when applied to populations of psychiatrically ill persons who have committed violence in the past. "Neither the court nor the state of Texas has cited a single reputable scientific source contradicting the unanimous conclusion of professionals in this field that psychiatric predictions of long-term future violence are wrong more often than they are right."[76] Yet, in logic that defies reason, the Court majority did not expressly disagree with the APA's assertion, but rather posited that since psychiatrists are not incorrect *all* of the time, they are thus correct *at least some* of the time! The Court felt that relevant unprivileged evidence "should be admitted and its weight left to the fact-finder, who would then have the benefit of cross-examination and contrary evidence by the opposing party."[77]

Another notable U.S. Supreme Court dissent also comes from 1983. In *Buttrum v. Georgia*, a capital sentencing appeal, Justice Thurgood Marshall wrote, "[e]ven if I accepted the prevailing view that the death penalty can constitutionally be imposed under certain conditions, I would vacate the death sentence imposed in this

---

74. Firestone, Marvin, *Psychiatric Patients and Forensic Psychiatry, in* LEGAL MEDICINE, 5th ed. New York: Mosby (2001), p. 479.

75. 551 P.2d 334, 345.

76. 463 U.S. 880, 921.

77. 463 U.S. 880, 898.

case. . . . It is well recognized that predictions of violent behavior are generally unreliable even under the best of circumstances."[78]

And for sheer stinging eloquence in refuting the science of prediction goes the award to a Florida state court in *Fischer v. Metcalf* from 1989: "unlike other branches of medicine in which diagnoses and treatments evolve from objective, empirical, methodological foundations, psychiatry is at best an inexact science, if, indeed, it is a science [at all]. . . ."[79]

To the author and many others, how largely discredited scientific opinion can still pass the first of the three elements of 28 U.S.C.A. §702 in federal courts in the post-*Daubert* era remains a mystery. Despite those clear requirements, and notwithstanding that which has been written on the general lack of reliability of forecasts, there still remains case law that supports the use of predictions, along with other accounts that uncomfortably equivocate.

In the supportive category, the ink had barely dried on *Daubert* when in 1997 the U.S. Supreme Court heard *Kansas v. Hendricks.* As he was nearing the end of his prison term, Hendricks was petitioned by the state of Kansas to be civilly committed under that state's sexually violent predator statute. The state alleged that Hendricks had a "mental abnormality or personality disorder" that made him likely to engage in predatory acts of sexual violence in the future.[80] Hendricks agreed that he thought about molesting

---

78. 459 U.S. 1156, 1157; *see also* Cocozza, Joseph & Steadman, Henry, *The Failure of Psychiatric Predictions of Dangerousness*, RUTGERS L.R., no. 29, 1974, pp. 1084–88; *see also* Ennis, Bruce & Litwack, Thomas, *Psychiatry and the Presumption of Expertise: Flipping Coins in the Courtroom*, CAL. L. REV., no. 62, 1974, pp. 693–705.

79. 543 So. 2d. 785, 787.

80. About the nonpsychiatric descriptor "mental abnormality," a somewhat tautologically defined legal term that forensic mental health professionals have long strained to give meaning: what exactly is a mental abnormality? It's not entirely clear. For example, the New York definition states that it is "a congenital or acquired condition, disease, or disorder that affects the emotional, cognitive, or volitional capacity of a person in a manner that predisposes him or her to the commission of conduct constituting a sex offense and that results in that person having serious difficulty in controlling such conduct." Thus, embedded in this very definition is the "fact" that the abnormality "causes" the proscribed behav-

children when he was under stress. Once released from prison and committed to the state hospital, however, Hendricks appealed the commitment, saying that it represented for him double jeopardy. The Court disagreed, and, in upholding the constitutionality of the Sexually Violent Predator Act, noted that, at the trial court level, the state presented predictive testimony from the chief psychologist at the state hospital to the effect that the defendant was likely to commit sexual offenses against children in the future if not confined. The Court felt that the possibility of future dangerous acts was enough and that there was no requirement of *total* or *complete* lack of control of behavior in order to have Hendricks and those like him committed.

An example of uncomfortable equivocation came from within the Fifth Circuit Court in 2003. In *Saldano v. Cockrell,* which was marked by especially egregious overreaching testimony, an expert for the prosecution testified in an offender's penalty phase that, based on the expert's use of an assessment instrument that included 24 elements deemed to be predictive of future dangerousness, the expert believed that the convicted murderer would likely again be violent if given the chance. Two of the 24 elements in the assessment were race and ethnicity (the convict was Hispanic). The prosecution expert testified that Hispanics were proportionally overrepresented in the Texas prison system, and to him that suggested a predilection toward criminal behavior among that population. Under cross-examination, the expert admitted that economic, educational, and vocational issues could also explain this apparent over-representation of Hispanics in Texas' prisons. Oddly, the defense attorney did not object to the prosecution expert's testimony, though the defense did offer its own expert testimony to attempt to refute race and ethnicity as predictive factors.

The prosecution's closing argument in the sentencing phase of *Saldano* stated, "our expert told you [that there is a probability that the convict will be dangerous in the future], and you can have *confidence in his opinion beyond a reasonable doubt* because of his *qualification* and his *background* and his *expertise*. . . . [His assess-

ior. *Available at* http://www.criminaljustice.ny.gov/legalservices/ch7_som.htm; *see also* Knoll, James, *The Political Diagnosis: Psychiatry in the Service of the Law*, Psychiatric Times, May 13, 2010, p. 13.

ment instrument] is a formula *recognized in the field* as to what would constitute dangerousness in a person" (emphasis added). After two remands, the convict was later granted relief from the resultant death sentence based on the constitutional error of employing race and ethnicity as forecasting elements in the assessment instrument; the flawed predictive science itself was apparently not at issue. If that was not bad enough, the prosecution's closing statement stressed to the jury the veracity of that very same flawed science, with powerful descriptors such as "confidence," "qualification," and "expertise," and then further misled by emphasizing without cited evidence claims of recognition of the predictive instrument from within the profession itself.[81]

What Is One to Do?

> Those who have knowledge don't predict. Those who predict don't have knowledge.
>
> —Lao Tzu[82]

Despite past U.S. Supreme Court decisions that have refused to strike the use of prediction, many still hope for a case before the Court that will address directly on point the seeming inconsistencies regarding *Daubert*, §702, and admissibility of predictive testimony. Just such a scenario presented itself in 2010 in the form of

---

81. 267 F. Supp. 2d 635, 639. If you think the *Saldano* case is an aberration, you are mistaken. More recently, the case of Texas death row inmate Duane Buck came to national media attention. Buck, who is black, was convicted of murder and assault and sentenced to death. The U.S. Supreme Court issued a rare stay of execution in 2011 when it was revealed that a psychologist testifying at sentencing said that, while Buck would not pose a threat to society if incarcerated for life, blacks and Hispanics in general are statistically more likely than whites to commit future crimes. Though the defense argued that the jury was unfairly influenced by this testimony, the high court later refused to hear the case and the stay has since been lifted. *See* Totenberg, Nina, "Supreme Court Declines Duane Buck Death Row Case," National Public Radio, Nov. 7, 2011. *Available at* http://www.npr.org/2011/11/07/142113748/supreme-court-declines-duane-buck-death-row-case (retrieved Dec. 30, 2011).

82. Sixth-century B.C.E. Chinese philosopher and founder of Taoism. *Available at* http://thinkexist.com/quotation/those_who_have_knowledge-dont_predict-those_who/214313.html (retrieved Dec. 10, 2011).

United States v. Comstock.[83] Graydon Comstock was a federal prisoner who was serving a three-year sentence for possession of child pornography. He was certified as a sexually dangerous person six days prior to his release and was accordingly informed that he then would be committed to a civil facility for treatment. This was to occur under the tenets of the 2006 Adam Walsh Child Protection and Safety Act, 18 U.S.C. §4248. The act authorizes the federal government to seek (essentially open-ended) civil commitment of any "sexually dangerous person" who is felt to be suffering from a mental disease or defect and who is in the custody of the attorney general due to incompetence, or who is already adjudicated and in the custody of the Bureau of Prisons and nearing release. Comstock was deemed to fulfill the latter criterion.

Inmate advocates questioned whether §4248 fell outside constitutionally allocated powers of the federal government. Additionally, there was concern over due process, and whether the mechanism employed to determine sexual dangerousness was even valid. After Comstock and four other inmates filed suit, one amicus brief noted that "neither clinical predictions, nor actuarial assessments, nor any combination of the two has proven sufficiently accurate on a consistent basis to form the necessary legal foundation for the forcible, potentially indefinite detention authorized by §4248. Such science may have a valid place in certain clinical contexts, but it is ill-suited and insufficiently accurate to meet the demands of due process required here" (emphasis added).[84] In 2007, a federal district court had ruled in Comstock's favor regarding both the question of federal powers and of due process. Then, in January 2009, a three-judge panel of the Fourth Circuit Court had unanimously affirmed the lower court's decision on federalism but interestingly made no comment regarding due process.

Unfortunately and predictably, in May 2010, the U.S. Supreme Court decided *Comstock* based solely on the issue of federalism, stating that the national government does, in fact, have the author-

---

83. 560 U.S. ____ (2010), 551 F. 3d 274.

84. *Cited* in brief of amici curiae, National Ass'n of Criminal Defense Lawyers and National Ass'n of Federal Defenders, at 17; *see* United States v. Graydon Comstock et al., 560 U.S. ____ (2010), 551 F.3d 274, Nov. 4, 2009 (No. 08-1224).

ity under the Necessary and Proper Clause of the Constitution to direct the civil commitment of individuals already in federal custody. The decision did not rule on any other aspect of the constitutionality of 18 U.S.C. §4248 because the federalism issue was the only one properly before the high court at that time.[85]

Nothing was said about how statistically unreliable are such predictions and risk assessments. The perplexity continues for now.

~~~~~~~~~~~~~~~~~~~~~~~~~~~~~~

One textbook designed to help mental health professionals testify in court offered this suggestion: "[a] frequent line of cross examination is to attack what the expert witness is doing as unscientific. [In] dealing with that attack, one must indicate that one has never maintained that clinical psychology or psychiatry is a highly refined science [but instead is] . . . regarded as a highly refined craft." The text goes on to remind the reader that he is present in court to render an opinion, nothing more and nothing less.[86]

This may be true in theory, but expert testimony is probably rarely perceived as "just an opinion" by juries. As the reader noted previously in *Saldano*, the manner in which information is presented, and the accolades and spin that often accompany the information, can influence juries. To say nothing explanatory—that is, to render an opinion, not more and not less—leaves the jury to be impressed by credentials and professional titles and stature and puffery, and thus accords the flawed science more validity than it deserves. However, to preface one's argument with detailed accounts about how unreliable such predictions are essentially emasculates any testimony the expert later provides. This approach is tantamount to throwing out the proverbial baby with the bathwater, and possibly sways the jury as much against the proffered information as relative silence may sway the jury in favor of it.

Mental health practitioners are a vital resource for our legal system, but they serve best when they are not asked to overreach. If expert opinion testimony is imperfect, and if mental health professionals do no better than laypersons in predicting long-term behavior, then removing those mental health professionals from the opinion

---

85. *Id.*

86. Shapiro, Dan. Forensic Psychologic Assessment 218 (Boston: Allyn & Bacon, 1991).

process would hardly diminish the end result. Removal would, however, render the process more intellectually honest. Instead of calling on an expert to bloviate, let the clinician educate the court about aspects of mental health and mental illness, the adequacy of treatment, and the problems inherent with noncompliance, and even provide information on demographic risk factors. Then, stop the testimony there and avoid the next opinionated step into "the wonderland of clairvoyance."[87] Such an approach would lie solidly within the purview of both *Daubert* and §702. Along this line, Thomas Szasz, M.D., a prominent skeptic and psychiatrist himself, presciently offered that "a legal procedure is infinitely more humane, reasonable, and protective of human rights than any psychiatrist's conclusion."[88]

At the beginning of this chapter, passing reference was made to predictions of future dangerousness in both the longer and shorter term, without offering definitions. Unlike predictions of the former variety, those of the shorter term usually have greater accuracy. This is the sort of prediction that clinicians are often called to make when someone needs involuntary hospitalization when having an acute crisis or requires forced medication because they are refusing treatment and deteriorating markedly in the here-and-now.

For short-term predictions, accuracy is almost certainly not due to any expertise that the clinician uniquely brings to the table, but rather is based on common sense. Take, for example, a patient who is restrained and trying to bite, kick, and spit as the hearing is being convened—he is probably dangerous in the short term. A layman would know this, as would any clinical professional, and yet while both may know it, only the latter is permitted to proffer the expert opinion testimony in court. Most trainees see these sorts of emergency hearings early and often in their schooling, and I suspect that the relative ease with which the attending psychiatrist or psychologist makes such judgment calls tempts many into later advancing

---

87. Carbone, J.S., *Into the Wonderland of Clairvoyance: Faulty Science and the Prediction of Future Dangerousness*, in MALINGERING, LIES, AND JUNK SCIENCE IN THE COURTROOM 565 (Youngstown: Cambria Press 2007).

88. Jancin, Bruce, *Szasz Hailed in U.K. for 'Questioning Spirit,'* CLINICAL PSYCHIATRIC NEWS, vol. 38, no. 9, Sept. 2010, p. 10.

their own predictions of distant future behavior far beyond their professional or scientific ability.

The deprivation of liberty based on misapplied scientific principles results in a diminution of our legal system and the rights afforded by our Constitution. Instead, the system and the professional disciplines of mental health are both served best when, to again paraphrase Crichton, science is not tricked out for public policy aims.

Take-Home Pearls

- Unaided predictions of future dangerousness—what some have called nothing more than likeability tests—are of no better accuracy when proffered by mental health professionals than by laymen.
- Actuarially based predictions of future dangerousness can delineate certain known risk factors for violence, and enjoy slightly improved predictive outcomes, but they arguably still fall short of the standards of proof required by our legal system.
- The continued admissibility of suspect scientific predictive testimony seemingly runs afoul of *Daubert* and §702 but still occurs regularly.
- The shorter the term of the prediction, the better the apparent accuracy, but this is probably due to common sense more than any special skills the mental health clinician brings to the table compared the man on the street.

Chapter 9

Summary

These pages contain a whirlwind of information covering ancient history and the present; current controversies and opinions; scientific advances and pure quackery; objectivity and subjectivity; politics and public policy; terminology and nomenclature; and outdated, updated, and revised modes of management and treatment. In addition to details of the text, the bulleted pearls at the end of each chapter hopefully provide a quick and painless review of the key points being discussed.

And yet there remains a tremendous amount of material that has not been covered in detail, or at all, in this work and that very much relates to issues of mental health—topics such as sex offender management, substance abuse and dual-diagnoses, child and adolescent matters, informed consent and refusal, documentation, restoration of mental capacity to proceed to trial, and landmark court cases come to mind.

All of this reflection brings a closing thought: my own discipline of psychiatry, and those of the other allied mental health professionals, has the potential to benefit a host of those who suffer in silence and incomprehension. Yet for all its potential good, the discipline is replete with examples of (unnecessary) misunderstanding and confusion. This is one reason why many people still view the specialty with suspicion.

This work, then, is not actually finished, but just beginning. More advances in knowledge will come, and more improvements in treatment will follow. It is my sincere hope that readers—students and practicing attorneys alike—will be motivated to pursue further study on their own and gain an even greater familiarity with the quantum of mental health and mental illness.

Glossary

AIMS—Abnormal Involuntary Movement Scale, a checklist of symptoms used by clinicians to monitor whether patients taking certain classes of medications (usually antipsychotics) are developing, or experiencing an exacerbation of, neurological side effects.

Affect—The objective (external) facial expression seen by others; contrast with Mood.

Anhedonia—The subjective inability to experience pleasure.

Anticholinergic—An adjective describing any substance that blocks the physiologic action of the neurotransmitter acetylcholine; anticholinergic substances can produce side effects such as dry mouth, blurry vision, constipation, and urinary retention.

Antisocial—One of the cluster B personality subtypes, characterized by behavior that lacks empathy, is usually predatory, and deviates markedly from accepted societal norms; see Sociopathy and Psychopathy.

Anxiolytic—Any substance or intervention that lessens anxiety.

Atypical (Antipsychotic)—An umbrella term used to describe the newer, second-generation antipsychotic medications; contrast with Neuroleptic.

CATIE—Clinical Antipsychotic Trial of Intervention Effectiveness, a vast multicenter study that first raised serious questions about the purported advantages of atypical antipsychotics over older agents.

Character—The totality of behavioral and emotional traits, attitudes, perceptions, and habits that guide one's ability to manage stress and function interpersonally. While individuals may be unique when taken *in toto*, clusters of closely related character facets across a spectrum are well documented; see Personality.

CBT—Cognitive Behavioral Therapy, a widely practiced form of psychotherapy based on the idea that our own thoughts, and not external stimuli, are the direct cause of feelings and subsequent behaviors. This approach enables the patient to change thinking patterns, and thus feelings and behaviors, even if the external situation does not or cannot change.

Cognitive Dissonance—The discomfort experienced when conflicting beliefs, values, or emotions simultaneously coexist. To allay the guilt or anger that can result, some individuals subconsciously employ one or more different defense mechanisms; see Rationalization.

Compulsion—An irresistible, persistent impulse to perform an act; contrast with Obsession.

Delusion—A false belief that persists despite incontrovertible evidence to the contrary. A state of non-reality; see Psychosis, Hallucination, Illusion, IOR.

Depersonalization—The pathological process of experiencing a strangeness and unfamiliarity with one's own identity or behavior; this can be seen in those with psychotic disorders such as schizophrenia, and sometimes in drug reactions.

Derealization—A sensation of altered reality; this can be seen in those with psychotic disorders such as schizophrenia, and sometimes in drug reactions.

DDx—Differential Diagnoses, a list of possible conditions that might explain a constellation of presenting symptoms, usually organized from most likely to least likely, and employed by clinicians as a template when undertaking an initial evaluation.

DSM—*Diagnostic and Statistical Manual of Mental Disorders*, the so-called "psychiatric bible" of diagnostic parameters and codes; the manual is currently in its fourth edition, with the fifth edition planned for release in 2014; see *ICD*.

Dopamine—One of several primary neurotransmitters found in the brain and suspected to be involved in the genesis of aspects of mental illness.

ECT—Electroconvulsive Therapy, the application of an electrical current to the brain of a patient for the purpose of triggering a (nonconvulsive) seizure, which in many cases is beneficial in treating otherwise intractable major depression.

Electrolytes—Electrically charged ions (e.g., sodium, potassium) that are found in blood and that regulate most metabolic processes; medications can alter the relative concentrations of electrolytes and produce undesired physiologic effects.

Euthymia—A state of neither depression nor euphoria, but rather a mood that is considered neutral; an adjective often used in mental status exams.

FOI—Flight of Ideas, a nearly continuous flow of rapid speech and thoughts that jumps from one topic to the next, usually based on some (vaguely) discernible associations, but in severe cases is so disorganized as to be incoherent; see LOA.

Hallucination—The perception of a stimulus with no external cause, seen in both psychotic disorders and conditions involving delirium or intoxication; they can affect any of the five senses, though visual and auditory hallucinations are the most common; a state of non-reality; see Psychosis, Illusion, Delusion.

Hypomania—A state of motor, cognitive, and emotional excitement and agitation that does not quite fulfill the elements of full-blown mania; see Mania.

Hysteria—An archaic term for what today would be called anxiety or an agitated depression; see Neurosis.

ICD—*International Classification of Diseases*, a global diagnostic classification of human pathology overseen by the World Health Organization; attempts have been made for years to synchronize *DSM* codes with those from the mental illness section of the *ICD*, at present without complete success; see *DSM*.

IOR—Ideas of Reference, the belief that casual events or remarks are intentionally aimed at an individual when in fact they are not; for example, when a person believes that a TV newscaster is sending messages specifically to a single viewer; see Delusion.

Illusion—A misperception that is based on actual external stimuli (as opposed to a hallucination that is based on no actual external stimuli). An example is a tree that moves in the wind at night but is perceived as a person lurking in the darkness; this is not necessarily a psychotic condition, as it is based on actual external stimuli; see Hallucination, Delusion, Psychosis.

LOA—Loosening of Associations, a condition similar to FOI, but with less apparent association between topics; see FOI.

Mania—A state of extreme excitement and agitation manifested by both mental and physical hyperactivity; at its most severe, it can be accompanied by psychosis; see Hypomania.

Melancholia—An archaic term for what is currently called depression.

MSE—Mental Status Examination, an important part of the clinical psychiatric assessment process. It is a detailed description of a patient's current state of presentation, with specific references to appearance, cognition, reality testing, behavior, affect, speech, thought process, thought content, and apparent insight and judgment.

MMSE—Mini-Mental Status Examination, a brief 30-point questionnaire that is used as a screening tool for the presence or progression of cognitive impairment. If warranted by the screening, more sensitive neuropsychological tests can be administered; see Psychological Tests.

MMPI—Minnesota Multiphasic Personality Inventory, arguably the most commonly employed psychological test for identifying character structure and pathology; while not diagnostic per se, it can suggest tendencies that are maladaptive in certain individuals; see Psychological Tests.

Mood—The subjective (internal) emotional state of an individual; contrast with Affect.

Neuroleptic—An umbrella term used to describe the older, first-generation antipsychotic medications; the term comes from "neuro" and the Greek "lepsis," meaning to take hold; contrast with Atypical (Antipsychotic).

Neurosis—An archaic term for what today would be called anxiety or an agitated depression; see Hysteria.

Neuropsychological Testing—Written and performance-based instruments that go into greater depth in evaluation of higher cognitive functioning, memory, visual-spatial abilities, and communication skills than do standard psychological tests; neuropsychological tests can focus on possible genetic, developmental, traumatic, and environmental etiologies; see Psychological Testing.

Neurovegetative—Describes symptoms that are both cognitive (guilt, distraction) and somatic (insomnia, loss of libido, decreased energy, poor appetite, restlessness) and are often seen in those suffering from major depression; see Somatic.

Nomenclature—A naming system used in a particular discipline.

Norepinephrine—One of several primary neurotransmitters found in the brain and suspected to be involved in the genesis of aspects of mental illness.

NOS—Not otherwise specified, a descriptor employed in the *DSM* for those presentations that meet a number of diagnostic elements, but do not fulfill the full criteria for the disease state in question.

Nosology—The science of classification of diseases; see Taxonomy.

Obsession—A persistent and disturbing preoccupation with an often unreasonable idea or feeling; contrast with Compulsion.

Paraphilia—A recurring, sexually arousing mental image or behavior that involves unusual and often socially unacceptable practices (e.g., sadism, masochism, fetishism, pedophilia).

Personality—The totality of behavioral and emotional traits, attitudes, perceptions, and habits that guide one's ability to manage stress and function interpersonally. While individuals may be unique when taken *in toto*, clusters of closely related personality facets across a spectrum are well documented; see Character.

Pharmacodynamics—The study of how drugs act on the body; contrast with Pharmacokinetics.

Pharmacokinetics—The study of how the body metabolizes drugs; contrast with Pharmacodynamics.

Phobia—An exaggerated and often disabling fear that usually is illogical but often related to a symbolic object or situation.

Phrenology—Pseudoscience from the nineteenth century that espoused that bumps, indentations, and general contours of a patient's skull could be diagnostic of mental illness, sociopathy, or, in the alternative, genius.

Psychodynamic—Describes insight-oriented processes that interpret subconscious emotions that often arise in childhood but persist into adulthood and can affect later coping and behavior.

Psychological Testing—Written and performance-based instruments that evaluate basic intellectual, emotional, academic, and personality functioning; see MMPI, MMSE, Neuropsychological Testing, Psychometrics.

Psychometrics—A branch of psychology dealing with the use and application of mental measurements and trends; see Psychological Testing.

Psychomotor—Describes activity that has both emotional and bodily components (e.g., restlessness).

Psychopathy—A term, often used interchangeably with sociopathy, describing perceptions and behaviors that are without empathy for others, usually predatory, and that deviate markedly from accepted societal norms; see Sociopathy and Antisocial.

Psychopharmacopeia—A compendium describing available mental health drugs, chemicals, and medicinal preparations, especially one issued by an officially recognized authority.

Psychotic—Describes loss of contact with reality, often characterized by the presence of hallucinations and delusions; see Delusion, Hallucination, Illusion.

Psychosocial—Describing aspects of the human condition that are both psychological and social in nature.

Psychosurgery—Operations performed on the brain (e.g., lobotomy) for the purpose of treating psychiatric symptoms.

Psychotropics—Describing agents, usually medications, that act on the mind.

Rationalization—An attempt to justify otherwise unacceptable desires by concealing through superficially reassuring but incomplete or incorrect explanations. This can be a conscious or subconscious process and may encourage irrational behavior (e.g., wanting to smoke and focusing exclusively on the statistics of not developing lung cancer while ignoring the known risks of respiratory illness); see Cognitive Dissonance.

Serotonin—One of several primary neurotransmitters found in the brain and suspected to be involved in the genesis of aspects of mental illness.

Sociopathy—A term, often used interchangeably with psychopathy, and describing perceptions and behaviors that are without empathy for others, usually predatory, and that deviate markedly from accepted societal norms; see Psychopathy and Antisocial.

Somatic—Of, relating to, or affecting the body (as opposed to the mind).

Somatiform—An umbrella term for a group of mental disorders characterized by physical symptoms that cannot be fully explained by a somatic evaluation.

Subconscious—Existing in the mind and usually affecting thoughts, emotions, and behavior, but not immediately available in the conscious state.

Taxonomy—The science of classification; see Nosology.

TD—Tardive Dyskinesia, a neurological disorder characterized by involuntary and disfiguring movements of the mouth, tongue, trunk, and limbs that occurs as a possible side effect of prolonged use of antipsychotic medications.

Teratogenic—Of, relating to, or causing congenital (birth) defects.

Thought Content—The subject matter of cognition; in those with psychotic disorders, content can be delusional or involve hallucinations of any of the five senses.

Thought Process—The flow of cognition; in those with psychotic disorders, process can be disorganized and involve flight of ideas, loosening of associations, and nonsensical segue between subjects.

Appendix

For Further Study

In olden times (before the mid-1990s), researching a subject of interest meant spending all day going through card catalogues and squinting at microfilm in sometimes cavernous and uninviting libraries. Now, the Internet has rendered such pursuit a relative pleasure to be undertaken from one's home or office without concern for hours of operation, eating policy, or dress code.

Needless to say, just because something appears on the Internet does not make it accurate. For that reason, the reader is cautioned to frequent websites from reputable private, government, and academic entities only.

With that caveat in mind, the following are some online resources that are potentially helpful for those wishing to read further on mental health topics. These are, naturally, only the tip of the proverbial iceberg.

The **United States Food and Drug Administration** maintains a website at http://www.fda.gov/drugs/default.htm that has much information on drug recalls and safety, clinical trials, pending medication approvals, the status of generics on the U.S. market, and other news stories of a pharmaceutical bent, both psychiatric and nonpsychiatric.

The **Centers for Disease Control and Prevention** has a modest online mental health section but nevertheless provides useful information on the demographics of suicide as well as traumatic brain injuries. It can be found at http://www.cdc.gov/InjuryViolence Safety.

The website of the **World Health Organization**, at http://www.who.int/topics/mental_disorders/en, is particularly interesting as it presents mental illness from a global perspective, and has numerous links to other pertinent Internet sites. The WHO also is the current guardian of the *International Classification of Diseases*; information on that work can be located at http://www.who.int/classifications/icd/en.

The **National Library of Medicine of the National Institute of Health** includes the databases PubMed and MedLine, both of which can be employed to find literally thousands of peer-reviewed articles on mental health topics. On the website is also a link to information on pharmaceutical clinical trials. It exists at http://www.nlm.nih.gov.

Also under the National Institute of Health umbrella is the **National Institute of Mental Health**, the website of which is http://www.nimh.nih.gov. That page has easily accessible educational resources, data concerning ongoing research, and contact information for community outreach programs for those with mental illnesses.

Official government reports on contemporary mental health challenges, along with links to cited references, can be accessed at the website of the **U.S. Surgeon General** at http://www.surgeongeneral.gov.

Substance Abuse and Mental Health Services Administration (SAMHSA) promulgates information on research grants and recent publications, along with statistics on mental illnesses and chemical dependency and abuse in the United States. It can be found at http://www.samhsa.gov.

Written in plain English with an easy-to-use searchable database, the federal government's **Department of Health and Human Services** maintains a cyber FAQ section on common mental health concerns. Its address is http://answers.hhs.gov/categories/84.

The **Bazelon Center for Mental Health Law**, based in Washington, D.C., is a nonprofit organization named for the late federal judge David Bazelon of the court of appeals for the D.C. circuit. The center's attorneys and advocates pursue a progressive mental health agenda, mostly at the federal level. The center emphasizes the protection of children and adults with mental illnesses through efforts aimed at legislation, policy, access to services, and liaison with state and local supporters. Its website, and further information on its mission, can be found at http://www.bazelon.org.

Pharmaceutical Researchers and Manufacturers of America (PhRMA) is a professional and trade organization that represents the country's leading drug and biotech companies. It works to support public policies that encourage research and development of new medicinals, both psychiatric and nonpsychiatric. Though a site reflecting the for-profit aspects of health-care delivery, PhRMA has interesting newsfeeds and also links to a number of member companies' own websites. As with any commercial sources, though, caveat emptor: http://www.phrma.org.

WebMD is said to be the leading health-related Internet portal in the United States, and its subsidiary **Medscape** is aimed primarily at physicians and other health-care providers. Accessing the content is free after registration, and one can find there peer-reviewed articles, blogs and commentary, patient education materials, news-feeds, and a medication database. Mental health and other aspects of health care are represented. Medscape is located at http://www.medscape.com.

The online location of *Clinical Psychiatry News*, a free monthly newspaper for psychiatrists that is published by Elsevier, a global corporation that also publishes *The Lancet, Cell, Nelson's Pediatrics*, and *Gray's Anatomy* is ttp://www.clinicalpsychiatrynews.com. It informs on recent clinical developments, research, professional opinion, pending legislation, and matters of interest regarding the business of psychiatric practice.

Finally, almost all professional organizations maintain web presences with varying degrees of educational materials posted for both members and the public. The website of the **American Psychiatric Association** can be found at http://www.psych.org. At that sitem one can access the online bookstore, psychiatric news clips, and a wealth of information on the ongoing process of creating the *DSM-5*. The **American Psychological Association**, at http://www.apa.org, likewise has tabs with information on a number of mental health issues, especially those pertaining to psychotherapy.

And there are state and sometimes municipal or county chapters of both the American Psychiatric Association and the American Psychological Association that can be referenced for additional news of local interest.

Happy reading!

Bibliography

_____. *Amici Curiae, United States v. Comstock, et al.* National Association of Criminal Defense Lawyers and National Association of Federal Defenders.

_____. Chlorpromazine and Mental Health: Proceedings of the Symposium Held by Smith Kline and French Labs., June 6, 1955. Philadelphia: Lea & Febiger, Inc., 1955.

_____. *Diagnostic and Statistical Manual of Mental Disorders.* 2d ed. Washington, D.C.: The Committee on Nomenclature and Statistics of the American Psychiatric Association, 1968.

_____. *Diagnostic and Statistical Manual of Mental Disorders.* 3d ed. Washington, D.C.: American Psychiatric Association, 1980.

_____. *Diagnostic and Statistical Manual of Mental Disorders.* 3d rev. Washington D.C.: American Psychiatric Association, 1987.

_____. *Diagnostic and Statistical Manual of Mental Disorders.* 4th ed. Washington, D.C.: American Psychiatric Association, 1994.

_____. *Diagnostic and Statistical Manual of Mental Disorders.* 4th ed., primary care. Washington D.C.: American Psychiatric Association, 1995.

_____. *Diagnostic and Statistical Manual of Mental Disorders.* 4th ed., text rev. Washington, D.C.: American Psychiatric Association, 2000.

_____. "Do All Men Think All Women Are Like This?" *Inside UVa.* Vol. 20, no. 19 (November 15, 1990).

_____. Foreward. *Physicians' Desk Reference.* 57th ed. Montvale: Thomson Medical Economics, 2003.

_____. *Homosexuality and Sexual Orientation Disturbance: Proposed Change in DSM II*. December 1973. Approved by the Board of Trustees of the American Psychiatric Association. APA Document Reference no. 730008.

_____. "'Hyperdiagnosis' Found Pervasive." *Psychiatric News* (December 3, 2010).

_____. "Liability for Physical Harm, Affirmative Duties, Duty to Third Persons Based on Special Relationship with Person Posing Risk," § 41, *Restatement (Third) of Torts*, tentative draft. St Paul: American Law Institute Publishers, 2005.

_____. *Merriam-Webster's Medical Dictionary*. Springfield: Merriam-Webster Mass Market, Inc., 2006.

_____. "Modified MMSE Screens More Accurately for Dementia." *Clinical Psychiatry News*. Vol. 38, no. 8 (August 2010).

_____. "New Data Blur Typical-Atypical Drug Distinctions." *Clinical Psychiatry News*. Vol. 38, no. 8 (August 2010).

_____. *New International Version Bible*. Grand Rapids: Zondervan, 1984.

_____. Patient Access to Treatments Prescribed by Their Physicians. Position statement of the Board of Trustees of the American Psychiatric Association, July 2007.

_____. "Prefrontal Lobotomies." *Life* (March 3, 1947).

_____. "Prescribing Bills Proliferate Despite Numerous Defeats." *Psychiatric News*. Vol. 44, no. 14 (July 17, 2009).

_____. "Proof of Qualification for Commitment as a Mentally Disordered Sex Offender." *American Jurisprudence Proof of Facts*, 3d ed. Vol. 51 (September 2005).

_____. *Statistical Manual for the Use of Institutions for the Insane*. Washington, D.C.: National Committee for Mental Hygiene (1918).

_____. *The Diagnostic and Statistical Manual [of] Mental Disorders*. Washington, D.C.: American Psychiatric Association Mental Hospital Service (1952).

_____. *The Newcastle Reporter.* Vol. 1, no. 6 (March 26, 1857).

_____. *The Visitor, or Monthly Instructor.* London: The Religious Tract Society (1841).

_____. *Treatment of Attention Deficit/ Hyperactivity Disorder.* U.S. Department of Health and Human Services (December 1999).

Albert, S., et al. "Faking Psychosis on the Rorschach: Can Expert Judges Detect Malingering?" *Journal of Personality Assessment.* Vol. 44, no. 2 (April 1980).

Akiskal, Hagop. "Biomarkers for Mental Disorders: A Field Whose Time Has Come." *Psychiatric Times.* Vol. 28, no. 11 (November 8, 2011).

Arehart-Treichel, Joan. "Higher Levels of Lithium Linked to Lower Suicide Rates." *Psychiatric News.* Vol. 46, no. 12 (June 17, 2011).

Arehart-Treichel, Joan. "Surprising Accord Found in Psychiatric Testimony." *Psychiatric News.* Vol. 46, no. 3 (February 4, 2011).

Argyropoulos, Spilios, et al. "Brain Function in Social Anxiety Disorder." *The Psychiatric Clinics of North America.* Vol. 24, no. 4 (December 2001).

Aviv, Rachel. "God Knows Where I Am: The Annals of Mental Health." *The New Yorker.* Vol. 87, no. 15 (May 30, 2011).

Beecher-Monas, Erica, and Garcia-Rill, Edgar. "Danger at the Edge of Chaos: Predicting Violent Behavior in a Post-*Daubert* World." *Cardozo Law Review.* No. 24 (2003).

Beecher-Monas, Erica. "The Epistemology of Prediction: Future Dangerousness Testimony and Intellectual Due Process." *Washington & Lee Law Review.* No. 60 (Spring 2003).

Beitman, Bernard. *Integrating Psychotherapy and Pharmacotherapy.* New York: W.W. Norton, 2003.

Bell, Robert, et al. "Suffering in Silence: Reasons for Not Disclosing Depression in Primary Care." *Annals of Family Medicine.* Vol. 9, no. 5 (September/October 2011).

Bellak, Leopold. *Dementia Praecox*. New York: Grune and Stratton, 1947.

Benbadis S. R. *Psychogenic Non-Epileptic Seizures, The Treatment of Epilepsy: Principles and Practice*, 4th ed. Philadelphia: Lippincott, Williams & Wilkins, 2005.

Bender, K. J. "Bidirectional Relation Between Schizophrenia and Epilepsy." *Psychiatric Times* (October 6, 2011).

Bernstein, Carol. "Meta-Structure in DSM-5 Process." *Psychiatric News* (March 4, 2011).

Blau, Theodore. *The Psychologist as Expert Witness*. New York: Wiley & Sons, 1984.

Bloch, Sidney. "A History of Psychiatric Ethics." *The Psychiatric Clinics of North America*. Vol. 25, no. 3. Philadelphia: W.B. Saunders Co. (September 2002).

Board, Belinda Jane. "Disordered Personalities at Work." *Psychology, Crime, and Law*. Vol. 17, no. 11, 2005.

Boschert, Sherry. "Computer Based CBT Brings Immediate Mood Improvement." *Clinical Psychiatry News* (May 31, 2011).

Boschert, Sherry. "Guided TMS Not Effective for Hallucinations." *Clinical Psychiatry News* (October 11, 2011).

Brown, E.M. "Why Wagner-Jauregg Won the Nobel Prize for Discovering Malaria Therapy for General Paresis of the Insane." *History of Psychiatry*. Vol. 11 (December 2000).

Butcher, James, et al. *Abnormal Psychology*. 13th ed. Boston: Pearson Education, Inc., 2007.

Butcher, J. N., Dahlstrom, W. G., Graham, J. R., Tellegen, A., and Kaemmer, B. *The Minnesota Multi-Phasic Personality Inventory-2 (MMPI-2): Manual for Administration and Scoring*. Minneapolis: University of Minnesota Press, 1989.

Cade J. F. "Lithium Salts in the Treatment of Psychotic Excitement." *Medical Journal of Australia*. No. 2 (1949).

Carbone, J. S. *Into the Wonderland of Clairvoyance: Faulty Science and the Prediction of Future Dangerousness, Malingering, Lies, and Junk Science in the Courtroom.* Youngstown: Cambria Press, 2007.

Carlat, Daniel. *Unhinged: The Trouble with Psychiatry—A Doctor's Revelations about a Profession in Crisis.* New York: Free Press, 2010.

Cartwright, Samuel. "Report on the Diseases and Peculiarities of the Negro Race." *DeBow's Review—Southern and Western States.* Vol. XI. New Orleans, 1851.

Chowdhury, Uttom, et al. "Clinical Implications of Brain Imaging in Eating Disorders." *Psychiatric Clinics of North America.* Vol. 24, no. 2 (June 2001): 229.

Coates, Reynell. *Popular Medicine.* Philadelphia: Cary, Lea, and Blanchard, 1838.

Cocozza, Joseph, and Steadman, Henry. "The Failure of Psychiatric Predictions of Dangerousness." *Rutgers Law Review.* No. 29 (1974).

Cody, Patrick. "Historical Places of Note Await Psychiatrists Throughout the U.S." *Psychiatric News* (May 3, 1991).

Cohen, P. "Child Development and Personality Disorder." *Psychiatric Clinics of North America.* Vol. 31, no. 477 (2008).

Conti, N. A. "Benedict Augustin Morel and the Origin of the Term 'Dementia Praecox.'" *Vertex.* Vol. 14, no. 53 (2003).

Cook, W. G. *Insanity and Mental Deficiency in Relation to Legal Responsibility.* New York: E.P. Dutton and Co., 1921.

Crighton, David. *Psychology in Prisons.* Chapel Hill: BPS Blackwell, 2008.

Csernansky, John. *Schizophrenia: A New Guide for Clinicians.* New York: Marcel Dekker Inc., 2002.

Coons, P. M., Milstein, V., and Marley, C. "EEG Studies of Two Multiple Personalities and a Control." *Archives of General Psychiatry.* Vol. 39, no. 7 (July 1982).

Curtis, Adam. Interview of Robert Spitzer seen in the documentary "The Trap," part 2 (March 2007).

Daban, C., Martinez-Aran, A., Cruz, N., and Vieta, E. "Safety and Efficacy of Vagus Nerve Stimulation in Treatment-Resistant Depression—A Systematic Review." *Journal of Affective Disorders*. No. 110 (2008).

Dalal, P. K., and Sivakumar, T. "Moving Towards ICD-11 and DSM 5: Concept and Evolution of Psychiatric Classification." *Indian Journal of Psychiatry*. Vol. 51, no. 4 (2009).

Dean, Eric. Shook Over Hell: Post Traumatic Stress, Vietnam, and the Civil War. Cambridge: Harvard University Press, 1997.

De Virville, Adrien. *Histoire de la Botanique en France*. Paris: Sedes, 1955.

Dhossche, Dirk. "Suicidal Behavior in Psychiatric Emergency Room Patients." *Southern Medical Journal* (March 1, 2000).

Diamond, Bernard. "The Psychiatric Prediction of Dangerousness." *University of Pennsylvania Law Review*. No. 123 (1975).

Dickey, Colin. *Cranioklepty: Grave Robbing and the Search for Genius*. Cave Creek: Unbridled Books, 2009.

Digby, A. "The Changing Profile of a Nineteenth-Century Asylum: The York Retreat." *Psychological Medicine*. Vol. 14, no. 4 (November 1984).

Doren, Dennis. *Evaluating Sex Offenders: A Manual for Civil Commitment and Beyond*. New York: Sage, 2002.

Doroshow, Deborah. "Performing a Cure for Schizophrenia: Insulin Coma Therapy on the Wards." *Journal of the History of Medicine and Allied Sciences*. Vol. 62, no. 2 (2007).

Doyle, Arthur Conan. "The Sign of Four." *The Complete Sherlock Holmes*. Vol. 2. New York: Barnes and Noble Classics, 2003.

Dupaquier, Michel et al., eds. *Statisticians of the Centuries*. New York: Springer-Verlag, 2001.

Edersheim, Judith. "Off-Label Prescribing." *Psychiatric Times*. Vol. 26, no. 4 (April 14, 2009).

Ellenford, Mary. "A History of Lobotomy in the United States." *The Pharos* (Summer 1987).

Ennis, Bruce, and Litwack, Thomas. "Psychiatry and the Presumption of Expertise: Flipping Coins in the Courtroom." *California Law Review*. No. 62 (1974).

Fabrega, Horacio. "Culture and History in Psychiatric Diagnosis and Practice." *Psychiatric Clinics of North America*. Vol. 24, no. 3 (September 2001).

Firestone, Marvin. "Psychiatric Patients and Forensic Psychiatry." *Legal Medicine*. 5th ed. New York: Mosby, 2001.

Folks D. G., and Freeman, A. M. "Munchausen's Syndrome and Other Factitious Illness." *Psychiatric Clinics of North America*. No. 8 (1985).

Fountas, K., Smith, J., and Lee, G. "Bilateral Stereotactic Amygdalotomy for Self-Mutilation Disorder: A Case Report and Review of The Literature." *Stereotactic and Functional Neurosurgery*. Vol. 85, no. 2/3 (January 12, 2007).

Frances, Allen. "Are College Students Getting Sicker? No, Diagnoses Change Faster Than People." *Psychiatric Times* (January 11, 2011).

Frances, Allen. "Biomarkers Oversold in Medicine: Implications for Psychiatry." *Psychiatric Times* (June 8, 2011).

Frances, Allen. "Defending Psychiatry from Reckless Attacks." *Psychiatric Times* (March 31, 2011).

Frances, Allen. "Drug Companies Peddle Female Sexual Dysfunction." *Psychiatric Times* (February 14, 2011).

Frances, Allen. "DSM 5 Badly Off Track." *Psychiatric Times* (June 26, 2009).

Frances, Allen. "DSM 5 Will Medicalize Everyday Worries into Generalized Anxiety Disorder." *Psychiatric Times* (April 11, 2011).

Frances, Allen. "Opening Pandora's Box: The 19 Worst Suggestions for DSM 5." *Psychiatric Times* (February 11, 2010).

Frances, Allen. "Psychiatry Should Stay Comfortable in its Own Skin: No Good Comes from Overselling Our Science Base." *Psychiatric Times* (May 13, 2011).

Frances, Allen. "PTSD, DSM-5, and Forensic Misuse." *Psychiatric Times* (September 30, 2011).

Frances, Allen. "Rape, Psychiatry, and Constitutional Rights Make for Very Bad Law." *Psychiatric Times*. Vol. 27, no. 9 (September 1, 2010).

Frances, Allen. "Solving The Problem of Questionable Diagnoses Grandfathered Into DSM." *Psychiatric Times* (February 10, 2011).

Frueh, B. C., Hamner, M. B., Cahill, S. P., Gold, P. B., and Hamlin, K. "Apparent Symptom Over-Reporting Among Combat Veterans Evaluated for PTSD." *Clinical Psychology Review*. No. 20 (2000).

Frueh, B.C., and Kinder, B.N. "The Susceptibility of the Rorschach Inkblot Test to Malingering of Combat-Related PTSD." *Journal of Personality Assessment*. Vol. 62, no. 2 (April 1994).

Gallagher, Robert, Ben-Povath, Yossef, and Briggs, Sylvester. "Inmate Views About the Purpose and Use of the MMPI-2 at the Time of Correctional Intake." *Criminal Justice and Behavior*. Vol. 24, no. 3 September 1997).

Ganellen, R.J. et al. "Can Psychosis Be Malingered on the Rorschach? An Empirical Study." *Journal of Personality Assessment*. Vol. 66, no. 1 (February 1996).

Garrison, Martha, and Schneider, Carl. *The Law of Bioethics: Individual Autonomy and Social Regulation*. St. Paul: Thomson-West, 2003.

Geller, Jeff. "A History of Private Psychiatric Hospitals in the U.S." *Psychiatric Quarterly*. No. 77 (Spring 2006).

George, M. S., Lisanby, S. H., Avery, D. et al. "Daily Left Prefrontal Transcranial Magnetic Stimulation Therapy for Major Depressive Disorder—A Sham-Controlled Randomized Trial." *Archives of General Psychiatry*. No. 67 (2010).

George, Mark, et al. "Vagus Nerve Stimulation: A Potential Therapy for Resistant Depression?" *Psychiatric Clinics of North America*. Vol. 23, no. 4 (December 2000).

Geppert, Cynthia, and Taylor, Peter. "Should Psychiatrists Prescribe Neuroenhancers for Mentally Healthy Patients?" *Psychiatric Times*. Vol. 28, no. 3 (April 1, 2011).

Gibbs, Patricia A., and Rowe, Linda H. *The Public Hospital, 1766-1885*. Williamsburg: The Colonial Williamsburg Foundation, 1990.

Goff, J. F. "Alcoholism: Disease or Willful Misconduct?" *Journal of Psychiatry and Law*. Vol. 18, no. 59 (1990).

Goldstein, Jan. *Console and Classify: The French Psychiatric Profession in the Nineteenth Century*. Cambridge: Cambridge University Press, 1987.

Granados, Alex, and Stasio, Frank. "Defining Mental Health, The State of Things." National Public Radio, February 24, 2011.

Grant, B.F., et al. "Co-occurrence of 12-Month Alcohol and Drug Use Disorders and Personality Disorders in the United States: Results from the National Epidemiologic Survey on Alcohol and Related Conditions, National Institute on Alcohol Abuse and Alcoholism, National Institutes of Health." *Archives of General Psychiatry*. Vol. 61 (April 2004).

Grob, G.N. "Deinstitutionalization of the Mentally Ill: Policy Triumph or Tragedy?" *New Jersey Medicine*. Vol. 101, no. 12 (2004).

Grossman, Linda, and Wasyliw, Orest. "A Psychometric Study of Stereotypes: Assessment of Malingering in a Criminal Forensic Group." *Journal of Personality Assessment*. Vol. 52, no. 3 (1988).

Grossman, Robert. "Neuroimaging Studies in Post Traumatic Stress Disorder." *The Psychiatric Clinics of North America*. Vol. 25, no. 2 (June 2002).

Haddad, Jane, and Cohen, Fred. *Training in Correctional Mental Health*. Tucson: Correctional Mental Health Specialists, 1999.

Hammond, Marilyn. "Predictions of Dangerousness in Texas." *St Mary's Law Journal*. No. 12 (1980).

Hansen, Mark. "Depravity Scale May Help Judges and Juries During Sentencing." *ABA Journal* (July 1, 2011).

Hare, Robert. "Psychopathy and Anti-Social Personality Disorder: A Case of Diagnostic Confusion." *Psychiatric Times*. Vol. 13, no. 2 (February 1, 1996).

Harris, Gardiner. "Talk Doesn't Pay, So Psychiatry Turns to Drug Therapy." *The New York Times*, March 5, 2011.

Hayes, Emily. "Non-Psychiatric Prescribing Fuels Rise in Antidepressant Use." *Clinical Psychiatry News* (August 5, 2011).

Heinze, Michaela. "Developing Sensitivity to Distortion: Utility of Psychological Tests in Differentiating Malingering and Psychopathology in Criminal Defendants." *Journal of Forensic Psychiatry & Psychology*. Vol. 14, no. 1 (April 2003).

Hellerstein, David. "From Cinderella to Straw Man? Supportive Psycho-therapy in the 21st Century." *Psychiatric Times*. Vol. 28, no. 8 (August 11, 2011).

Herman, Ellen. *The Romance of American Psychology*. Los Angeles: University of California Press, 1995.

Hiscock M., and Hiscock C. K. "Refining the Forced-Choice Method for the Detection of Malingering." *Journal of Clinical and Experimental Neuropsychology*. No. 11 (1989).

Hodgins, Sheilagh, ed. *Mental Disorder and Crime*. Newbury Park: Sage Publications, 1993.

Horsley, J. S. *Narcoanalysis*. New York: Oxford University Press, 1943.

Jackson, John Z. "When It Comes to Transplant Organs, Demand Far Exceeds Supply." *New Jersey Law Journal*. No. 170 (2002).

Jackson, R. L., Rogers, R., and Sewell, K.W. "Forensic Applications of the Miller Forensic Assessment of Symptoms Test (MFAST)." *Law and Human Behavior.* Vol. 29, no. 2 (April 2005).

Jancin, Bruce. "Dueling Borderline Guidelines Spark Debate in U.K." *Clinical Psychiatry News*. Vol. 38, no. 8 (August 2010).

Jancin, Bruce. "PTSD 'Not A Given' After Mass Catastrophes." *Clinical Psychiatry News* (May 2011).

Jancin, Bruce. "Szasz Hailed in U.K. for 'Questioning Spirit.'" Clinical *Psychiatric News*. Vol. 38, issue 9 (September 2010).

Jancin, Bruce. "Theta Burst Stimulation Promising for Refractory Schizophrenia." *Clinical Psychiatry News* (April 8, 2011).

Johnson, Sally. "Dead Right, Dead Wrong, or The Jury Is Still Out: The Complex Worlds of Violence and Mental Illness." *Department of Psychiatry Grand Rounds*. University of Maryland Medical Center (December 2, 2010).

Johnson, Sandra, et al., eds. Health Law and Bioethics. New York: Wolters Kluwer, 2009.

Jones, Franklin. "Military Combat Psychiatry: A Historical Review." *Psychiatric Annals*. Vol. 81, no. 17 (August 1987).

Kadosh, R. Soskic, S., Iuculano, T., Kanai, R., and Walsh, V. "Modulating Neuronal Activity Produces Specific and Long-Lasting Changes in Numerical Competence." *Current Biology*. Vol. 20, no. 22 (November 4, 2010).

Kales, Anthony. *Evaluation and Treatment of Insomnia*. New York: Oxford University Press, 1984.

Kaplan, Arline. "Blood Tests for Schizophrenia and Depression: Not Ready for Prime Time." *Psychiatric Times*. Vol. 28, no. 11 (November 8, 2011).

Kaplan, Harold, and Sadock, Benjamin. *Comprehensive Textbook of Psychiatry*, 5th edition. Baltimore: Williams & Wilkins, 1989.

Kaplan, Harold, and Sadock, Benjamin. *Pocket Handbook of Psychiatric Drug Treatment*. Baltimore: Williams & Wilkins, 1993.

Kapur S. "Schizophrenia." *The Lancet* (August 22, 2009).

Karlsson, Hasse. "Understanding the Mechanisms—How Psychotherapy Changes the Brain." *Psychiatric Times*. Vol. 28, no. 8 (August 11, 2011).

Kashy, D. A., and DePaulo, B. M. "Everyday Lies in Close and Casual Relationships." *Journal of Personality and Social Psychology.* No. 74 (1998).

Kashy, D. A., and DePaulo, B. M. "Who Lies?" *Journal of Personality and Social Psychology.* No. 70 (1996).

Kellner, C. H., Knapp, R., Husain, M. M., et al. "Bifrontal, Bitemporal and Right Unilateral Electrode Placement in ECT: A Randomised Trial." *British Journal of Psychiatry,* No. 196 (2010).

Kellner, Charles. "Electroconvulsive Therapy: The Second Most Controversial Medical Procedure." *Psychiatric Times.* Vol. 28, no. 1 (February 8, 2011).

Kernberg, Otto. *Severe Personality Disorders: Psychotherapeutic Strategies.* New Haven: Yale University Press, 1993.

Kessler R.C., et al. "Lifetime and 12-month prevalence of DSM III-R Psychiatric Disorders in the United States—Results from the National Comorbidity Survey." *Archives of General Psychiatry.* Vol. 51, no. 1 (1994).

Kessler, R. C., et al. "The Epidemiology of Generalized Anxiety Disorder." *Psychiatric Clinics of North America.* Vol. 24, no. 1 (March 2001).

Kessler, R. C., Berglund, P., Demler, O., et al. "The Epidemiology of Major Depressive Disorder: Results from the National Comorbidity Survey Replication." *JAMA.* Vol. 289 (2003).

Kim, Michelle, et al. "The Warrington Recognition Memory Test for Words as a Measure of Response Bias: Total Score and Response Times Cutoffs Developed on 'Real World' Credible and Non-Credible Subjects." *Archives of Clinical Neuropsychology.* Vol. 25, no. 1 (2010).

Kinon, B.J., Potts, A.J., and Watson, Susan. "Placebo Response in Clinical Trials with Schizophrenia Patients." *Current Opinion in Psychiatry.* Vol. 24, no. 2 (2011).

Kirsch, Irving. *The Emperor's New Drugs.* New York: Basic Books, 2010.

Kleinman, A. "Triumph or Pyrrhic Victory? The Inclusion of Culture in DSM IV." *Harvard Review of Psychiatry*. Vol. 6, no. 4 (1997).

Kleinplatz, P.J., and Moser, C. "Politics versus Science: An Addendum and Response to Drs. Spitzer and Fink." *Journal of Psychology and Human Sexuality*. Vol. 17, no. 3/4 (2005).

Knoll, James. "The Political Diagnosis: Psychiatry in the Service of the Law." *Psychiatric Times* (May 13, 2010): 13.

Knoll, James. "The Suicide Prevention Contract: Contracting for Comfort." *Psychiatric Times* (March 1, 2011).

Kramer, Peter. "In Defense of Antidepressants." *The New York Times* (July 9, 2011).

Kunen, Seth, and Stamps, Leighton. "Psychiatric Comorbidity in Emergency Department Patients: Why Is It Being Missed by ED Physicians?" *Psychiatric Times*. Vol. 25, no. 12 (October 1, 2008).

Laegreid, L., Olegard, R., Walstrom, J., and Conradi, N. "Teratogenic Effects of Benzodiazepine Use During Pregnancy." *Journal of Pediatrics*. Vol. 114, no. 1 (January 1989).

Landsdale, Edward. "Used as Directed? How Prosecutors are Expanding the False Claims Act to Police Pharmaceutical Off-Label Marketing." *New England Law Review*. Vol. 41, no. 159 (2006-07).

Larson, Erik. *The Devil in the White City*. New York: Vintage Press, 2004.

Levin, Aaron. "Campus Shooting Follow-Up Shows New Approach Needed." *Psychiatric News*. Vol. 46, no. 19 (October 7, 2011).

Lieb, Klaus, et al. "Pharmacotherapy for Borderline Personality Disorder." *British Journal of Psychiatry*. Vol. 196 (January 2010).

Lieberman, J.A., and Tasman, Allan. "The Mood Stabilizers." *Handbook of Psychiatric Drugs*. Chichester: Wiley & Sons, Ltd., 2006.

Long, Leonard. "Rethinking Selective Incapacitation: More at Stake Than Controlling Violent Crime." *University of Missouri Kansas City Law Review*. No. 62 (autumn 1993).

Lopez, Alan, et al., eds. "Global Burden of Disease and Risk Factors." Washington, D.C.: Oxford University Press, 2006.

Lyons, A., and Petrucelli, R. *Medicine, An Illustrated History.* New York: Abradale Press (1987).

MacDonald, Michael. *Mystical Bedlam: Madness, Anxiety, and Healing in Seventeenth-Century England.* New York: Cambridge University Press, 1981.

Mahoney, Diana. "Poor Adherence Boosts Antidepressant Dosing." *Clinical Psychiatry News*, vol. 38, no. 11 (November 2010).

Marin, R. S. "Apathy: a Neuropsychiatric Syndrome." *Journal of Neuropsychiatry and Clinical Neuroscience.* No. 3 (1991).

Mayes, R., and Horwitz, A.V. "DSM-III and the Revolution in the Classification of Mental Illness." *Journal of the History of Behavioral Science.* Vol. 41, no. 3 (2005).

McIntyre, J. S., et al., eds. *Psychiatric Evaluation of Adults, APA Practice Guidelines for the Treatment of Psychiatric Disorders.* Washington, D.C.: American Psychiatric Association, 2000.

McQueen, M. P. "Health Costs: More Autism Coverage." *Wall Street Journal* (March 6, 2011).

Mendelsohn, Robert. *The Confessions of a Medical Heretic.* Chicago: Contemporary Books, Inc., 1979.

Meninger, Karl. *The Human Mind.* New York: Alfred Knopf, 1947.

Merson, M. H., et al., eds. *International Public Health: Diseases, Programs, Systems, and Policies.* Boston: Jones and Bartlett, 2005.

Miller, N., and Chappel, J. N. "History of the Disease Concept." *Psychiatric Annals.* vol. 21, no. 4 9 (April 1991).

Miller, F.G., and Colloca, L. "The Legitimacy of Placebo Treatments in Clinical Practice." *American Journal of Bioethics.* Vol. 12, no. 9 (2009).

Miller, Norman. *The Principles and Practice of Addictions in Psychiatry.*" Philadelphia: W.B. Saunders, 1997.

Millon, Theodore. *Masters of the Mind: Exploring the Story of Mental Illness from Ancient Times to the New Millennium.* New York: John Wiley & Sons, 2004.

Millon, Theodore, et al. "Historical Conceptions of Psychopathy in the United States and Europe." In *Psychopathy: Antisocial, Criminal, and Violent Behavior.* New York: Guilford Press, 1998.

Mills, Shari, and Raine, Adrian. "Neuroimaging and Aggression." In *The Psychobiology of Aggression.* New York: The Haworth Press, 1994.

Mills, S. R. "The Recognition Memory Test in the Detection of Malingered and Exaggerated Memory Deficits." *Clinical Neuropsychologist.* No. 6 (1992).

Mintz, Daniel. "Psychodynamic Psychopharmacology." *Psychiatric Times* (September 9, 2011).

Mojtabai, Ramin, and Olfson, Mark. "Proportion of Antidepressants Prescribed Without a Psychiatric Diagnosis Is Growing." *Health Affairs.* Vol. 30, no. 8 (August 2011).

Monahan, John. "Mental Disorder and Violent Behavior: Perceptions and Evidence." *American Psychology.* No. 47 (1992).

Monahan, John, Steadman, Henry, et al. *Rethinking Risk Assessment: The MacArthur Study of Mental Disorder and Violence.* New York: Oxford University Press, 2001.

Monahan, John, and Steadman, Henry. *Toward a Rejuvenation of Risk Assessment Research, Violence and Mental Disorder.* Chicago: University of Chicago Press, 1994.

Moon, Mary Ann. "Off Label Use of Atypical Antipsychotics Minimally Effective." *Clinical Psychiatry News* (September 27, 2011).

Moon, Mary Ann. "Worldwide Bipolar Disorder Prevalence Estimated at 2.4%." *Clinical Psychiatry News* (March 7, 2011).

Moran, Mark. "Monotherapy after Polypharmacy Effective for Some Patients." *Psychiatric News.* Vol. 46, no. 11 (June 3, 2011).

Moran, Mark. "Neurobiological Secrets." *Psychiatric News.* Vol. 46, no. 8 (April 15, 2011).

Moran, Mark. "Using Antipsychotics Off Label Often Brings Little Benefit." *Psychiatric News.* Vol. 46, no. 20 (October 21, 2011).

Morse, Stephen. "Crazy Behavior, Morals, and Science: An Analysis of Mental Health Law." *Southern California Law Review.* No. 51 (1978).

Mossman, Douglas. *Dangerousness Decisions: An Essay on the Mathematics of Clinical Violence Prediction and Involuntary Hospitalization.* University of Chicago Law School Roundtable, 1995.

Nakamura, David. "Loughner Ruling Creates Potential Obstacles on Path to Trial in Arizona Shootings." *The Washington Post* (May 27, 2011).

Newman, Andy. "Analyze This: Vincent Gigante, Not Crazy After All Those Years." *The New York Times* (April 13, 2003).

Oliver, John. *Sexual Hygiene and Pathology: A Manual for Physicians.* Philadelphia: J.B. Lippincott Co., 1955.

O'Malley, C.D. *Andreas Vesalius of Brussels, 1514-1564.* Berkeley: University of California Press, 1964.

Osbaldeston, Tess Ann, transl. *Dioscorides' De Materia Medica: A New English Translation.* Johannesburg: Ibidis Press, 2000.

Othmer, E., and Othmer, S. *The Clinical Interview Using DSM IV-TR: Fundamentals.* Vol. 1. Washington, D.C.: American Psychiatric Publishing, Inc., 2002.

Otto, M.A. "DSM Workgroup Examines Proposed Separate Diagnosis for Suicide Disorder." *Clinical Psychiatry News* (April 22, 2011).

Ovsiew, Fred, and Munich, Richard, eds. *Principles of Inpatient Psychiatry.* New York: Wolters Kluwer, 2009.

Owens, David. "How CATIE Brought Us Back to Kansas: A Critical Re-Evaluation of the Concept of Atypical Antipsychotics and Their Place in the Treatment of Schizophrenia." *Advances in Psychiatric Treatment.* No. 14 (2008).

Paola, Suzanne. "Up From the Falling Sickness." *Helix* (Winter 1990-91).

Parker, Gordon, and Fletcher, Kathryn. "Debate: What's the Evidence for the Evidence-Based Treatments of Depression?" *Psychiatric Times* (September 8, 2011).

Pearce, J. M. "S. Leopold Auenbrugger: Camphor-Induced Epilepsy—[A] Remedy for Manic Psychosis." *European Neurology*. Vol. 59, no. 1/2 (2008).

Perry, G. G., and Kinder, B. N. "The Susceptibility of the Rorschach to Malingering: A Critical Review." *Journal of Personality Assessment*. Vol. 54, no. 1/2 (1990).

Perryman, Kent. "Shocking Treatment." *Sierra Sacramento Valley Medical Society Newsletter*. Vol. 58, no. 1 (January/ February 2007).

Petrila, John, and Swanson, J. W. *Mental Illness, Law, and a Public Health Law Research Agenda*. Program on Public Health Law Research, Princeton. Robert Wood Johnson Foundation, 2010.

Phillips, James. "DSM 5: When to Change and When Not to Change." *Psychiatric Times* (January 25, 2011).

Phillips, James. "How to Use the DSM." *Psychiatric Times* (January 26, 2011).

Pies, Ronald. "Misunderstanding Psychiatry and Philosophy at the Highest Level." *Psychiatric Times*. Vol. 28, no. 9 (September 2011).

Piper, A. and Merskey, H. "The Persistence of Folly: Critical Examination of Dissociative Identity Disorder, part II—The Defense and Decline of Multiple Personality or Dissociative Identity Disorder." *Canadian Journal of Psychiatry*. Vol. 49, no. 10 (2004).

Porter, Roy. *Madness: A Brief History*. New York: Oxford University Press, 2002.

Pozgar, George, ed. *Legal Aspects of Health Care Administration*. Boston: Jones and Bartlett, 2007.

Preskorn, Sheldon. "Avoiding SRI Discontinuation Syndrome." *Psychiatric Times* (June 2011).

Prigatano, G.P., et al. "Digit Memory Test: Unequivocal Cerebral Dysfunction and Suspected Malingering." *Journal of Clinical Neuro-psychology*. Vol. 15, no. 4 (July 1993).

Purcell, T.B. *Factitious Disorders and Malingering, Emergency Medicine: Concepts and Clinical Practice*, 5th ed. St Louis: Mosby, 2002.

Quinsey, Vernon, et al. *Violent Offenders: Appraising and Managing Risk*. Washington, D.C.: American Psychological Association Press, 1998.

Raab, Selwyn. "Mob Boss Who Feigned Incompetence to Avoid Jail Dies at 77." *The New York Times* (December 19, 2005).

Rasmussen, Keith, et al. "Electroconvulsive Therapy in the Medically Ill." *Psychiatric Clinics of North America*. Vol. 25, no. 1 (March 2002).

Ray, Isaac. *A Treatise on the Medical Jurisprudence of Insanity*. Boston: Charles Little and James Brown, 1838.

Regnier, Thomas. "Barefoot in Quicksand: The Future of 'Future Dangerousness' Predictions in Death Penalty Sentencing in the World of *Daubert* and *Kumho*." *Akron Law Review*. No. 37 (2003).

Reinhart, Melvin, and Shafii, Mohammad. "Profound Regression Following Two Electroconvulsive Treatments." *Canadian Psychiatric Association Journal*. Vol. 12 (1967).

Resnick, Phil. "Detecting Malingered Mental Illness." Presentation to the American Psychiatric Association Annual Conference, Honolulu, Hawaii, May 2011.

Riley-Smith, Jonathan. *The Crusades, Christianity, and Islam*. New York: Columbia University Press, 2008.

Roberts, Michelle. "Experts May Have Found a Way to Detect Alzheimer's Years Before Symptoms Appear." BBC News, December 22, 2010.

Rogers, Rayna. "Multiple Personality and Channeling." *Jefferson Journal of Psychiatry.* Vol. 9, no. 1 (1991).

Rogers, R., ed. *Clinical Assessment of Malingering and Deception.* 2d ed. New York: Guilford Press, 1997.

Rogers, R., et al. *Structured Interview of Reported Symptoms.* Odessa: Psychological Assessment Resources, 1992.

Rogers, R., Kropp, P. R., Bagby, R. M., Dickens, S. E. "Faking Specific Disorders: A Study of the Structured Interview of Reported Symptoms." *Journal of Clinical Psychology.* Vol. 48, no. 5 (September 1992).

Rubenstein, Sarah. "Feds Delay ICD-10 for Two Years." *Wall Street Journal* (January 15, 2009).

Rush, John, ed. *Handbook of Psychiatric Measures.* Washington, D.C.: American Psychiatric Publishing, 2000.

Rutkow, Lainie, et al. "Prescribing Authority During Emergencies." *The Journal of Legal Medicine*, no. 32 (July 2011).

Saxena, Sanjaya, and Rauch, Scott. "Functional Neuroimaging and the Neuroanatomy of Obsessive-Compulsive Disorder." *Psychiatric Clinics of North America.* Vol. 23, no. 3 (September 2000).

Sayani, Daniel. "CDC: Antidepressant Use Up 400% in Past Decade." *The New American* (October 21, 2011).

Schatzberg, Alan, et al. "American Psychiatric Association Response to Frances Commentary on DSM 5." *Psychiatric Times* (June 29, 2009).

Schatzberg et al., eds. *Manual of Clinical Psychopharmacology*, 6th edition. Washington, D.C.: American Psychiatric Press, 2007.

Scherr, Alexander. Daubert & Danger: The 'Fit' of Expert Predictions in Civil Commitments, Hastings Law Journal, no. 55, 2003.

Schneider, Sarah. "Allen Frances Gave Us the Asperger's 'Epidemic' Just Like Al Gore Gave Us the Internet." *Shift Journal* (January 6, 2011).

Schreter, Robert. "Alternative Treatment Programs." *Psychiatric Clinics of North America.* Vol. 23, no. 2 (June 2000).

Schretien, David, Brandt, Jason, Krafft, Laura, Van Gorp, Wilfred. "Some Caveats in Using the Rey 15-Item Memory Test to Detect Malingered Amnesia." *Psychological Assessment*, vol. 3, no. 4 (December 1991).

Scott, Charles, and Gerbasi, Joan, eds. *Handbook of Correctional Mental Health.* Washington, D.C.: American Psychiatric Publishing, 2005.

Selvin, Beatrice. "Electroconvulsive Therapy—1987," *Anesthesiology.* Vol. 67, no. 3 (September 1987).

Shapiro, Dan. *Forensic Psychologic Assessment.* Boston: Allyn and Bacon, 1991.

Sharfstein, S. "Big Pharma and American Psychiatry: The Good, the Bad, and the Ugly," *Psychiatric News.* Vol. 40, no. 16 (August 19, 2005).

Shaw, Ian, ed. *The Oxford History of Ancient Egypt.* New York: Oxford University Press, 2000.

Shorter, Edward. A *History of Psychiatry: From the Era of the Asylum to the Age of Prozac.* New York: John Wiley & Sons, 1997.

Shulman, K. I., and Walker, S. E. "Refining the MAOI Diet." *Journal of Clinical Psychiatry.* Vol. 60, no. 3 (March 1999).

Shultz, S. M. *Body Snatching: The Robbing of Graves for the Education of Physicians in Early Nineteenth Century America.* Jefferson, McFarland & Co., 1992.

Simon, Robert, and Gold, Liza. *Textbook of Forensic Psychiatry.* Washington, D.C.: American Psychiatry Publishing, Inc., 2010.

Singer, H. D., and Krohn, William. *Insanity and Law: a Treatise on Forensic Psychiatry.* Philadelphia: Blakiston's Son & Co., 1924.

Skaggs, Clayton. "Kansas' Sexual Predator Act and the Impact of Expert Predictions: Psyched Out by the *Daubert* Test." *Washburn Law Journal.* No. 34 (Spring 1995).

Slovenko R. *Psychiatry in Law/ Law in Psychiatry.* New York: Brunner-Routledge, 2002.

Smith, Jennie. "SSRIs May Not Be Safer Than Tricyclics in Elderly." *Clinical Psychiatry News* (August 2, 2011).

Smith R. "In Search of 'Non-Disease.'" *British Medical Journal*. Vol. 324, no. 7342 (April 2002).

Solomon, D.A., et al. "Multiple Recurrences of Major Depressive Disorder." *American Journal of Psychiatry*. Vol. 157, no. 2 (February 1, 2000).

Spiegel, Alix. Creator of Psychopathology Test Worries About Its Use. "All Things Considered." National Public Radio, May 27, 2011.

Spiegel, Alix. What's a Mental Disorder? Even Experts Can't Agree. "All Things Considered." National Public Radio, December 29, 2010.

Spitzer, Robert, and First, Michael. "Classification of Psychiatric Disorders." *Journal of the American Medical Association* (October 19, 2005).

Stahl, Stephen. *Essential Psychopharmacology*. New York: Cambridge University Press, 2000.

Stahl, Stephen. *Psychopharmacology of Antidepressants*. London: Martin Dunitz, Ltd., 1998.

Stahl, Stephen, ed. *Psychosis and Schizophrenia: Thinking it Through*. Carlsbad: Neuroscience Education Institute, 2010.

Stambor, Zak. "Psychology's Prescribing Pioneers." *Monitor on Psychology*. Vol. 37 (2006).

Stone, Alan. *Mental Health and the Law: A System in Transition*. Washington, D.C.: U.S. Government Printing Office, 1976.

Thomas, John. "Deep Brain Stimulation Surgery for OCD." *Psychiatric Times*. Vol. 28, no. 9 (September 2011).

Tokitsu, K. *Miyamoto Musashi: His Life and Writings*. Boston: Weatherhill, 2004.

Tombaugh, T. N. "The Test of Memory Malingering (TOMM): Normative Data from Cognitively Intact and Cognitively Impaired Individuals." In *Psychological Assessment*. Vol. 9, no. 3 (September 1997).

Turney, Brent. "Dangerousness: Predicting Recidivism in Violent Sex Offenders." *Knowledge Solutions Library* (March 1996).

Tward, Aaron, and Patterson, Hugh. "From Grave Robbing to Gifting: Cadaver Supply in the United States." *JAMA*. Vol. 287, no. 9 (March 6, 2002).

Vance, Charles. "Malingering in a Forensic Context." Presentation to the Forensic Fellowship Conference, Dorothea Dix Hospital, Raleigh, N.C. (November 17, 2009).

Vedantam, Shankar. "A Political Debate on Stress Disorder: As Claims Rise, VA Takes Stock." *The Washington Post* (December 27, 2005).

Walsh, B.T., Seidman, S.N., Sysko, R., Gould, M. "Placebo Response in Major Studies of Depression." *JAMA*. Vol. 287, no. 14 (2002).

Warner, Jessica. "Addiction Fatigue Syndrome: The End of an Intoxicating Idea." *The Globe and Mail* (December 17, 2010).

Watson, Thomas. *Lectures on the Principles and Practice of Physic*. Philadelphia: Blanchard and Lea, 1853.

Weissman, Sidney. "Are We Training Psychiatrists to Provide Only Medication Management?" *Psychiatric Times* (June 2011).

Wendling, Patrice. "Most Depressed Patients Admit to Lying to Their Doctors." *Clinical Psychiatry News* (October 2011).

Whitaker, Robert. "The New York Times' Defense of Antidepressants." *Psychology Today* (July 10, 2011).

Willcox, Walter, ed. "Natural and Political Observations Made Upon the Bills of Mortality." Baltimore: The Johns Hopkins University Press, 1939.

Yates, Deanna, et al. "Should Psychologists Have Prescribing Authority?" *Psychiatric Services*. No. 55 (2004).

Yehuda, Rachel, and Davidson, Jonathan. *Clinician's Manual on Posttraumatic Stress Disorder*. London: Science Press, 2000.

Youssef, H.A., et al. "Evidence for the Existence of Schizophrenia in Medieval Islamic Society." *History of Psychiatry*. Vol. 7, no. 25 (March 1996).

About the Author

John S. Carbone is currently the Chief of Psychiatry and Director of Mental Health Services for the prison system of the North Carolina Department of Public Safety. Before assuming this leadership role, Dr. Carbone practiced for more than two decades in direct patient care and in psychiatric consultation-liaison capacities in both public and private settings, including mental health clinics, state and community hospitals, multi-specialty offices, and forensic facilities in Virginia, West Virginia, Tennessee, and North Carolina.

Dr. Carbone not only has extensive experience in medicine, but adjuvant expertise in both law and business, having earned J.D. and M.B.A. degrees. He is admitted to practice law before the State Bar of New Mexico, the U.S. District Court for the District of New Mexico, and the U.S. Court of Appeals for the Federal Circuit. He is a Diplomate of the American Board of Psychiatry and Neurology since 1995, and a Fellow of the American College of Legal Medicine since 2007.

Index

defined, 125
FDA sanctioning of, 125
prevalence of, 125
physician assistants, 122
psychiatrists, shortfall of, 122
psychologists, preclusion from,
123
state laws covering, 122
types of, 127–29

R

Reil, Johann, 11
review of systems in psychiatric
diagnoses
Rorschach Inkblot Test, 157
malingering, use in detecting, 157
purpose of, 157
Rush, Benjamin, 120
diagnostic textbook, authorship
of, 12

S

Sakel, Manfred, 113
Saldano v. Cockrell, 195–98
Schildkraut, Joseph, 131
schizoaffective disorder, 80–81
as both psychosis and mood
disorder, 80
defined, 80
simplified criteria for diagnosing,
81
schizoid personality disorder, 93
psychosis, type of, 78
simplified criteria for diagnosing,
93
schizophrenia, 77–78
American Psychiatric Association,
definition of, 77
defined, 77
simplified criteria for diagnosing,
79
substance abuse, impact of, 78

substances causing behaviors
resembling, 78
schizophreniform disorder, 79
psychosis, type of, 79
simplified criteria for diagnosing,
79
schizotypal personality disorder,
93–94
characteristics of, 94
psychosis, type of, 78
simplified criteria for diagnosing,
93
seasonal affective disorder, 36
Sexually Violent Predator Act, 195
shared psychotic disorder, 82
defined, 82
simplified criteria for diagnosing,
82
Sharfstein, Steven, 25
somatiform disorders, 166. *See*
conversion disorder; hypochondriasis; pseudologia fantastica;
somatization disorder
somatization disorders, 168
subconscious perception of
impairment, 168
symptoms of, 168
Spitzer, Robert, 21, 24
Diagnostic and Statistical Manual
revisions, 21
Stahl, Stephen, 123
Structured Interview of Reported
Symptoms, 156
malingering, detection of, 156
substance-induced mood disorder
simplified criteria for diagnosing,
68
symptoms of, 68
suicidal tendencies, 50
documentation in mental status
exams, 50
suicide prevention contracts, use
of, 50